Rumi Speaks
Through Sufi Tales

Krish Khosla

KAZI Publications, Inc.

© 1996, ABC International Group, Inc.

All rights reserved. No part of this book may be reproduced, stored in a retrieval system, or transmitted, in any form or by any means, electronic, mechanical, photocopying, recording or otherwise, without the prior written permission of the Publisher.

Library of Congress Cataloging-in-Publication Data

Khosla, Krish. Rumi Speaks Through Sufi Tales.
  I. Khosla, Krish. II. Title
PK6480.E5S45   1996
891'.5511--dc20   94-36971
                                    CIP
                                      NE
ISBN:1-56744-516-0

Published by
ABC International Group, Inc.

Distributed by
KAZI Publications, Inc.
3023 W. Belmont Avenue
Chicago IL 60618
Tel: 7732-267-7001; FAX: 773-267-7002

Contents

Introduction ix
   Music and Whirling xii
   Rumi's Literary Output xiii
   The Present Work xv
   The Essential Unity of Prophets and Saints xviii
   The Essential Oneness of Faiths xviii

1 Prophet Moses and the Pharaoh 1
   The Conception and Birth of Moses 1
   The Two Miracles of Moses 5
   The Spirit and Dragon Symbolism 7
   The Way to Real Knowledge 8
   Mystic Bewilderment 8
   Divine Knowledge 9
   The Two Magicians of Pharaoh 11
   The Eternal "I-Hood" Without "I" 15
   Moses and Pharaoh in Dialogue 16
   The Percipient and the Spiritual Sense 19
   Moses Warns Pharaoh 20
   Moses Promises Four Gifts 22
   Paradise and Hell Are Interchangeable 23
   "I was a hidden treasure..." 24
   His Wife's Exhortation 25
   Pharaoh and His Vizier Haman 27
   Moses, Pharaoh, and the Divine Will 27
   Color and Colorlessness 28
   Food for the Spirit 32
   The Human Being's Spiritual Evolution 34
   The Day of Retribution 35
   The Divine Immanence 36
   The End of Pharaoh 38

2 Prophet Solomon and the Queen of Sheba 39
   Appearance and Reality 40
   The Queen Sends Gold to Solomon 42
   Solomon Returns the Gift 42

Spiritual Alchemy	44
The Philosophic Work in Alchemy	45
The Perfect Human Being	48
Solomon's Message to the Queen	49
Her Attachment to the Throne	50
The Divine Mercy Calls the Queen of Sheba	53

3 Prophet Joseph and Zulaykha — 55

Rumi Reports the Exhortation of the Diwan	57
Zulaykha's Love for Joseph	57
God's Zeal	59
Joseph Interprets a Dream	60
Joseph, His Guest, and the Mirror	60
Famine Strikes Egypt	64
Joseph's Dream Comes True	64
Jacob	65
The Brothers	65

4 Prophet Muhammad and the Sick Companion — 69

The Revival of the Sick Companion	70
Pain Is a Blessing	71
The Nature and Doings of the Animal Soul	71
The Devices of God, His Mercy and Wrath	72
Universal Intellect and Conventional Wisdom	74
The Prophet and the Sick Companion	74
The Higher Self	76
The Prayer of the Sick Man	76
Spiritual Birth	78
Good and Evil	80
The Prophet's Admonition	80
Spiritual Heaven and Hell	81
Seek Spiritual Kings	82

5 The Old Harper — 85

The Harper's Supplication	87
The Caliph Umar and the Minstrel	89
The Place of Music	91
The Penitence of the Harper	92
Intoxication and Sobriety	93

6 The Countrymen and the Townsman — 95
God the Real Object of Love — 98
The Bogus Saint — 102

7 Daquqi: His Visions and Miracles — 105
The Apparition of the Seven Candles — 107
The World of Archetypal Images — 108
The Candles Appear as Seven Men — 109
The Seven Men Appear as Trees — 110
The Seven Trees Become Seven Men — 112
Daquqi Leads Them in Prescribed Prayer — 113
The Real Essence of Prescribed Prayer — 115
A Ship in Distress — 117
Daquqi Intercedes for the Ship's Deliverance — 119
The True Heart — 120
The Disappearance of the Saints — 121
The Two Classes of Saints — 121
The Continual Quest for Saints — 122

8 The Lawyer of Bukhara — 123
Love Is Universal—Rumi's Doctrine of Monotheism — 128
The Lover of God — 129
The Doctrine of Reserve — 132

9 The Story of Ayaz — 135
The Ragged Apparel — 135
The Perfect Human Being — 136
The Shoes and the Sheepskin Jacket — 137
The Oneness of Lover and Beloved — 140
Liberation By Stages — 142
Ayaz's Chamber Raided — 144
The Origin of Sin — 145
The Sorcery of Love — 148
The Shaykh — 149

10 The Breaking of the Pearl — 151
Ayaz's Intercession and Supplication — 154

11 Compulsion and Freewill 161
Necessity and Freewill 162

12 Shaykh Muhammad Sarrazi of Ghazna 167

13 The Story of Bilal 175
New Year's Day Is Come 177
Bilal, the Prophet's Caller to Prescribed Prayer 183
The Doctrine of Reserve 184
Bilal's Death 185

14 The Sufi and the Judge 187
The Miracle of Prophets and Saints 187
The Sick Man 190
The Sick Worldling 190
The Sufi Abstains From Revenge 193
The Judge 193
The Sufi and the Judge 194
The Need for a Guide 197
Speech and Silence 198
The Sufi's Questions 199
The Judge's Reply 199
The Judge's Admonition 201
The Judge's Next Reply 202

15 The Dervish and the Hidden Treasure 205
The Dervish's Prayer 205
Duality the Basis of Creation 206
The Mystic and Unicolor 207
The Unicolor at the Resurrection 207
The Day of Slaughter 208
The Treasure Scroll 209
The Metaphor of the Reed 213
The Sea of Unity 214
The Hidden Treasure 215
The Dervish Turns to God 217
The Mystery of the Hidden Treasure 220

16 The Mouse and the Frog — 221
The Mouse as Lover — 223
The Mouse as Sinner — 225
The Sufi as the Son of the Moment — 225
The Flesh and the Spirit — 227
Mystical Clairvoyance — 227
Life, a Succession of Thoughts — 228
The Supplication of a Sinful Soul — 231
The End of the Mouse and the Frog — 232
Spiritual Congeniality, the True Basis of Friendship — 233

17 The Dervish and the Police Inspector — 235
All Gifts Are From God — 236
God Is Reflected Everywhere — 238
Khwaja, the Perfect Human Being — 238
In Life and Death, the Saint Is With God — 241
The Bailiff's Dream — 243

18 The Three Princes — 247
God's Zeal — 248
The Forbidden Fruit — 249
The Meaning of "If God Will" — 249
Form and Formlessness — 251
The Castle Cast Its Spell — 253
The Quest for Divine Beauty — 255

Notes — 257

INTRODUCTION

The great poet Jalal al-Din Rumi was born at Balkh in Persia in 1207. His father, Bahal Din Walad, was a noted theologian, preacher, instructor and a Sufi, whose erudite work, the *Marif* (*Gnosis*), deeply influenced Rumi's life and writing.

In 1219, dreading the onslaught of the deadly Mongol hordes that were sweeping down from the Northeast and nearing Balkh, Bahal-Din left the city with his family and proceeded on pilgrimage to Makkah. Stopping at Nishapur on the way, he met the eminent Sufi poet Attar who presented the young Jalal with a copy of his mystical poem, the *Asrar Nama* (*Book of Mysteries*), blessed him and said that he would soon be kindling a fire in the hearts of all lovers of God.

After performing the pilgrimage, the family settled in Rum, as Asiatic Turkey was then called, making Laranda, not far from Konya (Iconium), their first home in Turkey. Here Jalal was married to the accomplished Gawhar, daughter of one Sharif al-Din Lala of Samarqand. In 1226, his son, Sultan Walad, was born. Walad has left us some interesting material about his father.

A few years passed. The Seljuq King Alal-Din Kaiqubad and his learned Vizier Muin al-Din Parwana, invited Baha to Konya, the capital of the Seljuqs of Rum. There, he was received with much respect. Soon he settled down as a preacher and instructor. He was held in high esteem by the learned of the city and was given the title of Sultan al-Ulama (Sultan of the Religious Scholars).

Following his family tradition, Rumi studied the exoteric sciences and mastered them at a rather young age so that when his father died in 1230 or 1231 CE, although only around twenty-four years old, he was asked to take over his father's duties as preacher and instructor.

About a year after Baha's death, one of his old disciples, Burhan al-Din Muhaqqiq Tirmidhi, went to Konya, seeking shelter under the Seljuq King, a reputed patron of letters. He came to see his old master, but found to his dismay that he was no more. Meeting his son, Jalal, who must have been already well-acquainted with Sufism, he is said to have taken his spiritual training at his hand. The training continued until Burhan's death in 1240 CE. Thereafter, Rumi continued his outward life as a teacher and religious scholar, practicing austerity in private, building up the fire of Sufism within.

Much of Rumi's theosophy centers round the concept of the perfect human being (*insan-i-kamal*) who mirrors all the divine attributes, whose heart is the substance of which this creation is an accident, a secondary reflection. God said about Himself, "Neither the heaven nor the earth can contain Me, but I am contained in the true believer's heart"[1] in the heart of the perfect human being. "He is I" and "I am he," says God about the perfect human being.

Rumi was in search of the perfect human being. Three such men appeared in his life. The first was the wide-cloaked Shams al-Din, who came to Konya in 1244 CE. Said to be 'exceedingly aggressive and domineering in his manner', he was surnamed 'The Sultan of Mendicants, the Mystery of God upon the Earth'. Because of his flighty travels, he was nicknamed *paranda* (The Bird).

It is said that when the disciple is ready, the master appears. True, the real teacher is within us, but we are so deafened by the trumpet tones of desire that we cannot hear his voice. Though the external teacher cannot plant anything new in us, he can deliver the message of our inner teacher in a voice which our outer ear can hear. Rumi was now ready. The master appeared in the person of Shams—the literal meaning of which name is 'sun'.

The transformation of Rumi in Sham's company was almost miraculous. He broke from his past. His jurisprudence, theology, pedagogies all lay neglected. Dead to the world, he would remain closeted in spiritual communion with Shams. As his son Walad says of him, "The man of traditional knowledge became a lover, the adept a novice, the shaykh a learner."

Rumi thought lowly of poetry once, saying that whenever he thought of rhymed couplets for communication with God, He told him, "I will throw word, sound, and speech into confusion, so that without these three, I may converse with you."[2] But with Shams' coming, everything changed. Poetry lost its previous odium and became a living means of communication for him with the beloved. It began to flow like a heady wine from his innermost being. He blossomed into the greatest mystical poet of all time.

Rumi's disciples, however, bitterly resented their master's association with Shams, as it cut them off from him. He had donned the dervish cloak and stopped teaching. They threatened Shams with violence. Leaving Konya, Shams went and sought shelter in Damascus. This separation was heart-breaking for Rumi. Seeing his anguish, the disciples repented. He forgave them, and sent his son, Walad, to Damascus to bring Shams back to Konya. On his return, they were kind to him initially, but before long their anger flared upon again, and this time, around 1247 CE, he mysteriously disappeared never to be found again. Rumi weeps and wails for him in many an ode in his *Diwan* (collection of poems). Feeling weary of this world, Shams left at last for the world of the soul, he moans, 'left for eternity's tavern', a placeless place from whence none ever returned.

The second perfect human being was the gold-beater, Salah al-Din Zarkub, whom Rumi chose for his companion and deputee three or four years after Shams' final disappearance. He said that the Shams he was seeking had arrived in the form of Zarkub. The disciples resented this fresh intrusion, alleging that Zarkub was not qualified to teach. But as Rumi and he had been Burhan's fellow-pupils, and Burhan held Zarkub in high esteem, he was able to prevail on his disciples to accept him as their instructor. Zarkub worked in this capacity until his death around 1261 CE. His daughter, Fatima, was married to Rumi's son, Walid. Walad taught her to read the Koran.

The third perfect human being in Rumi's life was his disciple, Husam al-Din Ghalabi, whom he appointed as his deputee in succession to Salah. On Rumi's death in 1273 CE, Husam succeeded him as the head of the Mevlevi Order of dervishes founded by Rumi. After his death in 1284 CE, Sultan Walad succeeded to this post.

Rumi praises Husam's spiritual perfection to the highest heaven, and describes him as 'the key of the treasuries of the empyrean', 'the trustee of the treasures on earth'.

Husam was the inspirer of the *Mathnawi*. Rumi calls it the *Husami Nama*—the Book of Husam.[3] The entire *Mathnawi*, he says, in root and branch, is Husam's,[4] likening himself to a flute on Husam's lips wailing forth music made by him.

MUSIC AND WHIRLING

The *sama*—traditional music, chanting and whirling plays a special role for Rumi. He practiced it in the service for the dead. The dead were carried to their place of burial to the accompaniment of joyous hymn-singing, as the spirit's homeward journey was an occasion, not for sorrow, but for rejoicings and whirling.

The Sufi chants and whirls when in spiritual ecstasy or to induce such ecstasy. The whirling symbolizes the ecstasy of dying to self (*fana*) and of attaining to life eternal (*baqa*). The sound of music recalls to the Sufi's heart the primal voice of God, proclaiming His Lordship to the human souls in pre-existence [7:172]. It is a call to retrieve our original state with Him, when we were not separate beings, but were one with Him. It calls the inner self to love and knowledge of God. It is the prayer of His lovers. It trumpets the spiritual resurrection of the mystic. The music of the rebeck and the reed would inspire Rumi and exalt him to the plane of universal consciousness. Music has wondrous spiritual virtues. Rumi's followers came to be known in the West as 'the Whirling Dervishes' because of their special whirling dance.

RUMI'S LITERARY OUTPUT

Rumi's literary output is staggering in dimensions. His major works are two, both poetical. One is the *Diwan* containing 35,000 verses or more. It is known as the *Diwan-i-Shams-i-Tabrizi* —named after Shams and dedicated to his memory. The other is the *Mathnawi,* which is our main concern in this work, which contains about 26,000 verses. Nicholson in his introduction to the complete English translation says, "Judged by modern standards, the *Mathnawi* is a very long poem. It contains almost as many verses as the *Iliad* and the *Odyssey* together and about twice as many as the *Divine Comedy*."[5]

His prose works are three in number, of which we may mention one here, the *Fihi ma fihi* ('*In it is what is in it*'), as it is didactic in nature, covering common ground with the *Mathnawi* at times.

Rumi is mainly indebted to two famous *Mathnawi* writers, that is writers of poems with rhyming couplets, namely Sanai, whose best-known work is the *Hadiqat al-haqiqat* (*Garden of Truth*), and Attar with whose allegorical poem, the *Mantiq al-tayr* (*Conference of the Birds*), the West is not unfamiliar. According to Rumi, Sanai was 'the two eyes' and Attar 'the spirit' of Sufism. The third to influence Rumi was the great Andalusian Arab mystic Ibn al-Arabi who is said to be the father of Islamic gnosis.

The odes of Rumi are mainly descriptive of individual mystical states. They are visions, love and rapture, representing the ecstatic outpourings of a spirit drunk and drenched with God.

The *Mathnawi* is sober and serious. It is a store-house of

knowledge (*ilm*), gnosis (*maarifat*), and love (*ishq*). It has been described as 'the Koran in the Persian language' (Koranic verses are noted in brackets throughout the text).[6] In Rumi's words, "The *Mathnawi* is the proof of God's existence. The heart's parade with fountains and foliage, a drink to the patient, but a sorrow to the house of Pharaoh and unbeliever." His message is of timeless relevance.

The *Mathnawi* explains spiritual themes through the medium of tales, anecdotes and animal fables drawn from different sources to which Rumi gives a spiritual coloring and makes them his own. Thoughts hang together in free association. The main stories are interspersed. His style of free association is to interrupt a story with seemingly unrelated stories and then continue much later on in the story. The poetry has melody. Wine and the cup-bearer give it an intoxicating quality. Rumi's wine, whether in the *Mathnawi* or in the *Diwan*, is not any grape wine, but the wine of love and light brought straight down from the divine distillery. If the aim of spiritual intoxication is 'sobriety', a return to normal, and, in the higher states of attainment, to supra-normal consciousness, it may be said that at the last, intoxication is sunk in sobriety and the two become one as in the *Mathnawi*.

What makes the *Mathnawi* difficult to understand is that it is 'experimental' or experiential, not doctrinal. It does not set forth spiritual experiences and truths with the logical precision of a systematic treatise indicating step by step how the Sufi way leads from the stage of asceticism to that of nearness to God. It is a work of inspiration, a spontaneous outflow couched in the language of emotion and imagination. Spontaneity and inspiration have their own logic.

Prolixity and repetition are said to make the *Mathnawi* tiresome reading, especially its last two volumes. This may be true of the translation, but not so true of the original. The melody and rhythm of the original verses do not cease to please even on repetition, especially as the repeated ideas are generally attired in different words. But as the music of the original is difficult to reproduce in translation, repetition in the translation can be a bore. But as the *Mathnawi* is voluminous and its matter recondite, at times cryptic, repetition can be useful. Sometimes, the repetition is a commentary on the earlier reference, which is all for the better.

THE PRESENT WORK

Rumi's Sufi tales, from which sixteen have been taken for exposition of Sufism in theory and practice in the present work, are not mere legends or tales of the ancients meant to entertain but of so serious relevance today. Concerned with faith beyond all forms of faith, they are a timeless guide to the human being regardless of where he lives and what religious label he wears. In the eyes of one with spiritual experience, they are a description of the actual spiritual state of a saint or dervish. This state is equivalent to the presence of the shaykh or spiritual director who has the light of God in him, can reveal to us our inward self, and guide us towards God, if our hearts follow him.[7]

The *Mathnawi*, Rumi says, is 'the shop for Unity', and if anything other than God is found in it, it is only an idol, a means of attraction. Hence, anyone who delights in the tales and anecdotes without perceiving their inner significance has missed their purpose. He is a worshipper of false gods. The usefulness of every external object is always internal. It is latent like the beneficial quality in medicine.[8]

Rumi is the teacher par excellence. He uses the Socratic method of dialogue which is helpful as intelligent or proper questions, especially of a spiritual nature are not always easy to frame and ill-framed questions may not elicit proper answers. In the tale of "The Sufi and the Judge," the judge answers a host of questions asked by the Sufi, and says, "I know that you are not raw or foolish, but pure and enlightened and that your questions were asked not for your own benefit, but for the benefit of others." Similarly, in "The Story of Ayaz," the King asks him to explain why he mingled his soul's love with his old rustic shoes and sheepskin jacket—which were symbols of self-abasement—

as he wanted others to benefit by knowledge of their mystery.

Rumi's purpose is always didactic. "Even jesting is teaching," he says. "Listen to it seriously. Do not be taken by its appearance. To jesters, every serious matter is a jest. To the wise, all jests are serious."[9]

Often, Rumi himself becomes the unconscious mouthpiece of the divine word, which is the fountain head of all inspiration. The speech that issues from him in those inspired moments, is identical with the spirit of prayer. It finds its way easily into the hearts of all true believers, of all seekers of Truth.

The difficulty in Rumi's stories arises from the abstruseness of the subject matter. At times, as he says in the story of Ayaz, while the outward form of the story is suited to the imagination of those who can apprehend only the outward form, the transcendence of its real essence is such that its revelation is beyond the power of speech, reason or mental faculties.[10]

Words and feelings beyond words and feelings are best indicated by means of symbols, parables and analogies—whose inadequacy is no ground for disbelieving the reality of mystical experience. Rumi provides a spiritual fare which can assimilate according to his capacity.

What adds to the difficulty is the careless manner in which the tales are presented with little regard for the conventions of form. Also, as he says, they are at times begun in haste. Their spiritual meanings and implications are not properly explained. They are left without a moral or proper finish, without leading up to the unitive experience of the perfect human being which is the object of the *Mathnawi*.[11] As to what is missing in one place, it is generally found in another. With a little effort, one is often able to find his way to Rumi's meaning. It may be added that the best commentary on the *Mathnawi* is the *Mathnawi* itself.

The present selection seeks to follow the spirit of the original with a liberal borrowing of its language. The tales merely serve as pegs for hanging spiritual themes. The focus is on the hangings, not on the pegs.

What is of special interest is that, often, we see ourselves in the tales. Take our very first story, "Moses and Pharaoh." Many treat it as an old fable to be read and forgotten. But the story is only a mask. Both Moses and Pharaoh are in us. They have been with us from the time of Adam and will be with us until the resurrection. The message of the story is clear—we should seeks out these contraries. If we wish ourselves well, we must shun the black shadow of Pharaoh and free ourselves from dualism, plurality and from the allurements of desire. We should follow the light of Moses which is from yonder. That light is ever the same, but the lamp and the wick keep changing.

The tale of "Solomon and the Queen of Sheba" that follows speaks of 'spiritual alchemy' which is an apt description of Sufism itself. The Queen's love of her fabulous filigree throne is the same as our own love of worldly baubles, which glitter with gilding, not with the gold of God, and which one discards as of little worth when his spiritual eye is opened.

Do we not ourselves imprison Joseph, our higher self, an aspect of the divinity within us, in our narrow selfish selves, treat it cheaply and sell it for a mess of pottage? How often, like the Prophet's Companion, are we victims of the animal soul and pay the wages of sin—unless a prophet or saint saves us from ourselves? There is hardly a story that is not of relevance to our personal selves—perhaps of greater relevance amid the present-day tumult than at any time in the past.

The first four stories are concerned with four prophets, three with Moses, Solomon, Joseph, all pre-Islamic, but included in the Koran, and the fourth with Muhammad, the last seal of the prophets. The other stories are concerned with saints, dervishes and seekers of the Truth, except the story of "The Mouse and the Frog," which is the only animal story in this collection. But it is an animal story or fable in name only. Rumi gives it a spiritual coloring and makes it his own, similar in nature to his other stories.

THE ESSENTIAL UNITY OF PROPHETS AND SAINTS

It is well to remember that with Rumi the prophets are one in essence with God and hence with each other. Disbelief in any of them will make our belief in any one prophet imperfect. As God says of them, *"We make no distinction between any of them"* [2:136].

Nor are the prophets alone of one essence. With Rumi, there is hardly any difference between them and the saints, except for the former's prophetic mission. Knowledge by inspiration comes to both, but for the sake of differentiation, it is called revelation (*wahi*) when it comes to a prophet and inspiration (*ilham*) when it comes to a saint. Both experience the spiritual journey (*miraj*) and both have the power to perform miracles. But while the prophet's external evidentary miracles (*mujizat*) performed through inanimate objects—like the rod of Moses—involve an open breach of the natural order, the secret miracles and graces (*karamat*) of a saint operate secretly and directly in the heart of the disciple. The latter, according to Rumi, are superior in degree, as faith and gnosis are the product of direct spiritual experience. Their production by any evidentary or external means must of necessity be inferior. It should be borne in mind though, that saintship is the inward aspect of prophecy, so that every prophet is also a saint, although no saint is a prophet.

What is true of the saints is also true of the perfect spiritual guides. All perfect human beings are classified as saints. They all can scale the ramparts of heaven and be in God's own Jerusalem. They also are His elect.

This is not to say, however, that the prophets and saints or angels are equal. The rank of each depends on his spiritual proximity to God. This vast creation is an infinite aggregate of hierarchies.

THE ESSENTIAL ONENESS OF FAITHS

To Rumi, all faiths are one in essence. All paths lead to God. It is a mystery of divine wisdom that He reveals Himself in all forms of worship. Gilded idolatry is not a mockery or abomination, for the idol in essence is not unreal. The forms of worship differ only because the forms of His manifestation are infinite. The different faiths express only certain aspects of His nature which are necessarily inadequate. God created every creature in order that it would worship Him. He has laid down a special code of conduct and form of expression for every human being which is praiseworthy in relation to him although it may not be so in relation to others. Above all purity and impurity, He is not sanctified by our praise of Him. It is we who are sanctified. His ordainment of divine worship was a kindness to us.[12] Indeed, not only the human being, but, "there is not a leaf, but has its morning hymn."

Of every thought and belief, He is the essence, even of disbelief. There is no thought that is not from Him or is not about Him. Externalists can only seek and find one thing among the many, but not the one that is in the many or rather contains the many, but is none of all, and is the hidden ultimate of all faiths.

Rumi does not set much store by faith in mere rites and ceremonies which must be thrown off on the path. It is the correct inward attitude and understanding, the spirit, that counts, not words or forms. The world of mortal words is vain and void.

The last story calls for a brief comment. It is the story of the three princes who symbolize different grades of the same type of spiritual experience. The story finishes thirty-nine verses short of the end of the *Mathnawi*. The common criticism is that it 'is not fully concluded'. The two elder princes receive detailed notice, while the youngest is disposed of in a single verse, the last verse in the story, which says that he was the laziest of the three and won the prize completely—in the appearance as well as the reality. Certainly, an abrupt end and somewhat cryptic.

But the themes of laziness also occurs earlier in the *Mathnawi*, as in Book III, in the story of the poor man who prayed to God for a lawful livelihood without labor—so that he could remain inwardly active, addressing supplications to God, uninterrupted by external toil.

The last forty verses of the *Mathnawi* which follow the reference to the third prince are considered by some commentators, including Nicholson, to be a continuation of the story of the three princes, and by others, as a separate story—ending with a parable. Nicholson's comments in this context are not without relevance, considering the unfinished or abrupt nature of the last story also. He says, "The story should naturally have ended with a third episode depicting the supreme realization of unity by the youngest prince. The remaining forty verses of the poem are merely the prelude to a theme which Rumi may have felt himself unable to write or possibly preferred to leave unwritten."[13]

In any case, Rumi is not overly concerned with the frills and trappings of custom or convention. The very opening of the *Mathnawi* is hardly conventional. It exhorts the reader to listen how the reed tells its tale of separations from the reed-bed. No academics here. Rumi's sole concern is with the shoreless ocean of Truth where the end of the beginning are dreams.

Krish Khosla,
Dehra Dun
India

BIBLIOGRAPHY

Corbin, Henry. *The Man of Light in Iranian Sufism.* Translated by Nancy Pearson. Henry Viaud, 1971. Reprinted in 1978 by arrangement with Shambhala Publications, Inc.

Hujwiri, Ali B. Uthman al-Jullabi al-. *Kashf al-Mahjub*, the oldest Persian treatise on Sufism.) Translated by R. A. Nicholson. Gibb Memorial Trust.

Rumi, Jalalu'd-Din. *The Mathnawi*, translated by R. A. Nicholson. Gibb Memorial Trust.

1 Prophet Moses and Pharaoh

Pharaoh was a child of darkness. The Lord showed him in a dream the coming of one Moses who would destroy him and his kingdom. Pharaoh spoke to his dream interpreters and astrologers about this nightmare. They said, "We shall devise a plan and it will thwart his coming into this world."

It was not a common mortal whose coming Pharaoh sought to block. It was the coming of a prophet, the prophet Moses. God sends down prophets as His messengers, as preachers and instructors of mankind, as their spiritual guides and saviors, and, in some cases, as in this, also as transmitters of the Law. How could Pharaoh, a mere earthly king, just quintessential dust, hope to prevail against the will and omnipotence of God? But for Him, he himself would not have been born.

The Conception and Birth of Moses

Pharaoh's men waited until the arrival of the night of the conception of Moses. Early that day they arranged to bring out the Pharaoh's banquet and throne to the town square. They proclaimed that Pharaoh was graciously pleased to invite all the Israelites to the town square so that he might show them his face, which they were legally debarred from seeing under any circumstance, and extend kindness to them for the sake of divine recompense.

Intrigued by this invitation, the Israelites hastened longingly towards the town square. There Pharaoh showed his fresh and cheerful face, gave them affection and generous presents and promises of further bounty. He said, "For your own safety, sake, sleep in the town square tonight." They readily agreed and said that if he desired, they would stay there a whole month.

Happy at having separated the men from their wives on that crucial night, Pharaoh returned to the city at nightfall, attended by Imran, his treasurer, who, although an Israelite, was dear to him and enjoyed his complete trust. He told him to sleep at the door and warned him not to visit his wife that night. Imran said that his sole thought would be Pharaoh's pleasure.

Pharaoh left and Imran slept at the door. At midnight, Imran's wife went clandestinely to see him. Falling on him, she began to rain kisses on his mouth. This woke him up and amorously he asked her how she had come at that hour.

"From desire, and from the divine decree," she said. Imran did not battle with himself, but drawing her lovingly into his embrace, lay with her and the seed was sown.

He said, "A steel struck upon a stone and a fire was born which will wreak vengeance on the Pharaoh and his kingdom. I am the cloud. You are the earth. Moses is the plant. God is omnipotent. On the chessboard of life, both victory to the true believers and defeat to the hypocrites are from Him. We are utterly helpless. Moses was conceived when I lay with you. Tell no one a thing about this visit to me or we may be stricken with a hundred griefs." Soon, she was gone.

Loud cries were now heard coming from the people from the direction of the town square, which greatly upset Pharaoh. He rushed out barefooted and asked Imran what all the uproar was about. He said, evidently the people were dancing and rejoicing because of his bounty. This did not sooth Pharaoh's fears. He paced to and fro and passed a sleepless night.

It is said that when any prophet came into the womb, his star appeared in the sky. Thus, the star of Jesus was seen by wise men in the East. They went to Bethlehem, saw Jesus and presented him with gifts—gold, frankincense and myrrh. In the case of Moses also, who was earlier in time than Jesus, his star shot up in heaven when he entered his mother's womb. But it was not an occasion for rejoicing, worship or gift-offering, but for mourning and lamentation. The astrologers trembled in dread of Pharaoh's wrath. Predesti- nation had prevailed over their contrivance. Pharaoh's enemy had come into being.

At daybreak, with Pharaoh's command, Imran rode to the town square in order to ascertain the cause of the mighty tumult. He found the astrologers in mourning, their beards and hair plucked out, their garments rent, their faces torn. He asked, "Is all well? Why all this agitation and emotion?" They said that the dreaded unlucky star had appeared in the sky. They offered profuse excuses for the failure of their plan, their voices choked with emotion, their eyes filled with blood.

Imran, although glad at heart, feigned to be mad with grief and rage. Speaking very roughly, he accused them of treachery and greed. He said that they had vowed to set Pharaoh free from cares, but had deceived him.

Pharaoh, who had arrived and heard their excuses, also said that they were traitors and parasites. They made him spend riches on his enemies for nothing. For years they had been taking from him robes of honor and wealth and devouring the kingdom as they pleased. Was this their idea of loyalty and gratitude? He would hang them without mercy and rend them limb by limb.

Prostrating themselves before Pharaoh and seeking his pardon, the astrologers said that all these years they had warded off calamities successfully, except this one time. They besought his pardon. They said that they would observe by the stars the day of the enemy's birth and see that this opportunity was not lost. If they failed this time, he could gladly kill them.

Pharaoh spared them. He kept watching the days for nine months lest the hostile decree should overtake him again. He did not know that he who lies in wait to fight doom is doomed to failure. How can a painting strive with the painter?

After nine months, a strict proclamation was issued summoning the women with new-born babies to the town square, saying that just as Pharaoh had given robes of honor to the men the previous year, this year he would bestow treasures on the women and golden toys on the children.

Suspecting no guile, the women went joyfully with their babies to Pharaoh's pavilion. When all the women had gathered round him, his officers took away all the male children from their mothers and beheaded them so that Pharaoh's enemy might not grow up, that no disorder spread, and that he might continue to reign supreme.

Imran's wife, however, managed to stay away from the town square. The villainous Pharaoh sent midwives into the houses as spies in order to ensure that no baby had been surreptitiously kept back from this doom. After careful inquiries, they reported that a cunning, comely women—Imran's wife—had a newborn male child, but she did not come and bring him to the town square. The officers went twice to her house to investigate. Following the divine revelation, she threw the child amid the fire on the first occasion. As he was spiritually of Adam's stock, the Lord's words, *"O fire, be cool,"* which protected Abraham [21:69], protected him also. The second time they came, she threw him into the Nile. He was equally safe in the water as he had been in the fire. The officers went away, finding nothing, no trace of any child. The family of Pharaoh rescued the child and reared him for many years, whereafter the Lord caused him to be restored to his mother [28:10-13].

The blind-eyed Pharaoh kept killing thousands of new-born babies—he killed 70,000, it is said—while Moses remained safe in the upper chambers of his palace. The secret weapon of Pharaoh was a dragon that had swallowed the magicians of the kings of the world. But one greater than he was now born whose rod became a dragon that with God's help, as will be seen later, swallowed Pharaoh. *"Hand is above 'hand."* And, *"Over every lord of knowledge there is one more knowing,"* [12:76], right up to, "God unto Whom is the end" except, "there is no god but God and beside Whom all our devices are as naught."

But Pharaoh and his like are so blinded by conceit that they fancy themselves as God's equal, if not God himself. Some in self-justification argue that if they are being condemned for being desire's victim, God is no less a victim of desire—the desire to be 'known'—the desire for Self-manifestation as the one and the many. But this argument is based on a misunderstanding as the one and the many. This argument is based on a misunderstanding of the true nature of desire. Desire is part of the cosmic process. Without desire, there would be no life, no creation. To denigrate desire is to denigrate the creator.

Even on the human plane, one's desire for beauty and truth, or aspiration for attainment to God, is laudable and worthy of emulation. Desire becomes evil when it is egotistical or self-centered, when one deems oneself as separate and independent, and thinks that by hurting another, he can benefit without hurt to himself. The world of separateness, although a world of illusion, is a world of jealousy, strife and discord. A wise man knows that all that is without is but a reflection of all that is within his soul, nothing substantial or enduring. He knows that desire is the path to death, as in the case of Pharaoh. It is also the path to life, as in the case of Moses, who could hear the soundless sound of cosmic harmony. The same one life runs through all, inter-connecting everything.

THE TWO MIRACLES OF MOSES

At the destined hour, Moses began his prophetic mission. He said to Pharaoh, *"I am a messenger from the Lord of the worlds. I have come to you with a clear sign from Him."* When asked to produce it, he put his hand to his bosom and drew it forth. *"Behold, it was white with illumination*—'leprous as snow'. He *next cast down his rod and "lo! it was a serpent manifest"* [7:104-8].

The immediate operation of divine grace enabled Prophet Moses to perform these two miracles. His hand glowing with mystic light was a manifest sign of the splendor of divine attributes or of the light of God which was reflected from his heart and which he held in his bosom.[1]

The second miracle to whose symbolism we shall revert later, struck terror into the hearts of the beholders. They fled in panic in all directions. Many of them—25,000 according to some, seemingly an exaggerated figure—are said to have been killed in the stampede.

Pharaoh said to Moses, "By putting the people to flight and causing the death of so many, you have only earned their hatred. You are calling them to follow you, but you have no follower except your own shadow. There have been many impostors like you, but in our Egypt, they all have been exposed in the end. Your fate will be no different."

Moses said to Pharaoh, "Here I am despised, but in God's sight, I am loved, sought and approved. I admit nothing as co-partner with His command. If His command will spill my blood, I have no fear. On the day of judgment, you, not I, will be among the shamed. Glory belongs to God and His servants, but the infidels and hypocrites know it not."

Pharaoh: "I am the supreme authority at the moment. The people of the world have selected me, not you. Are you wiser than they? You are just a braggart. Do not delude yourself. I will assemble the best magicians of the world and expose your non-sense. But his needs time. Give me forty days and this will be done."

Moses: "I am not commanded to give you time. If you are powerful and I have no ally, what matter? He is the only real Helper and I am His slave. I will fight until He commands that

I should stop. He alone separates enemy from enemy."

When Pharaoh again said that he must give him a respite, an instant revelation came to Moses from God, "Gladly give him forty days' time. Fear not! Let him prepare a hundred diverse devices. I am not asleep. I will confound them all."

Moses gave the respite and left for his abode, the dragon following him, wagging its tail, wise and loving like the hunter's trained dog, but, in the air, wild and uncontrolled, rising above the Zodiac, terrorsome like the astrological dragon which was believed to cause eclipses. When Moses reached his people, he took hold of its mouth and it became a staff as before. Moses leaned upon it [20:21].

THE SPIRIT AND DRAGON SYMBOLISM

Rumi says that the dragon of Pharaoh is in us. It is the accursed animal soul. As we lack its unlimited resources and opportunities for self-indulgence within us, it is restricted in viciousness. Otherwise, it would act like a Pharaoh, as a mere fable, involving another, and feel offended if it is said to be our own story, of what passes in us. The accursed animal soul drives us far from God. "In the serpent see Iblis," says Rumi elsewhere.

In all these cases, the serpent or dragon symbolizes evil. But symbols change their meaning. Things pass into their opposites. To go back to the origin, in every ancient language, the word 'dragon' signified the being who excels in wisdom. The serpent with its own tail in it's mouth symbolized eternity. It watches the entrance to the realm of secret knowledge. The great dragon was the constellation of the dragon. The dragon symbolizing the spiritual initiator had respect only for the serpents of wisdom, not for the disbelieving collective mediocrity. This may explain the terrorsome postures assumed by the astrological dragon mentioned earlier in relation to the rod of Moses. The earliest adepts and hierophants, the human originals for whom it was claimed that they were initiated into the mysteries of nature by the universal mind represented by the highest angels, are even to this day called the 'dragons of wisdom'.

THE WAY TO REAL KNOWLEDGE

Moses wondered at God's eye-bandaging of the worldlings, these unbelievers. "Their eyes and ears are open and yet they cannot see the whole world flushed with the rosy light of the morning sun," he said within himself. "What shines wakeful day to me is midnight gloom to them. I am surprised at them. They are surprised at me. I took so much of the pure wine of Reality to them, but it meant nothing to them. That wine is for the pure in spirit, for those void of self. As they were blinded by self, how could they appreciate its worth? I took spiritual roses to them, but each rose was a thorn to them. Creation is based on contraries, although watered with one water [13:4]. One has to be a wakeful sleeper so that he may dream dreams in his wakeful state, and, asleep to worldly affairs, receive spiritual ideas. Speech, thought and recollection of created things are an enemy to such sleep. A mystic bewilderment is needed to sweep away thought and recollection.

MYSTIC BEWILDERMENT

This bewilderment is no ordinary bewilderment. In the famous 12th/13th century mystic Attar's *Mantiq al-tayr* (*Conference of the Birds*), bewilderment is the sixth of the seven valleys which the Sufi has to cross on the way to Reality. In this valley, as described by Attar, one is so sunk in God, so drunk with Him, that he forgets all, himself not excluded, forgets whether he is living or dead, manifest or unmanifest. He is neither a lover nor the beloved and has no awareness of love, except that he has a heart that is at once full and empty of love. His dazzlement arises from the infinite diversity of forms of His manifestation and from proximity to the divine light which is dark from excess of brilliance.

DIVINE KNOWLEDGE

God has said, *"Lo, unto Him we are returning."* The return to Him is like the homeward return of a herd of goats after their descent to the water. The leading goat, the first to get to the water, is now the last, and the lame hindmost goat is now the first. The prophets and saints became lame by giving up external knowledge, which quests outward and leads to worldly success, but knows nothing of the way to God which runs inward into the cave of self. The more perfect is one in exoteric knowledge, the more backward is he in reality, though more forward in appearance.

In the words of the Prophet, we are "the hindmost and the foremost," the last in appearance and the first in reality. For all created things the heavens themselves were but a preparation for the coming of the perfect human being, the roof and crown of creation. Why should then one seek to be in the front for the sake of passing worldly glory and fame, and not be lame, if lameness in the return journey to Him makes him the leader?

Whatever the academicians and intellectuals may think, the truth is that all the common means of knowledge are of little avail on the path to God. Sensual perception cannot transcend the world of the senses, the world of desire in its two fold aspect of attraction and repulsion, repulsion also is a form of desire, but in its negative aspect. Imagination and fantasy can run riot, giving to airy nothings a local habitation and a name. Nor can our much vaunted intellect do more than receive and perfect in some measure the second hand material supplied to it by the senses and imagination. It is subject to fantasies and can lose itself in the mist of speculation. It is the outward form of mystical knowledge, but a stranger to the archetypal ideas, or what Plato calls the 'eternal ideas', and needs guidance from the universal mind.

Philosophers tend to use the analytical method in their search for Truth. They select a limited number of elements from the unlimited number that constitutes this multitudinous universe and by careful observation and study, seek to ascend to a knowledge of the whole. But their basic material is far from adequate. The process of observation is not exempt from error. It is subject to the opinion of the observer and opinions vary and clash. Hence, lack certainty. The analytical method is entirely unsuitable for our purpose.

Divine knowledge is synthetic. It is a knowledge of the whole arising out of mystical experience or divine illumination needing no coil of premise and conclusion, no prop of sense and intellect, or of logic and philosophy—not even of sacred literature which may bring inner peace and bliss, but is an attachment for the soul, a bondage for the light of consciousness. It is a knowledge of the unity of life, of the harmony and interlinkedness of things. They are not separate and independent as is commonly believed.

In the esoteric school not even is the knowledge of the alphabet necessary. The Prophet is said to have been formally illiterate. But he was the supreme type of the perfect human being, illumined by universal intellect. Knowledge is in the soul and of the soul and in itself the soul. Inward regression is wisdom. Outward progression is folly. It is ignorance. The saint may not be honored in this world, but he is exalted in eternity. God knows best about His servants. He confers the treasure of gnosis on the perfect human beings, the saints, who have laid waste their bodily nature and live in mystical poverty and exoteric ignorance, lame and despised. A treasure of gold is safe if hidden in obscure ruins.

While the discursive intellect, as stated earlier, is not always reliable, the universal intellect is wholly exempt from time's wrongs. Hence Rumi's exhortation—sell discursive intellect and buy bewilderment in God. Abandon self, eschew traditional and exoteric knowledge—what "God has taught us" [2:31] alone is real. Let us seek it from Him who sets His favored ones on its quest and is the giver of knowledge. Seek an infinite cornerless corner of the illuminated heart, His passage-way, where it is inscribed in indelible letters of gold.

THE TWO MAGICIANS OF PHARAOH

When Moses went back home, Pharaoh remained with his people and sent for his advisors. They all thought it right that magicians of renown from all over Egypt should be summoned. He sent out messengers in all directions to them. Of all the magicians, two were regarded as complete masters who would travel mounted on a wine jar, even draw down the moon and produce milk from its beams and perform countless other incredible tricks. Pharaoh's message to them said that he needed their help, as two dervishes, Moses and Aaron, had marched against him and his palace carrying just a rod which became a dragon at the command of Moses reducing Pharaoh and his whole army to helplessness and lamentation. The remedy must be sought in magic, their only hope. Nothing else could save their lives from these two sorcerers.

When the two magicians received this message, fear and love descended on them. As they were one in spirit with Moses, their spiritual affinity with him made itself felt. They laid their heads on their knees—the knee is the Sufi's school—and began to meditate, seeking a solution to the problem that had arisen. Ascertaining from their mother the way to their father's grave, they went there seeking spiritual information, summoned his spirit, and acquainted it with Pharaoh's message and the calamity that lay in the rod of Moses. They asked the spirit whether the performance of the two dervishes was magic or something divine as they hoped, in which case they would bow down before them, and, in their company, become pure in spirit.

The spirit said, "I am not permitted to give a plain answer to your question although the mystery is not far from my eyes. I will show you a decisive sign so that what is unmanifest to you may become manifest. First, go and ascertain where Moses sleeps. When he is sleeping, go for the rod without fear if you are able. Moses is a magician. When a magician is asleep there is none to direct his magic. If you are unable to take it, take good heed. For he is God's messenger and is directly guided by

Him. Although Pharaoh may seize the world, he will fall headlong before Him, for who can prevail against God? Common sorcery is but trickery and deception. But God's magic, whether it takes the form of miraculous powers given to prophets and saints, or of illusions set up to tempt his foes to death and destruction, is true and real."

The two kissed their father's grave and went to Egypt. Guided by the people, they went to the palm grove where they found Moses sleeping among the date trees. His eyes were closed for spiritual relaxation, but his illumined heart was awake. He had all heaven and earth under his contemplation's gaze.

The eye of water and clay can see nothing spiritual. If one's heart is unilluminated, let him keep vigil and be in constant strife with his animal or carnal self. When his heart has been awakened, he sees by the light of God and contemplates all that exists. He may sleep without care for the seven heavens and the six directions will lay down their veil before the eye of his heart. The Prophet said, "My eye sleeps, but when is my heart asleep?" When Pharaoh is awake, what matter if the guardsman is asleep?

Seeing Moses asleep, the two magicians tried to steal the rod from the wakeful sleeper. Hardly had they made a move when the rod began to shake. Quivering upon itself, it turned into a dragon and rushed at them. Stricken with terror and panic, they fled, falling on their faces, tumbling over every slope. Seeing that this was beyond any magic, they became sure that Moses was heavenly. Later, fever and diarrhea seized them and death seemed near. They sent a man to Moses to beseech his forgiveness for what they had done, admitting that in testing him, they were motivated by envy and were sinners against God. He pardoned them. They regained their health and prostrated themselves before Moses. He said, "Your bodies and souls have become safe from hell. Although one in spirit with you, I could not make you out with your alien appearance,"—he pretended from politeness. [Pretended ignorance is not uncommon among Sufis]. "Come, as you are and fight for God." They kissed the earth and departed, waiting for an opportunity to fight for Him.

The rod of Moses was a wondrous rod. God once likened the Koran to this rod, the death of Muhammad to the sleep of Moses and promised Muhammad that the word of God would remain inviolate until the resurrection. Those who sought to change or annul the religion after his death were like these two magicians of Pharaoh who vainly sought to carry off the rod when Moses was asleep.

As arranged, the host of magicians from different cities gathered before Pharaoh and received robes of honor. He also gave them slaves, horses, cash, and goods and promised further most magnificent gifts if they proved superior to Moses in the trial.

They said, "We are champions in our art. None in the world can resist us." They pledged themselves to subdue the enemy and ruin his cause. Little did they know that it was a fight not against a mere rod, but against the light of Moses, against the light of God Himself.

The trial was now to begin. The magicians honored Moses by giving him precedence and seeking his command as to whether he would cast his rod first or they. This much show of respect earned them belief in the true faith.[2]

He said, "Throw." They threw their rods and cast a mighty spell on the spectators. Moses then cast this rod. It swallowed up the enchanting objects their sorcery had produced. They saw the tokens of the Lord in their defeat. The truth stood vindicated. Prostrating themselves, they said, *"We believe in the Lord of the worlds, the Lord of Moses and Aaron"* [7:121-122].

"How dare you believe in Him before I give leave?" said Pharaoh. You have plotted this plot in the city to drive people from it. I shall have your hands and feet cut off and then crucify you for flouting me and my gods" [7:123].

Pharaoh thought that this threat of punishment would shake them and fill them with terror and trembling, but he had miscalculated. He did not know that they were no longer the carnal souls he had imagined, but transmuted individuals. They had recognized the difference between their shadowy bodies and their real selves, their essence, which is beyond this world of illusion. As they had seen the origin of this bodily composition, they were unafraid of any bodily affections which belong to this insubstantial world of imagination. "This world," said the Prophet, "is the sleeper's dream." It is no harm if the body is mutilated in dreams. The clairvoyant eye of the mystic has beheld this truth. But ordinary mortals are lost in the sleep of ignorance. They are never awake and so are never conscious of reality. The sense objects they see in their waking hours and imagine as real are materialized images of the dream world, the world of archetypal images (*alam-i-mithal*), "where spirits are corporalized and bodies spiritualized."

They think they lose consciousness when they go to sleep, but this really is a second sleep, a transition from one stage of fantasy to another, a return to the intermediate world which is between the world of non-existence, of pure abstract ideas, and our narrow world of external existence, both sensible and spiritual.

Addressing Pharaoh, the magicians said, "We are living through God and have built ourselves an everlasting security. Come, do your worst! Rend this bodily raiment! There is One who will stitch it again. Death is not the end, but only the disintegration of the bodily particles. Thereafter, God draws the spiritual faculties of the deceased together and makes another body for them." As nothing gross or physical can exist in the spiritual world, the body fashioned after death is a 'bodiless body'. If He does not stitch the rent raiment, what matter? What could be sweeter than the naked embrace of the beauteous beloved?[3] People do not know that He is All-forgiving and says to him who believes in Him, "*Enter Paradise*" [36:25-26]. It was such ignorance that the Prophet had in mind when he said, "Oh would that my people knew."

THE ETERNAL "I-HOOD" WITHOUT "I"

Continuing, they said, "The Lord's munificence has bestowed on us a kingdom which, unlike yours, is living and majestic. Renounce this tattered mantle, this body, and renounce the Nile and Egypt by which you are deluded. There are a hundred Niles and Egypts within the Nile and Egypt of the spirit. Know that the spirit of the human being reflects the splendor of the divine attributes. The entire finite universe is but its reflection. You say to the people, "I as your Lord the supreme." You are ignorant of the real meaning of the words 'I' and 'Lord'. How should a Lord be trembling with uncertainty for that which is under his lordship—the world and the flesh? How should one who know that his real self is the eternal 'I-ness' of which this phenomenal body is only a shadow or reflection, be in thrall to body and soul? Behold, we are the real 'I' delivered from the unreal 'I', from the 'I' that is full of trial and tribulation, from the 'I' that is an insuperable hurdle to union with the light of God. Not if you will seek the real 'I', but if you die to consciousness and self, will the eternal 'I-ness' which you seek become your seeker, and you will rise from self-mortification to life eternal and diffuse spiritual light. Speculative thinking or intellectual philosophy cannot on the contrary reach it. On the contrary, it may land one in the heresies of incarnation and absolute nearness to God. Thanks to your malicious 'I-hood', such fortune has come to our lot. We are dying in desire of death. In gratefulness for your freeing us from the perishable abode, we are warning you that while we journey to heaven—a life hidden in the form of death—your abode, O Pharaoh, is a death hidden in the shell of life."

But all this admonition was wasted on Pharaoh. At the hour of amputation of their hands and feet, the magicians said, *"It is no hurt, for lo, unto our Lord we shall return"* [26:50]. But how should the tyrannical, sin-soaked Pharaoh know that by punishing them, he was delivering them from the pain of separation from God. He had no conception of the eternal I-hood which is the passport to the city of God.

The personal self or I of daily life and the individual enduring ego or the eternal I are not two, not separate and independent, but manifestations of the same mind. The difference between them is that while the personal I sees in the mode of plurality, deeming all objects as separate and independent, the eternal I, looking beyond the personal I, sees in the mode of unity, deeming all objects as harmoniously interlinked. The attainment of this eternal I-hood is hard and arduous. It is generally not possible without spiritual guidance, meditation and ascetic practices.

MOSES AND PHARAOH IN DIALOGUE

Spiritual reason is the opposite of sensuality while imagination is sensuality's beggar. Spiritual reason is the sterling gold of rational qualities, while imagination is its counterfeit. Without a touchstone, however, one cannot be clearly distinguished from the other. The touchstone is the Koran. The spiritual knowledge of the prophets. If one given to imagination comes in touch with a prophet, he may see himself and know that he is undeserving of even the lowest degree of his spiritual knowledge.

To Moses belonged spiritual reason. To Pharaoh belonged imagination or carnal reason. When they met, Pharaoh asked him, "Who are you?"

"I am reason, the messenger and the proof of God, the refugee against error," said Moses.

"Stop this ecstatic bombast. Tell me your ancient lineage and name," Pharaoh said.

Moses said, "My lineage is from His dust-pit. My original name is 'the meanest of His slaves'. From Adam and Eve downward, all my ancestors were His slaves. My original lineage is from earth and water and clay. To water and clay God gave a soul and heart. The origin of all of us, of all the proud also, is derived from earth. From the earth the earthen body receives nutriment. Upon the departure of the spirit, the body becomes earth once again in the terrible grave. There your power also will be interred with your bones."

Pharaoh said, "A more proper name for you is slave of Pharaoh and slave of his slaves—son of Imran, Pharaoh's slave, first nurtured through him, a rebellious slave who after committing a murder, fled from Egypt in order to escape my judgment. You are in exile and are despised and poor for not acknowledging debt and duty to me."

"The Lord has no partner or associate in His Lordship," said Moses. "His slaves have no master but Him. This creation is all His handiwork. He is my sole designer. None has a share in this work. You cannot even fashion an eyebrow, let alone know my soul. It is not I, but you who are the traitor and rebel, for you claim duality with God. It was only inadvertently, not for self's sake, that I killed a mere cur, one soulless, dead in spirit, but you killed thousands of innocent babes, the progeny of the prophet Jacob, in hope of killing me. God chose me out, despite you, and your plots against me came to naught."

"Granted what you say is true," said Pharaoh. "Is it your idea of gratitude for the bread and salt I gave you in your infancy that you should treat me meanly in public?" [26:18].

"Much worse will be the humiliation you will suffer at the resurrection," said Moses, "if you do not heed me in good and evil. I may seem to be ruining your work, but in reality, I am seeking to convert your disbelief into the bliss of faith. I am your ladder to heaven."

One should know that in this world of contraries, there can be no restoration without devastation, no wholeness without brokenness, no existence without non-existence. The soil has to be cloven before it can be cultivated and become an orchard or a cornfield. Bread gives strength only when broken. Grapes yield wine only when crushed. One has to die to self before he can be spiritually born. Not-being is the mirror of being. The death of the body is the life of the soul.

"The obligation of gratitude demands," continued Moses, "that I should deliver you from this vicious net of evil in which you have entangled yourself, have made yourself a slave of sensuality. Instead of keeping your soul separate from desire, you have fattened it with power and riches, and allowed this mere worm, your soul, to grow into a mighty dragon. I have brought a mightier dragon—the prophet's divinely-inspired breath—to destroy the dragon of your sensual nature. If you will follow my counsel and put your faith in God, you will be delivered from sensuality. Or else, the latter will bring your spirit into the mouth of hell."

Pharaoh said, "You are really a master sorcerer, for you have divided my people into two factions. Sorcery can drive holes even in rock and mountain."

Moses responded, "I am sunk in the message of God. Sorcery can never by associated with the name of God nor even with mine. The substance of sorcery is nothing but heedlessness of God, nothing but disbelief, while my transcendental prophetic spirit is the guiding light of revelation [42:52]. As you are evil thinking, you bear that evil thought against me."

As we are parts of this world, whatever be our mental state, we tend to deem all to be of the same kind as ourselves. If we are bestial, we deem even the noble as bestial. If we are whirling round and become giddy, we see the house whirling round though it is stationary. If we are happy, the world seems gay like a garden of roses. One may travel from China to Peru, but as his sole object of perception is generally color and perfume, just external phenomena, he will only see what is in accord with his disposition. He will feed on self-deception and illusion. He will see nothing spiritual anywhere. Bestial in nature, his spirit bound by secondary causes will never grow. Whatever is permanently rooted in one aspect, be it the fields of Elysium or the fountains of paradise, becomes ugly after a time. But to the mystic who has entered the earth of God, the boundless mystic anemone field which transcends all means and causes, everything gross or physical, and who has experienced a new creation at every moment, all in perpetual flux, changing changing, ever renewing itself, God reveals Himself in His infinite forms and aspects.

THE PERCIPIENT AND THE SPIRITUAL SENSE

Our perception is a measure of our vision of the truth of men and things. In everyday life, each percipient sense performs its own specific function and is ignorant of the functions of the other percipient senses. The eye can see beauty and all that is visible, but the ear can perceive no visible form—ugly or beautiful. The latter's art is the perception of sound. To the nose, sight and sound mean nothing. Its function is the perception of smell.

Again, the crooked sense has a crooked perception. He who sees double cannot see unity. As Moses would say to one who was squint-eyed and full of deceit and hypocrisy like Pharaoh: "You know no difference between you and me. Do not judge of me by your self, so that you may not see one as two, but judge me as I am, judge with my eyes, so that you may behold beyond this phenomenal world of manyness a spacious world with which I am spiritually one. Merge yourself in me, as a disciple merges himself in the master so that, delivered from sensuality and this illusive world, you may attain to vision of the truth, of unity beyond plurality.

Originally there was no relationship between seeing and the eye. The eye is not the source of vision. Luminosity does not reside in the white of the eye. If it did, how could forms become visible in dream. Initially, the eye was just embryonic flesh, with no vision. It is God's mercy that has given relationship to light and the eye. Sensuous light dwells in the eye and produces physical vision, but it is derived from God.

What is true of the eye and vision, is also true of the other sense organs and their faculties. No sense is the source of its peculiar faculty.

Nor are the five senses unconnected. Corresponding to the five external senses are five spiritual senses or five faculties of the soul. They are linked with one another, as they are derived from one source, the universal spirit. They serve to manifest the divine attributes, which are not separate but involved in one another, so that when one sense is freed from the body, the other senses also are similarly freed and they all unite in one sense. The eye becomes an ear to hear and the ear an eye to behold. Why only the senses? Bastami, the eminent 9th century Sufi says, "Every hair of a gnostic becomes a seeing eye." His body is all spirit.

Although God relates the unrelated, the relation of derivatives to their originals transcends understanding. Adam is of earth, but has no resemblance to it. If the fire had no spiritual eye, how did it show respect to Abraham and become *"cool and peaceful"* when Nimrod threw him into it [21:69]? If the mountain and rock were sightless, how should they have accompanied David as minstrels? If the Nile were sightless, how should it have distinguished between the Egyptians and the Israelites? [2:50]. If the wind were unseeing, how should it have destroyed the people of Ad? [69:6]. At the resurrection, the spiritual-eyed earth will relate its chronicles, and show us every good and evil we have done on earth [99:4, 7-8]. When God wills a thing, He says to it, *"Be,"* and it is [16:40]. This is clear proof that all elements, all objects we deem inanimate, are alive before Him and hear and obey Him in proportion to their perception—and have their morning and evening hymns.

MOSES WARNS PHARAOH

"The Lord of judgment has been sending you terrible visions," said Moses to Pharaoh, "suitable to your evil conscience, including that of sending me as a prophet with a rod and the light—the white hand of Moses, the light of God—to break your name and fame, so that you might know that He is omniscient and knows what cure is best for you. He is the healer of all incurable ailments. But you took no heed. Your physician and astrologer understood the meaning of the visions, but from motives of cupidity, knowing that you are not the kind to desire good counsel and are unreasonable and blood thirsty, gave you false interpretations. Of course, the ruler must not be effeminate, for effeminacy would render him ineffective as a ruler. He may shed blood in a righteous cause. But mercy should always precede his wrath, as it does with the Lord. But you harbor the devil in your breast and have wounded countless innocent hearts.

"Worldlings like you attack people of the other world, going as far as the frontier of generation and corruption to stop the coming of the elect spirits into this world. The infidels attack holy men when the latter do not attack them, so that for them, there is nothing to fear. But how can you block the frontier passes which God has created for procreation? You sought to block them, but despite you a captain came forth. Behold, I am that captain. I will break your power and pride. Mend your ways or the divine decree will crush you. But of what avail are my words? You are deaf to them. God has given everything its original nature. Some He has created to be the vessels of mercy, some to be the vessels of wrath. Good is rewarded with good. Good words from us are rewarded with divine blessings. Evil will be punished with evil.

"When wickedness blackens the heart, we should not become besotted here or grief will strike us in retribution for our besottedness unless His bounty intervenes. If we would have a pure and understanding heart, this can be gained by being observant, by means of meditation, knowing that God watches over us, and worshipping Him as though seeing Him. We will then see every moment the response to our actions—good for good, evil for evil—and will not have to wait for its revelation till the coming of the resurrection.

"If we aspire to mystic contemplation of the Lord, a higher spiritual experience than of the observant which former is reserved for the elect, we should keep polishing to clear it of darkness. Our polishing instrument is reason. The body is receptive to its polishing. When the heart is cleared of the rust of worldliness, it will become like a mirror and reflect all the divine attributes. Even in this world, we will then see, not as a mere fantasy, but by immediate vision, paradise and hell, the resurrection and all manner of forms of the unseen.

"But we are prayerless. Our sensuality has chained reason and made our nature sinful and dark. We have made war on God and the prophets and do evil on the earth, so that our doom on the day of resurrection will be painful and lasting [5:36-37]. We should tie up sensuality, so that reason may be untied."

Inspired from the unseen, Moses declared the secret thoughts and visions of Pharaoh, so that he might come to believe in the omniscience of God. He said, "God showed you from your own nature, not without purpose, what should befall you in the end. He showed you hideous forms in dreams from which you shrank back, although in reality they were your own form. The mirror reflects only what is before it, ugly or beautiful. Sometimes you saw in vision that you were disgraced or were in the jaws of a wild beast or were sunk in a torrent of blood. Now a voice came to you from heaven, now from the mountain, now for every inanimate thing that you were damned, eternally damned. You saw even worse things. I have told you just a little, but enough for you to know that I know the whole. How much longer will you flee from these evil signs? The doom they shadow forth has almost overtaken you.

"But all is not lost. Take heed! The door of repentance, which is one of the eight doors of paradise, is open to the human being until the resurrection. It is the only door that is always open. The other seven are sometimes shut and sometimes open. Seize the opportunity and repent."

Moses Promises Four Gifts

"Come, accept and implement one counsel from me, and take four gifts as recompense."

"What is that one counsel?" asked Pharaoh.

"That one counsel," said Moses, "is that you say publicly that there is no God but the Maker, that He is the Creator of heaven and earth and all that is therein, whose sovereignty is unlimited and He is without like."

PARADISE AND HELL ARE INTERCHANGEABLE

According to Rumi, paradise and hell and all pairs of opposites like good and evil, faith and unbelief, are aspects in which God manifests Himself to our consciousness. The spiritual person manifests His beauty and the carnal person, His wrath. The four fountains of paradise symbolize His beautiful attributes. The penal fires and freezing cold of hell symbolize His wrathful attributes. All these contraries like His attributes are unified in the divine essence. Their contrariness relates only to this world of appearance. Coming from a single indivisible source, they can be interchanged if God so decrees.

Pharaoh was aware of the possibility of this interchange and hoped that through the influence of the four paradisical fountains his evil qualities might be purified, so that he would take to noble actions which would turn his anguish of unbelief into the bliss of faith. With this hope, he said, "O Moses, tell me what four gifts you promise in recompense. Bring them before me. It is possible that by favor of those fair promises my unbelief will die. Perchance, by the reflection of the river of honey, this malice of mine may turn into honey. Perhaps by the reflection of the river of milk, my captive reason may receive nourishment. Perhaps by the river of wine, I may experience intoxicating delight from obedience to His command. Perhaps by the river of water, my barren body may gain freshness. Thus by the reflection of paradise and its four rivers, God may befriend me, and I may become His seeker. This will be in the same manner as at present, when by the reflection of hell, I have become fire steeped in His wrath. By that of its flames, I am as the flames. By that of its freezing cold, I am like that cold. I am the hell of the poor and the oppressed. Woe to them whom I find all of a sudden under by control."

Moses said, "The first gift is constant good health for the body. The second, a long life. After an unbreached happy life, you will go forth from this world, but not in pain, not against your will, but desiring death, seeing that there is treasure in the ruin of the body, that beyond this dark and woe-stricken world, is the camp of the divine king crowded with the army of light." As goes the Lord's command in the divine book, we should vie with one another in hastening—hastening towards God's own town.

"I WAS A HIDDEN TREASURE"

The reason for creation was God's desire for the manifestation of the 'hidden treasure' of His attributes. The human being is the culmination of creation, for he alone reflects all His attributes. Other creatures reflect only some, not all. But unless he manifests them as God has manifested them in him, he can not become perfect and fulfill the ultimate purpose of creation. The treasure is within him, in his soul and spirit, in his heart, but veiled by the body.

Hence, one has to destroy the house of the body in order to gain the treasure beneath. The invisible spirit within contains the splendor of the divine attributes. This cosmos is nothing but its image, its self-projection. If one does not destroy this house, it will of itself fall into ruin one day. As he has not earned the treasure by self-negation, it will not be his. God will withhold it. The spirit will receive that treasure as recompense for destroying the body. There is nothing for the human being in the other world except the recompense for that which he did here [53:39]. This Pharaoh was to discover for himself, but only when it was too late. We have not purchased this body. It is not our property. We have only hired it until death to work in during this period. But we are only keeping it going and fattening it with food and drink, delighting ourselves with colorful pictures and paintings, while two mines of treasure under it are buried unworked—those of spirit and reason which constitute the real nature of the human being. One should hasten and demolish the body, for, otherwise, when the bodily lease ends, he will gnaw his hand in grief, and say, "Alas, this shop, this body was mine. If I had died to self and not let myself be deluded by the false imaginings of my animal, carnal nature, the treasure would have been mine. Now the body and the treasure are gone and my hand is empty." But it is only when one seeks divine knowledge, which is the knowledge possessed by the prophets and saints that he can delight in dying to bodily senses and faculties, and be quit of grief.

"Enough," said Pharaoh, "Tell me the third gift I am eager to hear."

"The third gift is a dual empire, temporal and spiritual, free from adversity and opposition. Even when you are at war with God, He has given you this grand empire and such goodly gifts. Think how much grander will be the empire and how much better the gifts when you are faithful to Him."

"What is the fourth gift? Tell me quickly, for my patience is gone."

"The fourth is that you will enjoy eternal youth and virility, with hair ever black, cheeks pink and unfurrowed, and figure straight as a cypress. Although color and perfume are virtually of no worth in the eyes of prophets, I mention these gifts in keeping with the Tradition, 'Speak to men in measure with their understanding, not in measure with yours.' I speak to you as to a child."

"You have spoken well," said Pharaoh, but give me time to consult my wife."

HIS WIFE'S EXHORTATION

Pharaoh told his wife Asiya what Moses had said to him. She sprang up from her place and said, "Blessed are you, O black-hearted man! Moses has offered you a tiara of faith which will cover your multitude of sins. Hidden behind his words are many favors from God. It is as if He is showing solicitude for iblis. When that bounteous promise came and the Lord called you back with such kindness, it is a wonder that your heart did not burst for the sake of His favor, so that by your burst heart, you may, like the martyrs, experience bliss in both worlds."

True, this heedlessness of God is a manifestation of divine wisdom. Without it, with everyone full of God, who would run the affairs of this world and manifest His attributes? Other-worldliness would overthrow this-worldliness. There would be no good and evil for the soul of the human being to choose between. These contraries are necessary for His manifestation, and they provide the conditions for human probation and for the attainment of spiritual perfection. The heedless person must, therefore, endure. While he need not be contemplating Him all the time, why must he ignore Him altogether and make heedlessness a poison to spirit?

Where can one find such a gainful bargain as with God? The Prophet has said, "Whosoever belongs to God, God shall belong to him." It is stated in the Koran that God has purchased from the true believers their lives and possessions in return for paradise, so that they can buy whole rose nurseries with a single rose, hundreds of mines with a single groat. That groat is devotion to God.

"Our weak, unstable personality" she continued, "became existent as a fleeting reflection from the infinite eternal He of the Lord. When it dies to its separate personal self, it finds the universal self, which is the root and essence of our being. It belongs to Him and becomes eternal. It is like a drop of water which perishes from the effects of the sun, wind and earth. When it casts itself into the sea, it is delivered from their destructive influence. Its outward form is lost, but its essence is inviolate. Similarly, immersion in the sea of divine essence secures the sprit from corruption by earth and carnal desire. O you who are like a drop, cast yourself into the sea and feel safe in the hand of the sea! Fortunately for you, a sea has become the suitor for a drop. Buy and sell in God's name instantly. Give the drop and take a sea full of pearls. For the offer of Moses comes from the sea of grace. It is exalting you, one of the meanest, to the highest heaven. All other grace vanishes before this grace."

Pharaoh said, "I will talk it over with my advisor Haman, for a ruler must take counsel with his minister."

Asiya, who is said to have been true to her faith and praying for deliverance from him, tried to dissuade him from consulting Haman, saying, "What does one spiritually blind know about a man of God?"

But Pharaoh had no ear for Asiya's admonition. Congener always flies to congener. Jesus and Idris (Enoch) ascended to heaven, being homogeneous in intelligence with the angels. The infidels are homogeneous with satan and have learnt hatred, envy and countless other evils from him. As Pharaoh was homogeneous with Haman and both had the nature of hell, he went to Haman.

Homogeneity is a great attractor that shows one's real nature. One who is attracted to Haman is a slave of his carnal self. One who is attracted to Moses is a glorifier of God. If one is attracted to both, it is because both carnal self and reason are mingled in him. The two are at war. He should take heed and strive for the triumph of spiritual realities over the sensuous forms.

PHARAOH AND HIS VIZIER HAMAN

When Haman heard what Moses had told Pharaoh, he rent his shirt and broke into loud cries and sobs, saying, "How dare Moses utter such vain and impudent words before the ruler? You have conquered the world. Sultans from all over bring you tribute without dispute. The entire world worships you. To burn in a thousand fires is better than this, that the Lord should now become the slave's servant. Behead me first, so that my eye may not behold this servility in the ruler. May it never be that the earth should become the sky and the sky the earth." These evil words of the accursed Haman prevailed on Pharaoh to reject the gracious offer of Moses.

MOSES, PHARAOH, AND THE DIVINE WILL

Both Moses and Pharaoh were servants of God. But while Moses was guided aright, Pharaoh went off the path. God has implanted certain predispositions in us from which we cannot escape. In whatever we do we only fulfill His purpose. All actions proceed from His Essence and attributes. He is the sole actor and has the sole right to say, "I am."

Every person—the 'veriest scare-crow', the 'dullest clod-pole', the 'haughtiest feather-head'—has a bit of the divine light in him. Pharaoh could be no exception, but he was not destined to see it shine. In the solitude of the night, when he had none to call him, 'My Lord', or feed his ego, he would look within himself, become repentant of his evil ways and weep, crying, "O God, Your Will has illumined Moses and the same Will has darkened me. We both worship You and execute Your decree. I beseech you to make our crooked actions straight—mine and those of my like—and not to wreck my reputation."

God is not only Guide as He was to Moses, but also Misguide, as he was to Pharaoh. Creation is based on contraries. Our war and peace is not from us, but from between the fingers of God. He does what He pleases.

Again, Pharaoh would say to himself, "Do I not spend all night crying, 'O my Lord?' In secret, I grow humble and harmonious, but when I face Moses, why do I become different? My body and spirit are under His control. At one moment He makes me a kernel, at another moment a rind. At one moment a reflecting light. At another moment without light. Before the strokes of the bat of His decree, we are running like balls in space and in spacelessness." Pharaoh thus was in a state of change, an evil-doer by day and a supplicant by night.

According to Ibn al-Arabi, when God took Pharaoh's life, he was pure and sinless and had embraced the true faith. Some scholars reject this view. It would seem that what Ibn al-Arabi had in mind was the sameness of the source and destination of Moses and Pharaoh in the divine Essence, and their faithful execution of the divine will and decree in the phenomenal world, manifesting His contrary attributes of beauty and of wrath—attributes, although different of manifestation, here indistinguishably in the divine Essence. In this sense, both were faithful servants of God, both equally obedient to Him.

COLOR AND COLORLESSNESS

Using the color symbolism, Rumi says:

> Since colorlessness became the captive of color,
> One follower of Moses arose to war with another follower.
> When you attain to the colorlessness which you
>   first possessed,
> Moses and Pharaoh are at peace.
> Should you think of asking questions about this
>   mystery,
> I would say, when is the world of color devoid of
>   disputation?
> What is strange is that this color arose from that
>   which is colorless,
> And yet color arises to war with the colorless.[2]

In the colorlessness of spiritual unity, there is perfect harmony. But in the manyness of colors that arise from colorlessness and constitute the phenomenal world, color is in conflict with color. One follower of Moses is in strife with another follower. Each follows his name in their own different ways, not his essence which knows no variableness. But when denuded of color or form, they attain to their original colorlessness and are again in unity and harmony. Strife is not in the essence, not in unity, but in plurality, between form and form.

What is strange is how this color originating from that which is colorless should arise to war with the colorless? Is it the opposition of the phenomenal with the spiritual, of form with Reality? Or it is not really war, but as contrary is known by contrary, it is God's way of Self-manifestation through contraries, or His device to improve our understanding and discernment of good and evil by presenting the form and the formless Reality before us. Why rush to discord that harmony may be prized? Or is it just bewilderment, a state in which the intellect is ineffectual and the self is dead, a state sought by spiritual seekers. For it is in the wilderness of self-negation, of inmost self-regression, that the treasure of divine attributes is found, not in any outward flight of fancy or speculative thought.

The non-existent is ashamed of the existent. It was not the existent—the egoistic Pharaoh—that sought to flee from non-existence—the self-negated Moses—but the non-existent that was outwardly calling the existent to itself but was in reality repelling it. This was natural, as there is no spiritual affinity between the two. It is Reality's nature to repel illusion. It was his inward rejection by Moses that was the cause of Pharaoh's rebelliousness. The divine destiny fulfills itself in many ways.

There were moments when, under the influence of Asiya, Pharaoh felt like turning to faith, but was thwarted by destiny. On this occasion also, after she urged him to accept the offer of Moses, faith and felicity almost came to him, but Haman's evil counsel turned them back. May no ruler have a minister like Haman.

The human body, that is, one's bodily nature, is like a tree that is like the rod of Moses. Moses let the rod fall at the command of the Lord, and it became *"a snake sliding"* [20:18-20], the 'snake of eternity'. Similarly, if one obeys the divine command and does not follow his fleshly soul which is disposed to crookedness, but acts straight, his tree which is primal egoism and illusion, will be transmuted and deified and become like the burning bush of Moses, its boughs crying, *"I am God"* [28:30].

But it is only His command *"Be"* that can make such transmutation possible. That rod of Moses which became a snake was at first nothing but wood beating down leaves for his sheep. But later, when he took it up at his command, it became powerful. It defeated the hosts of Pharaoh and became their ruler. Moses smote the Nile with his rod and caused its water to become blood whenever an Egyptian would drink it. The locusts destroyed their sown fields and this afflicted them with famine and death. The Lord sent down these afflictions, so that they might heed [7:130-33].

Up went from Moses a spontaneous prayer to God, "Why all this torment for them, and this striving to convert them when you have made it known to me that they will never be disembraced from infidelity?"

God said, "Think not of the end, Moses, but deliver the message according to My command which is not without meaning. Through your persistent striving, the obstinacy and rebellious conceit of the infidels may be displayed, and also, God's guiding some aright and letting others be lost, may become manifest to all the sects. As the object of existence was the manifestation of these two attributes, it must be tested by exhorting to obedience and leading astray. The devil seduces to error. The shaykh guides aright. Both are His ministers. Both Moses and Pharaoh were subject to the divine will, like venom and antidote, light, and darkness. The Lord's gift of grace is mysterious. It is not necessarily in accordance with one's actions. It is above cause.

When the Lord's command straitened Pharaoh and his host step by step, till eventually, the whole Nile turned into blood, Pharaoh came personally to Moses, and, in all humility, said, "Pray do not repay evil with evil. We have no words of excuse. But I promise I will be obedient to your command with every fibre of my body. Pray for us, O spiritual king, so that your prayer may assuage His wrath."

Moses turned to the Lord and said, "O Lord, Pharaoh is deceiving me who am but Your agent in the deception with which You beguile Your enemies. He is deceiving Your deceiver. Shall I listen to him or give him deceit in return, so that he may know that his deceit is only derivative, and its source, like that of all human action, of all that is on earth, is from heaven?"

God said, "That our Pharaoh does not deserve that consideration. Just shake the rod so that what the locusts have destroyed may be restored. Let them turn back, so that the people may see the transformation wrought by Me. I have no need of means. They only serve as a veil so that people may attribute their success to the means they use or may pursue certain means to attain certain ends."

How should a cause proceed from itself without a spiritual cause? How should it succeed or fail except as He wills? Though Himself above all means and causes, He is the sole cause of causes and the sole determinant of their success or failure. The mystic's eye that sees nothing but God deems all secondary causes as illusion that belong to this phantasmagoria, this world of appearance. They do not belong to the world of Reality. We ourselves "are such stuff as dreams are made on." Indeed, of the entire cosmos, fantasy is the stuff. God normally lets the cause-and-effect phenomenon operate according to expectation in order that it may serve as the basis for the activity of mankind. The mystic only contemplates the immediate divine action.

FOOD FOR THE SPIRIT

The world is eating and is being eaten. To give but one example, the animal eats of the earth's herbage and grows fat. It is eaten by the human being and disappears. In turn, it becomes earth, and, as earth, it becomes a devourer of man.[3] The spirit of the common person also devours and is being devoured.

The human being does not live by bread alone. Bodily food and drink fatten the body, but hinder the fattening of the spirit. They are myrmidons of hell. Sensual desire is like an intoxicant that intoxicates the intelligence and stupefies the rational person. Wine is not the only intoxicant. Satan never drank wine. He was drunk with pride and disbelief. Drunk is he who sees that which is not. Copper and iron seem as gold to him. Sensuality blinds the spiritual eye and deafens the spiritual ear.

The human being in reality is spiritual intelligence. He is a person in virtue of his inward eye, the eye of spiritual intuition, the eye that sees the beloved and is the beloved's eye. Sensuality, disbelief, and the rest of him is but a mask that hides his reality. He should rend this mask, put on the garment of wisdom, and not lose his real self, the aspect of the divinity within.

As commanded by God, Moses moved his lips and the earth turned green with sweet herbage and precious grains. The famished people, spiritual, half-spiritual and bestial, fell to eating. They ate voraciously for a few days and their bellies were sated.

They understood that the Lord's bounty had saved them from starvation and death. But once the imperious necessity for food ceased, they forgot the Lord and His mercy. They reverted to infidelity and rebelliousness. As the Koran says, *"The human being grows insolent, for he thinks himself independent"* [96:6-7].

The fleshly soul is a follower of Pharaoh. When it is in want, it bows humbly before Moses, making supplication. When the want is satisfied, it waxes rebellious. Forgetting its sighs and cries, returns to its original infidelity and insolence. When the ass is unloaded, it kicks. Why then satisfy the animal soul? It is best to keep it hungry. Without hunger, it will never move towards God. It may weep and wail and repent now and then, but before long it will return to its usual unconsciousness of God. It will never become a true believer. Only when the fire of mortification has burnt up carnality will it become righteous. "Our birth is but a sleep and a forgetting."

The human being clings like Pharaoh to the illusion that this dream world is enduring and real because he has forgotten the world of Reality from which he has come and to which he will return—drawn up by the force of divine love, by centripetal attraction. This forgetfulness is not unnatural. When a person has been dwelling in a city for years and sees another city the moment he sleeps, he thinks that he was born and reared and has always lived in this dream city which has no real existence. No wonder the human spirit does not remember its original home and the many planes of being it has traversed during its descent to the world of matter. The perceptive faculty of the human being has been clouded by the dust of the journey, intoxicated by the wine of worldliness, and he has made no earnest effort to polish and purify his heart in order that his spiritual eye may be opened and he may see the beginning and the end of things.

This journey has indeed been a long journey for the human being, this journey from God. It is the evolution of the world spirit in countless forms, including the human, and is a journey which, not the Pharaoh in us, but a Moses or a spiritual adept can recall.

THE HUMAN BEING'S SPIRITUAL EVOLUTION

To give an idea of this journey, descending from the unmanifest spiritual cosmos, the spirit enters this manifested universe and goes through nine celestial spheres, each with a ruling intelligence: the starless sphere, (the sphere of spheres), the sphere of the fixed stars (Zodiac), and the commonly known seven planetary spheres, the last of which is the moon which is said to contain the four elements and then descends into this world as mineral. Dying to mineral, he becomes plant, whose functions are growth, assimilation and reproduction. But because of the opposition between them, he did not remember his past—except that the close clinging of greenery to rock and mountain may be due to his sub-conscious memories of his previous state. Dying to plant, he became animal, again with no remembrance of the past, except that spring with its flowers and greenery awakens sub-conscious memories of his association with his mother, the vegetal soul. Dying to animal, he became the human being as we know him with some qualities of the rock or mineral, the plant and the animal in him. The human being is the crown of creation. With his birth, to the biosphere, the envelope of life, has been added the nousphere, the envelope of thought.

New existences arise out of new deaths. Each new birth is for all purposes a forgetting of the past, except for sub-conscious memories of its ancestral association. The spirit evolves the form suitable to its evolutionary state. Our present state is not the last. We are parts of the whole. But on its own, the part cannot move. There has to be a drawing force. That drawing force is the whole. It is a reflection of divine love. All universals are God's ministers. The whole exerts its attraction upon its parts, the universal intelligence upon the particular intelligence, the master, who is identical with the whole, upon the disciple, although the latter may not be aware of it. Awareness of this pull comes when he has merged his individual intelligence in the universal intelligence, his individual self in the universal self of his master. The force of love impels all things towards unification in this world. The human being has fallen asleep in forgetfulness of his past states and in ignorance of his end, not knowing that there may be further migrations for him. Freed from his present human intelligence, which is full of cupidity and egoism, he may rise higher and behold myriads of wonderful intelligences. Ultimately, in complete self-fulfillment, he may attain the last of life for which the first was made.

THE DAY OF RETRIBUTION

The human being should have no doubt about his future. How should the Creator in His wisdom leave him in self-oblivion. He made him. How should He leave him in the dust? His love that has brought him so far will bring him again to wakefulness, so that, in self-wonder, he may say to himself how it was that he did not know that his grief and disease here was the effect of sleep, all fantasy and illusion. Yet, strangely enough, the sleeper regards the world, this sleeper's dream, as real, until a sudden death comes and he is delivered from mere opinion and falsehood. Dreams are true while they last. But there is no deliverance from retaliation for his actions. Whatever of good and evil he has done in his sleep will await him and own him at the last congregation. As joy and sorrow in dreams are commonly interpreted by their opposites, his laughter will be tears and tears joy on the day of interpretation. His disposition, if evil, will arise as a wolf and tear his limbs in anger—wolf, not in material form, but inwardly wolf reflecting his animal passions and propensities. It will not be a physical, but, as in Plato and oriental philosophy, a spiritual or allegorical metamorphosis.

The wrath and vengeance of God is His justice. The commission of a murder here attracts an immediate penalty, as the hidden interlinked world order that has been disturbed must disturb the disturbed in order to restore itself. But the penalty imposed in this world which God has called *"a play"* [6:32], is to allay civil strife. It is only *"a play"* compared with the retribution that is suffered in the other world. Thus, if the penalty for murder in the other world is like a castration, here it is only like a circumcision. Penalty is purifying.

THE DIVINE IMMANENCE

"Why worry about Pharaoh and his host?" God said to Moses. "Let these asses be fattened by self-indulgence. The ministers of divine wrath and vengeance are waiting for them like ravenous wolves. We make these asses their means of livelihood. You used your alchemical powers to make them human. You showed much favor and kindness in calling them to Me, but all to no avail. Let them revel in the sleep of ignorance so that when they wake up they will find themselves lightless and desolate. Their rebellious disobedience kept you in bewilderment. Hence they shall suffer much sorrow to the end that Our justice may step forth and measure out appropriate retaliation to the evil doer. For the king is always with them, knowing and seeing everything.

The analogy of intellect and body demonstrates His presence with us. The intellect oversees the body, though our perception cannot apprehend it, yet the perception of the intellect also is with us. If we ignore the intellect and do evil, the intellect apprehends the evil and rebukes us.

We forgot the intellect, but the intellect did not forget us. If it were not present and attentive, how should it rebuke us? And if our fleshly soul were not heedless of the intellect, would it have indulged in evil? Hence, we and our intellect are like the astrolabe by which we may know the proximity of the spiritual sun of existence. Our intellect is indescribably near us and is directionless. How should not the Creator of the intellect be indescribably near, for intellectual quest cannot find the way to Him. He is closer to us than our neck-veins, closer than ourselves.

The connection between spiritual essences and the phenomenal forms are mysterious. The motion in the finger, for example, without which the finger is useless, did not come from any direction. It leaves it at the time of sleep and death, but returns to it at the time of waking. Again, by what way, from which direction did the light of the eye come?

The world of creation is a world of directions and quarters. Its pomp and splendor are borrowed and temporary, but the spiritual or super-sensible world of the creative command *"Be,"* the world of the divine attributes, is non-spatial and directionless. Its pomp and splendor are real and everliving. Necessarily, more directionless is the commander, the creator of creation.

God is more intelligent than the intellect, more spiritual than the spirit. No created thing in heaven and earth is unconnected with Him, but how should that connection be described? Our thought can only think of uniting and separating, as dichotomy characterizes all human thinking and in the spirit there is not separating or uniting. Separation and union imply the existence of subject and object. They are incongruous with absolute unity. One may start from proofs furnished by the intellect, but although useful as a prelude to the spiritual quest, they cannot allay the thirst of the seeker of God as the intellect is ignorant of the way to His presence. "Do not seek to investigate the Essence of God," said the Prophet, "As in itself it is unknowable." On the way to Him are a hundred thousand veils or tiers. No thinker's speculation can be about Him. It can only be about some veil or some one thing among the many and its false identification with His Essence. This is irreverence. God dooms the irreverent who mistakes anything finite for infinity to fall headlong into self-conceit and worse. Creative of all, with all within Him, He is none of all. If one is earnest, one should contemplate His countless wonders. When from this contemplation he sees them and abandons his vain pride and egoism, he will know his own insignificance and become silent about Him. He will say from his soul that as the Lord is above reckoning and limit, He is above knowing and praise.

THE END OF PHARAOH

Pharaoh was the vessel of God's wrath. Grossly misguided, he and his people persisted in their evil ways. When the cup of their sin was full, retribution came. They sought to follow Moses and the Israelites across the sea. God made the bottom of the sea appear as dry land to Pharaoh. In the pride of his manhood, he drove into it, and, along with his host, was swallowed in the water.[4] Thus did the sea, symbolizing the intense spirituality of the prophet, overpower with deadly vengeance the brutish Pharaoh.

2 Prophet Solomon and the Queen of Sheba

The king and prophet, Solomon, famed for his knowledge and wisdom as well as for his worldly riches, had been taught the language of the birds by God. His hosts consisted of *jinn*, men and birds. Reviewing the birds, he found the hoopoe missing. "If he were among the absent," he said, "he would punish him with a terrible punishment. He would slay him, unless he could furnish full justification for his absence." But it was not long before he came and said to Solomon that he had come from Sheba. There he found that the people were ruled by a woman who had been given abundance of all things, whose throne was mighty, and she and her people worshiped the sun [27:24] instead of God.

This hoopoe, a noble bird with a stately crest, could see the water underground. He could tell its location, depth and source, and was of great use to Solomon in his travels in waterless wastes. He is celebrated for his role as Solomon's emissary to Bilqis, the Queen of Sheba. In the mystical poem, *Mantiq al-tayr (Conference of the Birds)* of the eminent mystical poet Attar, whom Rumi describes as the 'spirit of Sufism', the birds typifying the Sufi pilgrims elect the hoopoe as their leader in their quest for the fabulous bird Simurgh (*anqa* in Arabic), whose name is known, but not its reality, which is a symbol of the transcendental spirit, of God, the truth.

Solomon said to the Hoopoe, "We shall see whether you have spoken the truth or have lied. Take this letter of mine and cast it to the Sabaeans. Then turn away and see what reply they return." The hoopoe acted in accordance with this command.

Upon receipt of the letter, the Queen said to the chieftains that a noble letter from Solomon had been cast to her which was "*In the Name of God, the Merciful, the Compassionate*," and which said, "Do not rise up against me, but come to me like those who surrender."

God had bestowed on the Queen of Sheba the intelligence of a hundred men. Impressed by the eloquent and meaningful contents of the letter, she did not look down on the messenger. Her bodily eye saw it as a mere bird, but her spirit saw it as the fabulous bird, Simurgh [*anqa*].

APPEARANCE AND REALITY

The appearance and reality of existent things are two diverse aspects that hide the Essence. Because of this diversity, the intellect is at war with the senses, as Muhammad was with the ignorant infidels, who saw him as a common earthly mortal, and did not see in him the light of God, the prophetic nature that was revealed by the miracle that "*split the moon*" [54:1].

One should pour dust on the deluding sensual eye for it is the enemy of intellect and religion. God has called I 'blind' because it sees the foam and not the sea. It sees the present, not the future. The perfect human being is the Lord of the morrow and today and beholds all. His purified heart is a treasure of divine light. He may be before the sensual eye, but it sees only his earthly frame, nothing of that treasure.

If a speck of dust brought a message from the divine sun, and the illumined saint is such a speck, the visible sun would become its slave, as the sun is concealed in the speck, the saint. If a drop became a messenger from the sea of unity, that is, became a saint, the seven seas would become its captive, as the sea is hidden in the drop. When God taught Adam the Names giving him knowledge of the nature and reality of the named, and revealing to him all that shall happen unto everlasting, the angels who were wholly reason and spirit, bowed in homage before him at the command of the Lord. When a saint or a spiritually resurrected mystic, whose oculus cordis is opened, ascends or is borne aloft to God, the heavens tremble and split [84:1], so as not to block his ascension. Earth is gross and, therefore, settles beneath water. When it becomes God's envoy or a saint, the earthly body rises through divine love above the empyrean. The earth's subtlety is not the gift of water, but of the bounteous originator. God does what He will. From the heart of pain he raises the cure. From the very heart of darkness, he causes the light to to break forth. He exalts whom He will [3:26]. He commands the earthly Adam to rise above the starry heaven and the fiery satan, once His favorite, to go below the world's pedestal.

Understandably, in ancient times the sun was widely worshiped. It is visible to the naked eye. Its dazzling splendor is unequalled. Without its heat, no life, vegetal, animal or human is possible. Some philosophers believe that the human being is doomed to extinction in the death of the solar system. None can doubt the sun's existence.

But of God's existence there is no visible proof. He has no form, no like or opposite. He is the unseen seer. The sensuous eye cannot even see a saint, as his spirit is with God, veiled from human gaze. Leave alone seeing God, a person cannot even think of Him, that unthought thinker. He is not the four elements. He is their creator. He is not the first cause. Nor does He act from the necessity of His nature. He is independent of causality. Cause came into being by divine artifice yet He can render causes ineffective. He is the absolute Knower, Willer, Seer, etc. His fiat is absolute. He has the power of pre-determination. He dispels the illusion of secondary causes and alters His custom when He wills, saying to the sea, for example, "Be full of fire," [80:1, 6], or to the fire, "Go, be a rose-garden," as it became for Prophet Abraham at His command when Nimrod cast him into the fire. Or He says to the sun at the resurrection, *"Be joined to the moon,"* [75:9], and He makes both of them like black clouds. Or to the solid mountain, *"Be light as wool."* [101:5]. He is above 'how' and 'why', above conditionality.

While Solomon's letter touched the Queen's heart, she was not ready to renounce her scepter and crown and her many-splendoured life. She conferred with her chieftains and said, *"As is the wont of kings, they will come and ruin the township and turn the honor of the people to shame. I will send them a present and see what response it brings"* [27:34, 35].

THE QUEEN SENDS GOLD TO SOLOMON

The gift consisted of forty mules loaded with gold bricks. When the envoys reached Solomon's territory, the open plain, they found it all of solid gold. They rode a distance of forty stages on gold, until this noble metal had lost all worth in their eyes. They said, "Let us take the gold back. To bring gold to a land where the very soil is pure gold is nothing but folly." It was like bringing intelligence to God as a gift, where intelligence is utterly of no value. But again they said, "We are only slaves, bound to obey the Queen's command and take the gift, whether it is gold or earth, or take it back only if commanded by Solomon."

SOLOMON RETURNS THE GIFT

When Solomon saw the gift, he laughed and said, "I never sought worldly goods from you. I do not bid you bring me presents. I bid you come to me with submission, give up idolatry, embrace the true faith, and become worthy of the gifts I bestow. I have rare gifts coming to me from the unseen which human beings dare not even ask for. You despise the spirit which is priceless and instead worship the sun. The sun is our cook by divine command. To say it is God is folly. When He causes your sun to be eclipsed or it becomes invisible at night, when most calamities take place and one needs most protection, where is your object of worship? Where is the sun? Do you not then beg God to remove the darkness and give back the radiance?

"If you bow in sincere prayer before God, you will be liberated from the stars and become intimate with Him. I will then speak with you so that you may see a sun at midnight, the divine sun, that has no orientation, no direction except the pure spirit. Its rising does not depend on day or night. When it rises, that is day. When it begins to shine, night is night no more. As the speck is before the sun, such is the sun in the pure essence of the light of God. That light is the philosopher's stone, the immortal elixir, whose single impression fell on the primal vapor. The vapor became a star whose half a gleam struck on a dark patch. The dark patch became the sun whose single act gave Saturn its specific properties. In this way, the entire glittering spray of planets and stars and all the spiritual substances have come into being. That Light of lights is the origin and essence of all created things, earthly or heavenly. As is said in the Koran and in the Book of Genesis, '*God has only to say 'Be', and it is,*' no matter what it be."

The sensual eye is subject to the sun's vision. One should seek and find the divinely illumined eye of the perfect human being so that the flaming sun may become humble before its vision. For that vision is luminous while this vision is igneous, dark before light.

Solomon bade the envoys take the gold back to their Queen. What he sought, he said, was not gold, but the pure heart, the heart that loved God. For while, as was then believed, it was the sun's regard—or heat and cold in the mine—that produced gold, the lover's gold was his pallid countenance that was the object of the Lord's regard. How could the two be compared? He was hence calling them to protect themselves from his wrath by surrendering their souls to God. Their coming to him with gifts was already the result of the attraction he exerted on them. When they were drawn after him—as the lover is willy nilly drawn by the beloved—they would know that he was not unmindful of their good.

Showing affection and kindness to the envoys, Solomon said, "I will send you as envoys to your splendor-throned Queen. Go and tell her what a marvelous desert of gold you have seen so that she may know that we do not covet gold. We have gold from the gold-creator at whose will the entire earth would become gold. If you choose gold, then, on the day of resurrection when the earth and the heavens will be changed, you will find that God will make the earth silver for you, not golden, thus showing the vanity of worldly riches. You will see the guilty linked in fetters, their raiment of pitch, their faces covered by the fire [14:48-50]. We have no need of gold, as we can turn earthly beings wholly golden, making them spiritual. How shall we beg gold of you when we can transform you into spiritual alchemists? Renounce all, even the kingdom of Sheba. Kingdoms abound beyond this water and earth. Your sovereignty is illusion. You are not sovereign over your own sense and self, and so, how should you be sovereign over good and evil? You cannot even avoid graying with age. Lay your head before God. He will guide you. A single prostration before Him will give you an inward savor infinitely sweeter than a whole host of empires. No more will you then desire terrestrial kingdoms, but humbly beg God for the kingdom of that prostration."

Spiritual Alchemy

When Solomon said that he could turn the Queen's men into alchemists, he meant that he could give then knowledge of the sacred fire of the alchemists by which the lead of the personal mortal self is transmuted into the gold of the higher immortal self here and now, without having to wait until after death, as in exoteric religion. Possessing this knowledge, they would, while still in this body, become spiritual guides and saviors, or the fishermen of Jesus.

As Sufism seeks the transformation of the gross into the subtle and of the subtle into the deep divine, it is akin to the work of alchemy and may justly be described as spiritual alchemy.

The expression "the water of life" means the elixir of immortality. God says in the Koran, *"We made every living thing of water"* [21:30]. In Rumi, the water cleanses all impurities. It is brought back into the sea of the pure, its origin and returns to the earth cleansed by God of all trace of impurity.[1] According to Rumi, it is through salt that the bodies of the holy ones are transmuted and become pure.[3] Salt has wondrous properties.

THE PHILOSOPHIC WORK IN ALCHEMY

To turn to the philosophic aspect of alchemy, true selfhood is not separate, but is one and the same in all. All things are interlinked in a divine unity. If one identifies himself, as most of us tend to do, with the outer sense-objects, particularly his body, which is present in all his experiences and pursues selfish ends, deeming himself unconnected with others, he will only find that the dead gold of matter, the object of his quest, has expelled the living gold of the sun, the unitary light of consciousness, and by the reversed alchemy of desire driven him at the appointed hour to an unlovely leaden death.

The seeker of God must ignore the voice of desire, calm his senses and dissolve them in the mind. But as the mind has two aspects—the lower and the higher—and may look not up to the higher self, where dwells the cosmic unity and harmony, but to the lower self, the lower sense-world, with its plurality and strife, it must be dissolved in the light of the spirit, as the senses were earlier dissolved in the mind.

Acts, thoughts and feelings will continue to come and go, but they must be in accord, not with any social morality or convention, but with the unitary light within. Such accord presupposes knowledge which can discriminate between what is in tune with the divine harmony and what accentuates the sense of separateness. In the final initiation, the sacred fire bursts into flame, burning up all limitations.

When the false self is dead and the aspirant's whole nature

is subject to the higher self, the process of dissolution is complete. The aspirant is ready for the next phase of the alchemical operation which is the phase of sublimation. It is a process by which the lower principles which have been dissolved into the true center of being are caused to ascend in essence to the upper portion of the gold vessel, the higher self. It is a spiritual ascent, not spatial. There, under the formative rays of the stars, all the knowledge of the past, present and future is inscribed in their golden letters of light.

To return to the story, as God created this world in order that His attributes might become manifest. He had to have kings for the maintenance of order in this world and to serve as His instruments of wrath, which is His justice. He sealed their eyes so that crown and throne should be sweet to them, both as symbols of eminence and as a means of extraction of tribute from others. If they had tasted the wine of service to God, they would have, like Ibrahim ibn Adham, dashed their sovereignty to pieces and turned in servility to Him. But now there was no such temptation. Their heaven was placed in the senses. They should know that if by means of tribute they hoarded too much, ultimately, it will be left behind. Kingship and gold will not accompany their spirit on its onward journey.

It is best that one should give away gold and get collyrium for his eyes, so that he may see that this world is a narrow well. He should grasp the rope of patience and faith, "the rope of the Koran," and, overpowering the lower faculties, come to the top, so that the enraptured soul in triumph may exclaim, *"This is a youth for me,"* a perfect human being [12:19].

Unfortunately, in this world of illusion, most of us like children, cherish potsherds and colored pebbles as gold and riches. The knowers of God are a rare few. They become spiritual alchemists so that gold mines have no worth in their eyes.

Solomon said to the couriers, "Believe in religion and tell your Queen to hasten here. God summons all to the abode of peace." His Mercy is universal, and, like paradise, is for true believers and sinners alike. He bestows spiritual grace on the former and lets those without aspiration also come. It becomes aspiring and through high aspiration gain the gift of seeking wonderful felicity from Him.

In a threatening message to the Queen, Solomon said, "Come without delay or else, woe will betide you, and your own self will be your enemy. The hosts of the heavens and the earth are God's. He uses all kinds of created things as armies for carrying out His purposes. Do not persist in polytheism.

"You know that God is always with the prophets. Remember how in the time of the old Arab prophet Hud, the disbelieving tribe of Ad was destroyed by a fierce roaring wind [7:65-72]; 69:6). Recall how in the time of Noah, the deluge swallowed the unbelievers, including his own son [7:59-64]. Remember how the hosts of Pharaoh were drowned in the vengeful sea while the Israelites were given a safe passage [2:50]. Recall how the earth swallowed Korah of the folk of Moses, who fancied that he owed his rich treasure to his own knowledge, and not to God's kindness [28:76-81]. These are just a few instances of the kind of help which inanimate objects rationally gave to the prophets or the punishment they inflicted on the disbelievers at the command of the Lord.

"Every part of you, O Bilqis, all your members and faculties, are an army of God. At His command, eye-ache, tooth-ache and a whole host of other aches and pains mentioned in medical literature can wreak a hundred vengeances on you. Only in seeming, not in reality, is the army of your body under your command. You are amid His army. Be afraid. He is the soul of the soul of everything in creation. To oppose Him or be hostile to Him is utter folly.

"Remember also that on the day of judgment the mouths of sinners will be sealed. Their eyes, ears and skins will bear witness against them as to what they had been doing and earning on earth. They will become His army. God has given them speech as He gives to all things [36:65; 41:20, 21]. You will be entirely subject to His judgment and mercy on that day.

"Leave alone the armies of demons and genii who, at my

command, will break the ranks of my enemies. All God's armies are at my disposal. My counsel to you is that you relinquish your kingdom. For temporal sovereignty carries a hundred dangers, including fear for head, with fear for heart, fear for religion. Only when you have gained me, and with me, my spiritual aspiration, will you have gained the kingdom of this world as well as of God. You will then know that without me, you are as a soulless picture in the bath-house of the world." A picture even of a Sultan is only a picture which is unconscious of its own spirit and whose beauty is only for others.

"God has said, 'This world is a play and a pastime and you are but children.' So we are. Our wars are like children's fights, meaningless, foolish. We follow but conjecture or opinion, riding our hobby horses, and expect them to carry us to heaven. But subjective opinion is not knowledge. It cannot take the place of truth [10:36].

"The sensualist does not know his real nature. It is veiled by his bodily qualities. He regards himself as belonging to this phenomenal world, this world of forms, which, in his eyes, is real, and is other than God, existing independently in its own right. Ever chasing forms and phantoms, he lays waste his life. If for a moment he is alone, he is a misery to himself, not knowing that within him is the entire universe."

THE PERFECT HUMAN BEING

In Adam's body, a mere three cubits long, God displayed every thing that was contained in the tablets of destiny and the world of spirits and taught him the Names, that is, gave him knowledge concerning all that shall come to pass unto everlasting.[4] We are his progeny, but his true sons, his spiritual heirs, are perfect human beings who are God's viceroys on earth.

The perfect human being is the roof of creation. Steeped in the divine attribution, he is not only a lover of the universal, but is himself an aspect of the Universal. He is in love with himself as the subject and object of all love. He has become the substance of love. The is no duality. Or, as God alone is, God is loved by none but God.

Referring to the gnostic's—the perfect human being's—transcendence of all relations of otherness, and his finding all within himself, Rumi says,

> You are your own bird, your own prey and snare;
> > you are your own seat of honor, your own floor and roof.
> The substance is that which subsists by itself;
> > the accident is that which becomes its branch.
> If you are born of Adam, sit like him (and)
> > see your entire progeny within yourself.
> What is in the jar that is not in the river?
> What is in the house that is not in the city?
> This world is the jar, and the heart is like the river of water;
> > this world is the chamber and the heart is the wonderful city.[5]

As the logos, the perfect human being is the creative and sustaining principle of all things, sensible or spiritual. His heart is the substance of which this world or creation is an accident. The macrocosm is enfolded within his infinite spirit. All things derive their individual function and attributes from him. Though his essence manifests itself in all modes of individualizations, he is greater, for while they manifest only some of his attributes, he reflects them all. God is reported to have said, "Neither the heaven nor the earth or even the empyrean can contain Me, but I am contained in the true believer's heart,"[5] in the heart of the perfect human being.

SOLOMON'S MESSAGE TO THE QUEEN

Continuing, Solomon said, "As you will see when God opens your inward eye, I am a prophet sent by God to call the people to Him. My work for your conversion to the faith is only for His sake. I have no selfish interest in your person, beauty or kingdom. I am the slayer of lust, not its captive for the face of an idol. If there be any lust in me, I am ruler over it. Like Abraham, the Friend of God, and all the prophets, I am in my roots a breaker of idols. If I enter the idol-temple, the idols will prostrate before me—as they fell headlong and prostrate before Prophet Muhammad. Not I, but they will bow in adoration.

"This world with its lusts is an idol-temple for the prophets and the infidels alike. Both are within this burning crucible. But the holy people who have enslaved lust are like pure gold from the mine, which does not burn, but manifests its goldenness and laughs coquettishly in the fire in the crucible. The infidels are like the alloy, which at once becomes black therein.

"The body veils our inward reality. Misled by appearance, satan took Adam for mere clay and thought himself better than he. We all tend to suffer from this conceit and think ourselves superior to others. One should not regard Adam, the king of religion, as a handful of earth. How should some dust and ashes poured on the sun besmear its face? O Bilqis, seal the eye of illusion and self-deception, and, like a real queen, burn up your ephemeral kingdom."

HER ATTACHMENT TO THE THRONE

Solomon's message burnt into her sense and soul. Longing for the faith, she took leave of her kingdom and riches like lovers, although not without remorse for the past, and set forth on the spiritual journey to Solomon's kingdom. Her charming pages and handmaidens, orchards, and palaces, and flowing rivers, all now looked repulsive to her. Love's jealousy makes even the loveliest objects look unlovely. There is no god but God —*la ilaha illa 'l-lah*—and these phenomenal objects are not God. They are non-entities. Esoterically speaking, they are parts of the law of negation. No wealth or treasure was grudged by her. But there was one solitary thing which she found difficult to part with, and that was her mighty throne of filigree work, which she greatly prized and loved, as it was an emblem of her rulership and the means for the exhibition of her queenly perfection. It was to her what a pen is to a master penman or the tool to a master craftsman, insensible, not spiritually homogeneous, but metaphorically, a friend of the spirit within the human form. How should the spirit part without pain from the body, the exoteric senses and faculties which tell us whatever we know of the world of appearance? As no appearance is without reality behind it and no means which cannot lead from the knowledge of the outer to that of the inner, from the lower knowledge to the higher, appearance and means serve as a bridge from the phenomenal to the Real. These secondary means—the thrones, diadems and working tools—are the veils through which God is revealed to the intuitive eye. Everything that exists is connected with Him, and yet, unconnected.

Solomon, who was brimming with knowledge and wisdom and from whose heart a way had opened to her heart, discerned from afar that although she was following the path of resignation, the throne was exceedingly dear to her. He knew that when God bestowed grace on her and she became spiritual, the throne—representing the world, the flesh and the devil—which she loved, would lose all charm in her eyes. For when the spirit manifests itself from the unity, before its splendor, the body is utterly without splendor. But he did not wish her to feel hurt on account of the throne at the time of her meeting him. Hence, although the throne was unimaginably huge and impossible to take apart and transport by any normal means without breaking, he said, "Let it be brought here, no matter how! Let her childish wish be fulfilled. Later, this throne of delight will become a lesson, an object of repulsion, to her soul. It will make her realize from what a low state of lifelessness as queen to what a high state, the state of grace, has she arrived. When the pearl comes up from the depths of the sea, one looks with contempt on the foam, on the sticks and straws."

God is ever keeping the clay and semen before our eyes, as though to remind us that there was a time when the human being was a thing unremembered. He created him from a drop of commingled seed to test him. He gave him hearing, knowing.

He showed him the way, whether he was believing and grateful or believing and ungrateful. But the materialist forgets his lowly state and also disbelieves in any future state or in the resurrection. He is like the human embryo without heart and spirit that implicitly denies the existence of any higher state of being or of any world outside the womb. The human being, as he is, never anticipated his progression from mineral, plant and animal to his present state. He has been through countless resurrections. He loved every state through which he passed, forgot every past state and was sure that the present state was the last. God proved him wrong all through. His bringing him from the inanimate to the human state and investing him with intellectual and spiritual faculties is affirmation of his spiritual evolution from material origins and equally a rebuttal of his present denial of the resurrection, which arises from his ignorance and irrationality. The spirit has come from God, and will return to Him, its origin and home, at the end.

Speaking to his chiefs, Solomon said, "Which of you will bring me the throne of the Queen of Sheba?" A demon, a master magician, said that he would bring it before the king left the council. His Minister, Asaf, said that by means of the Greatest Name of God, he would bring it instantly before him. Miracle prevailed over magic. Simultaneously with his utterance, Solomon saw it set in his presence [27:38-40]. This was no surprise. With God and His lovers there is no past or future. There is no divisible time, but indivisible continuity, an eternal New, in which the creation is continually renewed. All events, all things, co-exist with no perceptible moment of non-existence, no gap between any two successive acts or events.

Solomon offered praise to God for this and countless other favors. Turning towards the throne, he said, "You are one that catches fools."

Many fools worship idols of wood or carved stone. Although both the idolater and the idol have no spiritual awareness, yet when the idolater becomes rapt in devotion, he feels some spiritual stirring and imagines that speech and signs proceed from the lifeless idol. Love and imagination are great sorcerers. When the idolater sincerely worships the false god, the Real God in His kindness extends some munificence to him, although not duly deserved. For His bounty is universal. Even the infidels partake of it according to their capacity.

THE DIVINE MERCY CALLS THE QUEEN OF SHEBA

The divine mercy's call came to the Queen of Sheba, "Come and behold God's Kingdom. Gather pearls of spiritual reality on the bank of His sea. Your sisters—the souls of prophets and saints—are enjoying the fullness of bliss in paradise. Come and join that goodly company. Why act like a ruler of the world which is but a carcase? (Tradition) Why proclaim with the flourish of trumpets, 'I am queen and mistress of the bath stove?' Admittedly, the bathstove is needed for the heating of the bath water in which the body is cleansed. It is like the worldly environment which has to be maintained for the trial and purification of the soul. But leave the dirty stokers, the heedless worldlings, the ignoble means which is their portion, and turn in devotion to God."

The sea of spiritual reality is our Solomon whose earthly body is in this world, but whose spirit is circling in the highest heaven. In him, we move unto everlasting. Solomon is beside us, but as we are slaves of worldliness, we are not free from relations of otherness. Not self-negated, we pay no heed to what he says. We are unworthy to perceive the divine attributes reflected in him. God is jealous of His Beauty. He spell-binds unworthy eyes so that they may not behold it. Knowledge of His jealousy is our savior.

It is said in the Koran that the Queen of Sheba came to Solomon's kingdom and saw the throne already there. This was surprise enough. When she entered the hall, she mistook the pavement of transparent glass for a pool of water. From fear of being splashed by it, she bared her legs in the presence of Solomon against all canons of modesty.[6] She had to suffer this shame, as her false imagination had attributed unreality to the reflection of the divine attributes in Solomon. Her soul now awoke and she penitently said, *"My Lord, I have wronged myself. I surrender with Solomon to God, the Lord of the worlds"* [27:42-44].

3 Prophet Joseph and Zulaykha

The prophet Joseph, son of Jacob, was the subject of his brothers' envy, as they believed that he and his brother were dearer to their father than they. They, therefore planned to get him out of the way. As a part of their evil design, they persuaded their father to let Joseph go out with them to the country for frolic and play. They took him out with them and cast him in the well. When they returned home to their father, they told him that while they were running races, leaving Joseph behind with their things, the wolf came and ate him up. They produced his shirt with false blood on it as proof.

This is not a mere tale, but a parable of our own life. When our lower faculties or self, symbolized by the brethren of Joseph, eclipse the higher faculties or the higher self, symbolized by Joseph, we are lured by the illusive delights of sense and, like Joseph, cast in the narrow well of the world. The light of our consciousness no more remains within, but streams out and gets entangled and lost in the sense objects, which are only the outward projections of their archetypes in the inner sense-world.

The Koran describes this earthly life as *"a mere play and a pastime"* [29:64], where we forget out hidden inter-linkedness and regard the sense-objects, our physical bodies included, as separate, independent entities. Under this illusion, each in his selfish pride and envy tries to outdo the other. In the present case, the wolf is said to swallow Joseph. His perfumed shirt of the spirit[1] is blood-soaked. But this wolf is no outward visible wolf. It is envy which is a big wolf in covert, surpassing all wolves in malignity, that swallows Joseph. It is the same wolf that led satan to disobey the Lord's command to him to bow to Adam.

Wolves abound in the human being. One should not doubt that according to the inexorable law of retribution, our evil dispositions will arise at the resurrection as so many wolves and tear our limbs in anger. As these wolves are the enemy of Joseph, our higher self, they must be killed and burnt while we are still in this body.[2]

Thus, the reference to wolves is not literal, but symbolic as in Plato and oriental philosophy. Rumi does not believe in metempsychosis. There has been no metamorphosis of the body among the Muslims, but only of the spirit.[3] It is the manifestation of one's 'foul inward disfigurement'.

Not that Jacob—a prophet in Islam—had no foreboding of evil. To a prophet or saint, such forebodings come from the unseen. But the divine destiny came and Jacob's prophetic vision was temporarily veiled. He gave them permission to take him out. When Joseph's brothers returned in the evening without him, he knew that their minds had been tempted to do something, but he did not know what had happened to Joseph [12:7-18].

While Joseph was in the well—and here God revealed to him his final fortune—a caravan happened to be passing by. When their water-carrier went to the well and let his pail down, Joseph clutched the rope firmly. It drew him out of the well—an example Rumi exhorts us to follow, saying,

> You are Joseph, full of beauty,
>   and this world is like a well,
> The updrawing rope is patient submission to the divine
>   command.
> O Joseph, the rope is come; clutch it with both hands,
>   do not be heedless of the rope, it is already late.

Praise be to the Lord that the rope has been let down,
   and grace and mercy have been mingled together,
So that you may see the new everlasting spiritual world,
   a world at once very manifest and hidden.[4]

RUMI REPEATS THIS EXHORTATION IN THE DIWAN

"O Joseph of the soul, wherefore remain in the body's well? Grasp the rope of the Koran and come up from the well of darkness."

It is no ordinary rope, but the rope of patience and faith, the rope of the Koran, which an aspiring soul must clutch firmly before it is too late, for it will draw up the spirit to heaven, back to its original home.

When Joseph came up, the water-drawer—the soul—said, "Good luck! Here is a handsome youth for me," a perfect human being, a prophet [12:19].[5]

Not knowing the transcendental worth of Joseph, they went and sold him for a paltry sum to the Governor of Egypt (Potiphar). This was nothing strange. Do we not ourselves imprison Joseph, the divinity, in our narrow self, treat him cheap and sell him for a mess of pottage, unless the Lord illumines our hearts, and the reality of Joseph dawns on us?

ZULAYKHA'S LOVE FOR JOSEPH

The Governor took Joseph home and said to his wife Zulaykha that the slave-boy might prove useful to them and that they might adopt him as their son [12:20, 21].

Joseph was a paragon of beauty. Zulaykha fell desperately in love with him. Her heart was so deeply pierced by love's shaft that she grew oblivious to her marital status and obligation. It was the overpowering sensual love which blinds the eye of reason. Its consequences were inevitable. As the great 14th century poet Hafiz says,

> From the daily waxing beauty of Joseph
>   I knew that love would drag Zulaykha out
>   from her protective veil. (Diwan)

Zulaykha tried her best to seduce him, but in vain. He would not even look at her. She had a chamber constructed in which all the walls were covered with paintings of herself so that when Joseph was called in, he found that wherever he looked, only the beautiful face of Zulaykha met his gaze. Nothing else was on view.[6] Joseph almost yielded. He cried out to God for help. "A signal of darkness" came and saved him from her wiles.

On another occasion, when Joseph was in her chamber, she bolted the door and solicited him. He would have fallen in with her desire, but, again, the Lord's mercy saved him. They ran to the door and she caught and tore his shirt from behind. At the door, they met the lord and master. She sought to lay the blame on Joseph for this incident. She said that the recompense for one who intended evil against another cannot but be prison or an evil doom. But as his shirt was torn from behind, it was obvious that, not he, but she was the pursuer and the guilty one.

Her love for Joseph was now public knowledge. Tongues wagged. Women in the city said that Governor's wife had been soliciting her slave-boy. She was love-smitten and in plain aberration.

When Zulaykha heard of their sly whispers, she asked them to a banquet. She gave to each of them a knife and told Joseph to come and attend to them. When the women saw the celestial beauty of Joseph, they forgot themselves in admiration of his face, and, unwittingly cut their hands in bewilderment, saying, "God save us! This is no mortal, but a gracious angel" —a clear warning that such is the fate of anyone who dare look on the Beloved without reverential love.[7]

Zulaykha said to the women, "This is the one you blamed me for. I asked an evil act of him, but he showed temperance and refused to carry out my command. The punishment for his disobedience is imprisonment."

As Joseph was really innocent, the menfolk deemed it fit to imprison him only for a short time.

While in prison, Joseph committed the sin of by-passing God and beseeching help from a fellow prisoner on the verge of release, saying, "When you are released from prison, make mention of me to the mighty prince, so that me too he may free from this prison."

GOD'S ZEAL

But how should one himself a prisoner give freedom to another prisoner? In truth, we are all prisoners awaiting the coming of death in this perishing abode, except the rare ones who are purified of selfhood and negated in divine ecstasy.

God alone is. All else is Not-being. And He is jealous of His unity. All action emanates from His Essence. Nothing happens except at His command. To seek light and guidance from candle and lamp when the sun in present is an act of irreverence, ungratefulness and self-will. If one whose prayer-niche is turned to mystical revelation, returns to the traditional faith, will it not be shameful and retrograde? Or when the king has bestowed on us the privilege of kissing his hand, is it not a sin if we prefer to kiss his foot?[8]

Joseph had sinned by forgetting the sole helper, the merciful Lord, and seeking the help of another. It was polytheism in a sense. Punishment was inevitable. The devil caused the fellow prisoner on his release and also those who should have ordered his release to forget all about Joseph. In consequence, he was left in prison for several years. The divine Judge said to him, "If the vulgar who are spiritually blind went into the world of darkness and tribulation, it would be understandable. But why you whose spiritual eye is open and who had seen the face of the Lord?" Hence, the judge of judges, whose sun of justice knows no obscurity or deficiency, punished him, saying, "Do not make your prop of rotten wood!"

It we are jealous, it is because God is jealous. His jealousy is superior. His jealousy is that He is other than all things. Jealous of His beauty, He spell-binds the unworthy, the unspiritual, so that they may not behold it.[9] Did not Jesus say, "Cast not pearls before swine?" His jealousy veils not only Him, but also His prophets and saints from the profane eye, which is deceived by appearances.[10] The excessive proximity of His splendor itself acts as a veil. If the holy ones observe the doctrine of silent reserve, it is because to divulge the mystery of union with Him is to incur His jealousy. The knowledge of His jealousy is a blessing, for it will make us adhere to the truth of the unity of being and place implicit trust in Him.

God punished Joseph, but as he was favored one, He kept him occupied with Himself so that his heart should not be pained by the punishment. He gave his soul such rapturous joy that the prison and its murkiness remained invisible to him.

JOSEPH INTERPRETS A DREAM

God had given Joseph the kingdom of interpretation of dreams. While, in prison, his inward eye opened. He saw and interpreted the well-known dream about the seven fat cows being devoured by the seven lean cows, saying that this meant that seven good years of harvest would be followed by seven lean years. He advised that some of the corn during the good years should be laid aside for use during the lean years. (The mystical interpretation of the dream is that the seven notorious cows, the flesh, were devouring the spirit's seven good cows) [12:46-48].[11]

The Governor was told of his interpretation. As suggested by Joseph, he asked the women who had cut their hands at the sight of his face as to what happened when they sought to seduce him. They said that he was blameless. Zulaykha also confessed that she had solicited him, and he was of the truthful.

JOSEPH, HIS GUEST, AND THE MIRROR

An old loving friend came to Joseph and became his guest. He spoke of his brothers' envy and injustice. Joseph, a truthful witness from the Lord, said, "O that was like a chain and he was the lion. The lion is not dishonored by the chain. If a lion had a chain on his neck, he still was the lord of all the chain makers. I do not complain of the chain or divine destiny." The perfect human being, the spiritual lion, like Joseph, is God's elect and superior to all earth-bound people.

When asked how he felt when he was in the prison and the well, he said, "Like the waning moon in the inter-lunar period. The new moon may be bent double, but it becomes the full moon at the end.

Every object in creation seeks perfection. We all come from God, the supreme perfection and to Him we all seek to return. It is the natural homing instinct. But none, high or low, not even a prophet like Joseph, can scale the snowy peak in one leap. The climb has to be gradual.

God Himself took six days to create this creation. Not without hurt and tribulation is any progress possible. Take the instance of a wheat grain which is the lowest form of soul life in matter. It is first cast under the earth from above. On account of its humility, it shoots up from the buried root as ears of corn, singing thanks to the Lord. It is then crushed in the mill and baked in the oven, crunched between man's teeth, and it serves as his nutriment. It was not his congener, but by suffering all this tribulation and negating itself, it became homogeneous with him. The animal spirit in the human being assimilates the inanimate bread. It becomes his mind, spirit and understanding. This gradual progression of the wheat grain is the work of love—of love of perfection, love that is universal. Nothing is, material or sensible, animate or inanimate, that is not hustling up for the waft of the divine spirit. The human being himself has been through mineral, plant and animal states before becoming human as he is today.

The seemingly insignificant wheat grain, now a living part of human kind, endowed with knowledge, will, in the fullness of time, also scales the empyrean with him, and, with him, lost in the divine love, enters the kingdom of God which is as much its home and destination as it is the human being's.

After Joseph had narrated his story to the guest, he said, "Now, good friend, what present have you brought for me? To come empty-handed to the doors of a friend is like going without wheat to the mill. God will ask the people at the congregation for judgment, '*Where is your present for the Day of resurrection? Or have you come to Us provisionless just as We created you at the first, and left behind all that We bestowed on you*' [6:95]? Or you had no hope of returning to Me and the promise of meeting Me on the day of resurrection seemed vain to you."

If one disbelieves in His promise of hospitality, he will get nothing but dust and ashes from His kitchen of bounty. And if he does not disbelieve, how is he entering the divine court empty-handed? One should sleep and eat a little less and bring his saving as a gift for his meeting with Him. He should be like those good-doers who would sleep but little of the night and ask for forgiveness in the mornings [51:17, 18] and worship Him as though they were seeing Him. One should not be idle, but pursue this inward activity, remaining outwardly inactive or stirring a little like the embryo so that the Lord may bless him with the perception of those who see by His light. He is then delivered from this narrow, womb-like world and goes into God's spacious earth [39:10], that immutable, infinite expanse of divine unity and transcendence, into which the saints have entered. In this constricted world, one has to bear the burden of the senses, the burden of fatigue, and is almost falling headlong from exhaustion. There, the heart suffers no oppression. No green tree dies or withers. No burden wears one down.

Every night, our senses sleep. We are borne aloft in a state of unconsciousness. This may be regarded as a hint of the state in which the saints are borne on high. They are like the Companions of the Cave, asleep even when seen awake and turning to and fro [18:18]. Good deeds and bodily actions proceed from them, but they are unconscious of either kind of action. The only actor is God. The human being is only the passive medium through which He acts and fulfills His purpose. A saint or gnostic whose personal will is steeped in His will has this mystical knowledge and is no burden-bearer. He is borne without his troubling to act, borne heavenward by the power of divine love.

To return to the story, "Come, where is the gift?" Joseph asked.

This demand confused the guest. He wept and said, "I sought many gifts, but none was worthy of you. If I brought my heart and soul to you as a gift, it would be like carrying coal to Newcastle. There is nothing which is not with you in full abundance. The entire creation is infolded in your infinite spirit. As your beauty has no peer, I thought it best to bring you a mirror clear like the light of a pure bosom, so that you may see your beauteous face in it, and when you do, you may think if me." And he produced the mirror from under his arm.

The mirror has no form of its own. Not-being is the mirror of being it assumes or rather reflects the form that is before it. In other words, it is not-being.

The Prophet said, "Seek not to investigate the Essence of God for in itself it is unknowable. Through His Names and Attributes which are its individualization, is His knowledge to be sought. As He manifests Himself only to the extent to which He is mirrored in not-being, not-being is the mirror of being. It is the material on which He works to display His perfection. His Essence is best revealed to itself in the perfect human being's non-existence, in his pure heart, which is empty of all phenomena, of all thought and recollection. It is no so revealed any elsewhere. Hence, Rumi's exhortation, "Bring not-being as your gift if you are not a fool."

In our day-to-day existence also, we see that non-existence and defect are the mirror that alone show the excellence of all crafts. Thus,

> If the garment is smart and well-made,
>   how should it enable the tailor to display his art?
> The doctor who sets fractured bones goes
>   only where there is a fractured foot.
> When there is no emaciated invalid, how should
>   the excellence of the art of medicine become manifest?
> If the baseness of copper is not evident,
>   how should the elixir manifest its magical power.[12]

Defects mirror the quality of excellence and perfection as hidden things are made manifest by their contrary. Light, for example, is made manifest by darkness. As God has no contrary, He is hidden. He who recognizes his deficiency progresses fast towards perfection. The conceit of perfection or self-admiration, on the other hand, will keep him rooted where he is, even drag him further back from perfection. There is no worse malady for the soul that this conceit. It cannot be eradicated without treading the inner path of sacrifice. We may regard ourselves as broken in spirit and pure, but the devil who disobeyed the Lord's command to bow to Adam, saying, *"I am better than he"* [7:11, 12], is in us all. The appearance of purity is deluding. Beneath it lies a host of vices and impurities which show up the moment the devil stirs one in trial.

Evil thoughts and love or worldly riches are the darkness of our spiritual states. It is best to find a sagacious shaykh or guide who well-knows the way and its twists and turns and give the hand of discipleship to his hand. Emanations of spiritual influence from him purify souls in measure with their capacity. Whatever purification we attain we must recognize as his work and not claim that it is ours.

FAMINE STRIKES EGYPT

When hard times came, as predicted by Joseph, his brothers came to him in dire distress. He gave them their measure of provision and told them to bring his youngest brother with them when they came next or there would be no provision for them. They brought him with them when they came again, and Joseph managed to keep him back.

JOSEPH'S DREAM COMES TRUE

Feeling the scathing pangs of separation from Joseph, his father Jacob had gone blind with weeping. At his behest, and from great need, the brothers returned to Joseph for more provision. Up until now they had not recognized him. He asked them, "Do you know what you did to Joseph and his brother in your ignorance?" Revealing his own and his brother's identity, he said, "Take this vest of mine and lay it on the face of Jacob. By its scent, he will become a seer again." This scent is a wondrous waft from the garden of universal reason. It is a remedy for sightlessness. It is a spiritual eye-opener, a life replenisher, and the guide to Eden and the Fountain of Abundance (*kawthar*). "You should then come to me with all your folk."

The brothers went back to their father. When they laid the shirt on him, his eyesight was restored. They then returned to Egypt. Joseph took his parents to himself. He seated them on the dais. His brothers fell down prostrate before him. Joseph said, *"This is the interpretation of my dream of old. The Lord has made it true. He has shown me kindness as he released me from prison and has brought you from desert after satan had caused strife between me and my brothers"* [12:100].

JACOB

Jacob, who is mentioned as a prophet in the Koran, was a lord of knowledge, but over every lord there is one more knowing—Joseph in this case. Jacob could taste the cup of God from the celestial face of Joseph. He inhaled the scent from his spirit and could see again. One who has not the beauty of Joseph must not strut with disdainful airs in his presence, for ugly is disdain in an unlovely face. Let him be like Jacob, fully acquainted with weeping and supplication. Let him not be a lacerating rock, but be earth, so that the breath of Jesus may resuscitate him and make him blessed as itself. Just as the orchard laughs only when the cloud weeps, it is only when the heart weeps that the Lord's mercy is roused and His bounty opens the spiritual eye. Self-abasement is divine. It is an elevator to Heaven.

THE BROTHERS

The brothers, typifying the lower self, were unable to perceive the scent of Joseph's vest because they were spiritually dead. Their higher self was calling them, but in vain. It was only when painful days came and the external illusory world collapsed around their ears that they were shaken out of their false self. It was then that they decided to visit Joseph, that is, turn towards the spirit. But still drowsed by the opiate of worldliness, they were unable to recognize Joseph, their higher self, until he revealed his identity. They then became self-accusing and penitent. They laid their heads before him. Their "animal soul" (*nafs-i-ammara*) had become the "reproachful soul" (*nafs-i-lawwama*). This was the limit of their climb. Much intense struggle for purification is required before the self-accusing soul can become the "inspired soul" (*nafs-i-mulhama*)—inspired with consciousness of good and evil, right and wrong—and the inspired soul can become the "tranquil soul" (*nafs-i-mutmainna*), and, if aspiring enough return to the Lord, content in His good pleasure, "*well-pleased, well-pleasing*" [12:53; 75:2; 91:7, 8; 89:27, 28].

Zulaykha had been faithful to Joseph all through. Long years of amorous languishment had roughened her bloom of youth. When she was ushered into his presence, he beamed on her, and she became young and beautiful anew.[13]

Love is love. It is one except that its object may be human or divine. True human love also leads us yonder. It is the bridge to the Real, as it excludes all otherness. It is pure. The miracle that Jesus wrought, resuscitating the dead by pronouncing the name of God, was manifested to Zulaykha through the name of Joseph, and her love of him, sensual at first, had become spiritual. She had found her true beloved. Void of self, she was filled with love for him. His name was sweet wine to her soul. Her offer of complete self-giving was prompted by love and reverence for Joseph who represented celestial beauty.

Like Sufis or lovers of God, Zulaykha would use erotic symbols. She would apply the name of everything to Joseph, the spirit, hiding his name in every other name and symbol. She told the inner meaning only to her confidantes. No matter how many names or symbols she piled up, her sole object was Joseph. If she said, "The wax is softened by the fire," this meant that her beloved was passionately fond of her. Or "dust well the furniture." This meant dust away the phenomenal forms which prevent union with the Essence. If she was hungry and uttered his name, she would instantly be filled with spiritual food. If thirsty, her thirst would be quenched with spiritual wine. This is what the beloved's name does. The common people are ever uttering the greatest Name, but it does not work this way with them, as their love is not true.

When the soul is one with God, to speak of God is to speak of the soul and to speak of the soul is to speak of God. Love devours everything except love. Rumi says,

> O heart, I searched from end to end and saw naught in you but the Beloved,
> Call me not an infidel, O heart, if I say, you yourself are He.[14]

4 Prophet Muhammad and the Sick Companion

A notable amongst the Companions of the Prophet Muhammad fell sick. That sickness reduced him to a skeleton. As the Prophet was exceedingly kind and generous, he went to visit him.

While such visits are good both for the ailing person and the visitor, they are of special value to the latter if he is a spiritual aspirant. For the serious aspirant is in perpetual quest of Sufis and saints, seeking them everywhere, even among the sick. For who knows, the sick person may be a pole (*qutb*), or if not a *qutb*, a friend of the Sufi way. Whatever his rank, one should attach himself to every holy person. Even if the ailing person is an enemy to him, the kindness of the visit will be all to the good for by kindness, many an enemy is made a friend, or at least, his enmity is reduced. In brief, we should seek the friendship of the entire Sufi community, of as many holy people as we can find. For united, we can break any attack by the enemies of the way. Union is always strength.

Unfortunately, most of us lack the spiritual eye, and so, are unable to distinguish between saints and simmers. Also, wretched quacks and charlatans abound, ever ready to lead us astray. But one must not despair of finding a true man of God. For a treasure does exist. One must be steady and persevering in his quest. Unblessed with spiritual intuition, he should think that the spiritual treasure is in everyone, including the sick, that no ruin is empty of it. He should seek in everywhere.

Visiting the sick is enjoined on the prophets also. Once Moses neglected this duty. God reproached him in a revelation, "Oh you whom I illumined with My light, I fell sick and you did not come to ask after Me."

Moses said, "O God Almighty, You are all perfection. What mystery is this that You were sick?"

The Almighty responded with, "I am he. His sickness is My sickness." Lover and beloved are not two independent entities. They are two facets of the single attribute of love.

If we aspire to sit with God, we must sit with the saints who are an extension of the shadow of God and whose heart reflects the formless infinite form of the unseen. If we are torn from them, we are in perdition. We have become a part without the whole. We have fallen far from God. The devil's cunning has severed us from them. Finding us alone and helpless, ensnared us body and soul. Hence, every moment, we must seek their shadow so that it may deliver us from lurid fantasies and false imagination and guide us towards the light of the spiritual sun, the true Light without whose shining, there could be no light on any level of being.

THE REVIVAL OF THE SICK COMPANION

When the Prophet saw his sick intimate, he was sweet and tender to him. As the perfect human being is in union with the creative *"Be,"* his holy breath revived him. He was created anew, so to speak. He said, "Sickness has brought me the good fortune that this sultan has come. With his coming, heath and ease have come to me. O blessed illness, anguish and nightly wakefulness! Behold, in my old age, of His grace and munificence, God has bestowed on me such sickness and back-ache that I cannot but start up from sleep every midnight and utter prayer and praise to Him, instead of slumbering all night like a buffalo. Through this sickness, which withers the body but freshens the spirit in me, the mercy of spiritual kings has been aroused. The fire of hell has been quenched by the light of the Lord, so that it threatens me no more.

PAIN IS A BLESSING

Pain is truly a treasure for there are mercies in it. When the body is broken by pain, the spirit is purified and strengthened. Unless God has seen advantage in pain, how should that absolute Mercy have created it? Patience is a virtue. The exercise of patience expands the heart with spiritual delight. Patient endurance of grief, sickness and pain is life's fountain and the intoxicating spiritual cup. Those crowning heights are in lowliness. Humility is exaltation. Brokenness is wholes. It is like autumn which implies and culminates in the spring. We should adapt ourselves to grief and desolation and seek everlasting life in dying to self.

THE NATURE AND DOINGS OF THE ANIMAL SOUL

The animal soul will say that this dying to self is only hurting oneself. It is bad. One should pay no heed to it, for all its doings are contrary to our spiritual progress. As will be seen later, it was the ultimate cause of the Companion's sickly plight and would have ended his life but for the Prophet's resuscitating visit. "Oppose it," has been the injunction of the prophets. In many a case, consultation with another person becomes necessary so as to avoid error and eventual repentance.

"Whom shall we consult?" the community asked.

"Take counsel with the intellect which is the leader," said the prophets.

"What if a woman with no judgment or clear understanding comes in?" they asked.

"Consult her, and do the opposite," they said.

"He who does not reject her counsel is ruined," said the Prophet.

One should know that the animal soul is the feminine principle and worse, for while woman is only a part of evil—as is man—the animal soul is wholly evil. If we consult this soul, no matter how plausible it may sound, the contrary of what it says is true. It is a great plotter of evil. If one finds it unconquerable and cannot cope with it, he should go and mix with a friend, and gain light and understanding. The human intellect is like a lamp. Paired lamps are brighter than a single lamp.

Astounding things arise from the guile and deceit of the animal soul. Its sorcery takes away the discerning faculties of the human being and robs him of spiritual strength. It keeps tempting one with false promises of a new heaven and earth—promises of the kind it has repeatedly broken in the past and shall continue making and breaking in the future. It is the sea whose spell shows only a little foam, but hides perilous depths. It is the hell that shows only a little heat, but hides the burning flame. Masking its deadly character, it appears feeble in the eyes of the righteous, so as to provoke a struggle in which its victory will be easy, unless one is favored by God. As may be recalled, the Prophet described the holy war against the infidels as the lesser battle, and that against the animal, carnal soul as the greater battle. The carnal soul is a veritable dragon, hard to conquer.

THE DEVICES OF GOD, HIS MERCY AND WRATH

God leads aright whomsoever He will and lets others go astray. Prophet Muhammad was shown divine favor in eternity so that temporal and spiritual victory seemed easy to him and his Companions. A vast host of infidels appeared small in his eyes. He set upon them, fearless of danger. As is said in the Koran, God eases to the state of ease the way of him who is God-fearing and believes in goodness. If the host had appeared numerous and formidable, the Prophet might have felt faint-hearted and faltered. In the battle of Badr, he threw a handful of gravel and it routed the dense hosts of Quraysh—in reality, not he but God threw. The Prophet was the passive medium. For the Prophet, God's causing the warfare to seem little was victory. God was his friend, guide and teacher.

4 Prophet Muhammad and the Sick Companion 73

But God's activity is deluding towards the infidels and others who are not pre-disposed to righteousness and disbelieve in goodness. Divine Wrath makes the way to defeat easy for them. It deceives them and causes a hundred seem but one from afar. The Prophet's sword—named *dhu'l faqar*—seemed but a dart, a lion seemed a mere cat. Inspired by a false sense of confidence, they were lead into battle so that God might catch them and they move towards hell by means of their own free act, of their own volition. He causes the prophets and saints to appear despicable in the eyes of the wicked although the entire world is under their sovereignty. He caused the sea to appear dry to Pharaoh. The sea, symbolizing the profound spirituality of the prophets and saints powers delegated to them overpowered Pharaoh and his host with a deadly vengeance [2:50].

How should the fleshly eye or carnal reason see? It looks at the shows of things, not through them into things. The eye becomes seeing by meeting with God. God is not every fool's confidant or guide. The fool sees deadly venom as candy, the ditch as the road. He sees not the same tree that the wise man sees. He does not see things as they are this creation. Every moment it is renewed by divine action. According to an ancient Jewish prayer, God, "Every day renews continually the work of creation"—a doctrine that was also held by the Dead Sea brotherhood.

We are not aware of this renewal because the renewal is of like by like. The change is too rapid for our perception. We consider this universe as continuous. God has kept it so fresh and enduring that the speculative materialist, relying on his partial, discursive intellect and verifiable outward data, says that the universe is eternal and self-created, thus making it co-external with God. Thanks to God, the prophets and saints, endowed with the all-knowing universal intellect, have taught us, and every spiritual man knows that "the whole living web of the divine tapestry," this vast fabric of the universe, is the handiwork of God woven in "the loom of time."

UNIVERSAL INTELLECT AND CONVENTIONAL WISDOM

The universal intellect appears in many guises. These hide its real nature. That is, it is hidden by its phenomenal manifestations. It flies heavenward, while our conventional ideas, our external knowledge, browse among the earthly objects. The mind, of course, is one, but it has a twofold aspect, the pure and the impure, impure when united with desire, pure when free from desire. The Godward flight of the intellect is inward. It is in the spirit.

External or conventional knowledge is borrowed, not ours. It may be the means of acquisition of worldly riches and fame, but of the way to the City of God, it knows nothing. The more one leans on exoteric knowledge, the further he is removed from the Truth. Exoteric or conventional knowledge is the bane of our soul. It is best to become ignorant of worldly wisdom which only enmeshes us in matter and embrace madness like the great Egyptian mystic Dhul-Nun, who, seeking refuge from the disgrace of the body-serving intellect, from the wickedness of the vile, and the infamy of the so-called sane, puposely went and became mad. It is best to flee from what delights the senses. Revile the sycophant. Be charitable. Eschew reputation. Accept disgrace and notoriety. We should do what takes us inward, not outward. We may recall that the Lord has spoken of those who *"have striven in (for) Us"* (Koran 29:69), not of those who have striven away from Him.

Prophet Muhammad, as we know, had no formal education. It is said that he never could write. But a myriad thoughts were in him like: What am I? What is this world? What is Life and what is death? Where do we go from here? What is the purpose of life? What should I do?

THE PROPHET AND THE SICK COMPANION

When the Prophet saw his suffering friend, he perceived that his sickness was caused by irreverence in prescribed prayer. He said to him, "Perhaps, from ignorance you said some-

4 Prophet Muhammad and the Sick Companion   75

thing foolish in your prescribed prayer whose consequences you are now suffering. Recall what you said when you were ached by the carnal soul!"

He answered, "I do not remember, but if you direct a spiritual breath towards me, it will instantly come to my memory."

The Prophet dwelt in light. From his illumining presence and aspiration, the divine light, which is all-seeing and before which there is no past or future, flashed forth from his heart into the sick man's heart. The words of the prescribed prayer forgotten came into his mind. He said, "I now remember the prescribed prayer, which I, insolent fool, uttered when I was sinking in sin. I was clutching at useless straws to save myself, while threats of dire retribution were coming from you to the sinners. Bound in unfastenable chains, seeing no help, no means of escape, no hope of repentance—which is from God to man—nor opportunity for revolt or fight against destiny, I, like the angels Harut and Marut, began to cry in grief to the creator. These two angels, who were sent down to earth and committed every kind of iniquity—dreading the last judgment—chose imprisonment in the pit of Babylon so that they might suffer in this world the pain and punishment of the other world. They were crafty, and what they did appealed to my sense. For the pain there is dreadful, and, in comparison, the pain here is light. The pain of smoke is lighter than the pain of fire. I, therefore, sought to follow their example."

But they suffered not only imprisonment in the pit of Babylon. It is said that the entire smoke of the world crams their brains and issues forth from their nostrils. Happy is not one who seeks to do what they did, but who wars against the flesh, and in order to gain deliverance from the torture of the other world, undertakes the pain of serving God in this world. But my good sense was muffled. I was saying, "O Lord, punish me quickly, so that I may be exempted from the greater pain of the other world. Thereupon, this dangerous sickness seized me, robbing my soul of all rest, leaving me no strength even to commemorate God or utter litanies. I have become unconscious of myself and of all good and evil. If I had not beheld your face and inhaled your reviving scent, I should have passed into painful death. You have shown me kingly sympathy and saved my life."

THE HIGHER SELF

It is well to remember that we are rooted in the higher self, and that self is the kingdom of God which Jesus said is within us. It is microcosmic. It is not more in one being than in another, but is the same and equal in all, so that, in this sense, the vital spiritual sense, all are born equal. When one ignores the higher self, that realm of Beauty, Truth and Goodness, as the Prophet's Companion did, and turns his attention to the lower self, the lunar world or the world of desire, and pursues the sinful joys of sense, the false delights of eye and ear, he incurs the displeasure of the higher self which has all that he is seeking without, which is only the shadowy projection of what is within. Neglected and left behind, that self pursues him with all the fury of a woman scorned. Not that the self had not warned him against the sin and folly of following after the wandering fires, but he did not heed the warning, or even hear it. And nothing goes right with him.

Gradually his strength fails, as the life-blood ebbs away from the wounds in his back made by the deadly arrows. He sinks exhausted on the ground. The remorseless hounds of fate which is himself come up speedily, and, destroying with their gaping mouths his personal form, bring about an enforced return to that unity of being which he has so long denied. The Prophet whose light served as life to the ailing Companion, warned him saying, "Never again utter such a prayer. Do not destroy yourself."

THE PRAYER OF THE SICK MAN

The sick man repented and vowed that never again will he brag rashly or show irreverence in prayer. He said, "This world is the desert of the Israelites and you are Moses. Because of our sin, we remain here in affliction. For years we travel and, at the end, we are still where we started. No progress, or hardly any. If Moses were pleased with us, we would be shown the way through the desert and also the farthest end. And if he were completely disgusted with us, no trays of food—no manna and quails [2:57] would have come to us, no springs would have rushed from a rock [7:160], nor would there by safety for us in the desert. No man is wholly white or wholly black, but a shade of grey. It is the shade that matters. If Moses were wholly disgusted with us, flames of fire would beat upon us. As he has become of two minds about us, he is our friend at times, and, at times, our enemy. At times his wrath becomes our possessor. At times, his clemency becomes our protector from affliction. How may it be that his anger shall again become clemency? This is within your power, O venerable one. I am deliberately using the name of Moses before you, as to praise anyone present is embarrassing."

Praying to God, he said, "Our covenant is subject to every gale of passion. It has been broken a hundred times while Your covenant is more stable and solid than a hundred mountains. Have mercy on our variableness, O Lord of mutations. We have seen ourselves and our shame. Spare us further trial, O king, so that You will have concealed our other acts of disgrace! You are boundless in beauty and perfection. We are boundless in crookedness and aberration. Direct Your boundlessness, O benevolent one, upon the boundlessness of the wrongness and error of wretches like us! Lo, of our material and spiritual resources, only a thread remains. We were a city and only a wall remains. Save, O save the remainder, O king, so that the devil's soul may not rejoice in full. As You have shown Your power, so now show Your mercy. If this prayer aggravated Your wrath, teach us how to pray, O Lord."

Continuing, the ailing man cited the case of Adam and said that on his fall from paradise, the Lord gave him permission to turn in penitence to Him so that he was saved from the devil. The devil regarded his guile as a hurt to Adam, but it became a curse to his own self. Who is the devil that he should triumph over Adam?

The divine curse warps the vision. It makes one self-conceited, envious and spiteful, so that he may not know that an evil act will at last return and strike the evil doer. He cannot see the master moves of the devil and know that love of rank and riches and other alluring sense-objects with which he beguiles us are a hurdle in the way of repentance and a barrier to the water of life.

The curse blinds one. If it did not, one would regard himself, his empirical self, as nothing, and his spiritual malady as a gangrenous and deadly wound. Pain would surge up within him and he would seek a remedy. Until mothers are stricken by the pains of childbirth, how should the child find a way to be born?

SPIRITUAL BIRTH

The Lord has placed the burden of trust in the human being— which to the orthodox is the essence of faith—with its commands and prohibitions. To the Sufi, the burden of divine love and gnosis is a trust which he stands pledged to fulfill. The Lord loves him. His heart is pregnant with love for Him. As Rumi says, "This body is like Mary. Everyone has a Jesus within him, but he is veiled by our self-conceit. How should the embryo be delivered until he longs for delivery and love pangs afflict his heart—until mother, his bodily nature, is in death throes and he is brought out from the veil of egoism and self-conceit. Self-conceit and love cannot co-exist."

To be without pain is to be a callous egotist, a self-glorifier, a usurper of the divine prerogative of homage. It is to say, "I am God," prematurely which becomes a curse to a vain boaster like Pharaoh. But the "I" of the self-negated martyr-saint Hallaj, which was no vain utterance but the truth, is a mercy from God. It is only when one fights and kills the carnal self through spiritual warfare that, phoenix-like, from the dead self, the undying universal self arises and one is spiritually born. Divine love cannot manifest itself except through the mortification of self.

But without the help of a midwife, no new birth is easy, if at all possible. In the case of spiritual birth, the wise counsels of the saint or shaykh are that midwife. As nothing but his shadow can help to slay that self, we should clasp his skirt with all our strength which can only be done by His aid for whatever strength comes into us is the effect of His attracting us towards Him. Whatever the soul sows is from the soul of the soul. All actions proceed from Him. We are only His instruments of action.

He is the one to give help. He is forbearing and long-suffering. Every moment, one should hope for His inspiring breath. If one has remained without Him for long, one should not despair or grieve. He is patient with sinners. He gives them a long rope. But when His mercy grips them, it does not let them escape. Never for a moment does His presence keep one absent from Him. His mercy eternally precedes His wrath so that by His mercy, the wicked or sinful may suffer affliction as a possible corrective. In other words, this affliction is afflicted not because God hates or despises one, but in order that he may abandon his evil qualities and conquer his bodily nature. He strikes not him, but the devil in him so that he may save himself from himself.

His acts of wrath are thus acts of mercy. They are aids to one's purification. Afterwards His grace comes in justification of His wrath saying that as he has cast off sin and emerged from the river of tribulation, washed and pure, he may enter into nearness with Him.[1] Nearness is thus manifested out of the essence of affliction.[2] If the servant of God complains to Him of grief and pain, He says, "Grief and pain have, after all, made you humbly entreating and righteous. Complain of the bounty that comes to you and removes you far from Me and makes you an outcast."[3]

Once there was a barren spell when the Prophet received no revelation. The idolaters mocked him saying that God now hated him. A revelation soon came that the Lord had not forsaken him, nor did He hate him, and the latter days of his life would be better than the first [93:3, 4]. True enough although it seemed ridiculous at that time, his latter years were of most wondrous illumination and success.

GOOD AND EVIL

If one says that evils also are from Him, that is true, but they are no detraction from His bounty. On the contrary, they are an evidence of His perfection. To take a parable, a painter paints beautiful as well as ugly pictures. Both kinds evidence his mastery. Ugliness in the painting is not the ugliness of the painter, but only the exhibition of the ugly by him. If he could not paint the ugly and invest it with every ugliness, it would be a reflection on his perfection as an artist. Hence, God creates both the infidel and the believer. Both manifest His Omnipotence and serve His purpose. Both bow down in worship before Him. The believer bows down willingly, because he is aiming at the Lord's pleasure, not personal gain. The infidel also worships Him, but his aim is selfish. His affirmation at the primal covenant came with reluctance, as if forcibly wrung from him. He looks after his heart, which God gave into the human being's keeping, but, motivated by self-interest, he claims to be its master. He becomes a rebel and sells the fortress, the heart, for for personal profit, forgetting that it belongs to God. It is to forget that body and soul, all belong to God. Like satan, he says to Him, "You have created evil, O You who are able to create both good and evil?" concealing his own role in evil. The faithful believer, on the other hand, says, "O king of beauty and fairness, You have freed me from all imperfections," saying nothing about his own efforts to fulfill the covenant.

All flow from one origin. All are His script and chart. The fault, like ugliness and infidelity, is a fault only in relation to us, not in relation to the creator, who is all wisdom. How should the pure spirit of the invisible see fault?[4]

THE PROPHET'S ADMONITION

The Prophet said to the sick man, "Say thus, 'O God, You that make easy that which is difficult, give good to us in this world and also in the other world. Make the journey that leads to union with You as pleasant as a garden. You indeed are our destination.'"

SPIRITUAL HEAVEN AND HELL

The Lord's favors are for the true believers. At the congregation for judgment, the believers will say to the angel —God's messenger, the prophet, saint or shaykh—"Is not hell the common road by which both believers and infidels pass [19:68-72)]? Here is paradise. We saw no smoke or fire on the way. When did we pass hell?"

The angel will say, "The verdant garden you saw in a certain place on the way, that was hell, a place of terrible penal fires, but which to you became gardens and greenery. As you have striven against your hellish soul and it has become full of purity and you quenched its fire for the sake of the Lord, as the flaming fire of lust in you has become the verdure of piety and the light of guidance to union with Him. as the fire of anger has become forbearance, the darkness of ignorance knowledge, and the fire of greed has turned to noble giving and that stinging envy to a rosary, as all these fires you quenched for His sake, and transformed your fiery soul into an orchard, and sowed the seed of fidelity in it, our Hell also to you has become greenery and roses and the horn of plenty."

What is the reward for good actions? As is said in the Koran, *"The reward for good is good"* [55:60].

"Did you not say," the angel will continue, "We are His devotees and are negating ourselves in His eternal attributes. Whether we are sane or insane, we are intoxicated with that divine cup-bearer and that cup. We bow to His writ and command. So long as He is in our hearts, our sole occupation is to serve Him and die for Him."

In the angel's speech, heaven and hell symbolize spiritual states, utterly non-spatial. They are the reflections or effects of the actions of the righteous and the unrighteous, of the believer and the infidel. Spiritual people in paradise display His beauty. The wicked in hell display His Majesty, Terror and wrath. The four fountains or rivers of paradise—pure water (*kawsar*), wine (*salsabil*), honey (*zanjabil*), and milk (*tasnim*)—symbolize His beautiful attributes. The penal fires and chains of hell symbolize His wrathful attributes. While the evil-doers are left burning in the flames of their lust, the righteous have no awareness of hell or of its smoke or fire.

SEEK SPIRITUAL KINGS

We should deem it incumbent on us ever to be in quest of the lovers of God, the shaykhs, those dwellers of paradise, who confer blessings on their devotees. If the seeker is illumined or has received capacity for the light, they will give him a home in the heaven of their heart, and reveal to him the divine mystery that is inscribed therein. Be then with your spiritual relatives. Find and cling to the full moon, the perfect human being if you are a segment of the moon. Why should a part keep away from its whole? What is this mingling with all these opposites?

There is absolute unity in God's eternal knowledge. Differences arose in emanation from latency into visible externality. This devolution, this individualization, is the cause of separation between the Whole and the parts. Of course, the parts are not parts in relation to the Whole, only as diverse created beings are they spiritually different. From one aspect opposed, from another, they are unified, all one from head to foot.[5] The lovers of the whole are not the lovers of the part. He who loves the part fails to attain to the whole. The part he loves will return to its own whole. The lover of the world is not the lover of the whole. He is like a lover of a sunlit wall who does not perceive that the radiance and splendor are from the sun, not from the wall on which he has set his heart. When the sunbeams return at sundown, he will be left in dark despair.

The vile soul is a fraud. It desires us to earn only that which is vile. If it desires us to earn something noble, there is always some trick behind it. It may be to deprive us of something nobler. So long as we are sold to the blandishments of the world, imperfection will remain our portion. Why then set store by the flattery and honeyed words of the common herd of men? Better for one are the flouts and flings of the spiritual lords. Let him bear them gladly so that through their spiritual influence, he who is nobody may become somebody. From the perfect human being's spirit comes felicity and robes of honor. Under his protective wing, body becomes soul. If you see anyone spiritually empty and destitute, know that he has followed not his master's desire, but the promptings of his animal self. To flee from the master is to flee from happiness.

We have learnt a trade to earn meat and raiment for our body. But of what avail will they be in the hereafter? We should learn a spiritual trade which will earn us God's forgiveness in the other world which is the world of recompense. The earnings of this world will bring us at the best, power and glory, but they are not enduring, and, as God has said, these earnings are children's play compared with the earnings of the other world [29:64]. This world is a playground, and death is the night. When we return with an empty purse, exhausted like a child who had set up shop and played the shopkeeper during the day for self-amusement, and returns home at night, hungry and alone. The earnings of religion are rich and lasting. They are love and inward rapture. They are receptive capacity for the light of God.

5 THE OLD HARPER

In the time of the Caliph Umar, there was a harper, a really wonderful minstrel. His enchanting voice and harpings were an ornament to any assembly. They would enliven and enrapture the dullest of souls. He was like Seraphiel whose trumpet blast at the resurrection will raise the dead to life.

The prophets also have spiritual notes, the inward voice of divine inspiration from which their message to people, their call to God, derives its inspiring power. But the fleshly ear cannot hear that soul-stirring voice, as that ear is defiled by vain prattle and all manner of iniquity. It cannot even hear the notes of the genii, though they belong to this world for the geni are a mystery to the human being. The notes of the heart are higher than those of the human being and genii. The heart is the passageway of the all-knowing God, while the human being and geni are imprisoned in the ignorance of the world. Neither can know the mysteries of creation except by His gracious will [55:33].

The saints are the spiritual children of the Prophet. They are the Seraphiels of our time. Their inward notes say in the beginning, "O you particles of negation, rise above this world of non-existence, above all this vain fancy and airy imagining. O you who are rotten and corrupt in this phenomenal world, know that your soul neither grew nor came to birth. It is everlasting." It does not perish with the perishing of the body.

From the saints come life and growth. At their voice which also only the ear of the heart can hear, the dead souls in the body's tomb start up in their winding sheets, and say, "This voice is apart from all other voices. To quicken the dead is only the work of the voice of God. We had morally died and had finished. The call of God came and we were spiritually resurrected."

The call, whether it comes unveiled or it comes veiled [42:51] from behind the burning bush as it came to Moses, it impregnates His true lovers and seekers. Gabriel, the holy breath, impregnated Mary, with a Messiah, a perfect child, which is the soul's new birth, the birth of one's true self.

Let them who are spiritually dead and rotten within turn back from this phantom world, this non-existence, and heed that voice. It is absolutely the voice of God although it comes from the larynx of a saint. God has said to him:

> I am your tongue and eyes,
> I am your senses, your pleasure and anger.
> Go, you are he of whom I have said, "By Me he hears
>   and by Me he sees."
> You are the divine consciousness. Why say you possess
>   the divine consciousness?
> As through bewilderment you have become
>   "one that belongs to God."
> "I am yours," "as God belongs to him who is His"
>   (Tradition)
> At times I say to you, "It is you," and at times I say, "It
>   is I." (Tradition)
> Whatever I say, I am the all-illuminating sun.
> The darkness of ignorance and sin which the heavenly
>   sun could not dispel, became from my breath
>   effulgent as morn.

This is the unitive state in which the divine and human aspects of the essence are interchangeable. At times, the divine attributes appear in which the human attributes have passed away. At times, God appears in the robe of human attributes. The divine consciousness is fully manifested in the saint, in the perfect human being for he is both creative and creaturely. He is creative, as he is the Logos, the equivalent of the creative "*Be*." The creation is but the secondary reflection of the divine attributes from the mirror of his heart where they are first reflected. Neither heaven nor earth could have borne the direct radiance of His attributes. For them it was excessive in intensity. A filtering medium was necessary and the perfect human being is that medium. He is creaturely, as he is the medium through which God sees Himself in the creation, His outer visible vesture and also creatures.

God taught Adam the Names directly. To the rest He taught the Names through Adam. Whether we receive this knowledge directly from God or through Adam, it is the same knowledge. Is not wine the same wine whether it is taken from the jar or from the cup into which it has been poured from the jar? "Happy is he," said the Prophet, "Who has seen me—the real me —and he that looks at him who saw me." If a lamp is lighted from a candle and another lamp is lighted from this lamp, and, in this way, a hundred lamps are lighted, it is the same light whether it is taken from the last lamp or from the candelabrum. We may receive the light of God from the earlier saints of from the last ones. It is the same light, the master-light of seeing on all levels of being.

God may say to the saint, "It's you," or "It's I," but whatever He says no saint or perfect human being becomes God. He is illumined by His light or has attained oneness with it, but he remains a human being. The Prophet is reported to have said, "I am the light of God and all things are of my light." He did not say, "I am God."

THE HARPER'S SUPPLICATION

To return to the harper, his wondrous voice was truly the delight of the world. It would charm the senses, awaken sudden dreams and fantasies in the hearer, and stupefy the mind of the spirit. But he was no saint. The years grew on him. He became old and infirm. His back was bent like a bow. His eyebrows drooped over his eyes. His enchanting voice that was the envy of the heavenly minstrel Venus became ugly and worthless. This was only natural. For with time, every lovely earthly thing becomes unlovely, except the voices of saints in the hearts of people. The trumpet blast of the resurrection is only an echoing sound of their breath. They are the soul of all mystical experience, as all thought and speech, the very savor of inspiration and revelation. The breath of the divine mystery is from them, from the attributes of God mirrored in their pure hearts, as the Logos, the origin of all created things.

Age seared the harper. He grew so weak that he was unable to earn anything, not even a loaf of bread. Turning towards God, he said, "O Lord, You have given me a long life and bestowed countless favors on this wretch. I have been sinning these seventy years, and, yet, never for a day have you withheld Your bounty from me. Today, I can earn nothing and am Your guest. I will play the harp for You. I am Yours."

He lifted his harp and, searching for God, wended his way to the graveyard of Madinah, uttering sighs all the way. He said, "I seek the price of silk from God for harp-playing (or harp strings)." He played the harp for long among the buried dead, and then, shedding tears, pillowing his head on the harp, dropped on a tomb. Sleep fell upon him. His soul left the harp. The harper flew away to the purely spiritual domain, to the vast plain of the soul. There, freed from the body and the anguish of the world, it sang of what had befallen it, saying, "How happy would I be if only they would let me stay in this garden and spring-time, drunken with this spacious region and mystic anemone field! I would be going about without head or foot, eating sugar without lip and tooth, frolicking merrily with the paradise dwellers, seeing a whole world with eyes shut, gathering basils and roses without a hand!"

His soul was plunged in honey. It had the fountain of Job to drink from and wash in—a fountain believed to have appeared under the feet of Job at the command of the Lord in which he washed his body and was cured of all affliction and made pure as the orient light [38:42-43]. In that plain of purity nothing gross or physical, no means or instruments, no external senses or limbs are required. The spiritual sense takes over and is all-operative and effective.

But God has created this world with a purpose. Heedlessness of Him is a part of the grand design. Blind to His mysterious purpose, and subject to hopes and fears, the heedless worldings run the affairs of the world and maintain the worldly environment which is necessary for the climb to spiritual perfection as well as for the of total consumption of the bodily existence of the saint or mystic by the rapture of love and longing. Without him, who would provide the guiding light? Forgetfulness of God is in great measure the pillar of the world.

This wide-extended material heaven and earth is so constricted in comparison with the spiritual heaven and earth that unfolded itself in the minstrel's dream that its constriction would stifle one's heart, while the spaciousness of the spiritual realm would open the wings of one's soul, enabling it to fly freely in the infinite of spacelessness. If this spiritual world and the way to it were manifest, no one would remain in this narrow sorrow-stricken world.

Not only the common mortals, but the spiritual adepts also who are lost in God are required to rise from self-negation to active consciousness of life in God, return, tell people what they have seen and experienced in that blissful state, and serve as their spiritual guides. They must display His attributes for the enlightenment of others, just as He has displayed them in their hearts.

THE CALIPH UMAR AND THE MINSTREL

The harper was in a broken state, but not alone, not abandoned by God. God sent such a sleepiness upon Umar that he was unable to stay awake. He fell into a state of bewilderment, saying, "This is unknown. It is from Above, and is, surely, not without purpose." He laid his head down and was soon overcome by sleep. He dreamt that a heavenly voice came to him from the unseen. His spirit heard that voice which is the divine origin and archetype of every sound. It is, indeed, the only voice, all the rest being but echoes. It is a voice which not only every man, Turk, Kurd, Persian and Arab has understood without ear, but even the wood and stone, each, according to its capacity, has understood, so that "Each bush and oak knows I am"—God alone has the right to say, "I am."

Every moment, the creative call of *alast* is coming from God, that is, "*Am I not (your Lord)?*" an affirmative question addressed at the primal covenant to the essences of all existents in creation at the time of their individualization in God's knowledge. They all replied, "Yes"and became existent [7:172] where the Lord is said to have brought forth from the children of Adam, from their loins, their seed, and made them affirm His Lordship, a verse which is variously interpreted. And every moment at His creative call, every object of potential existence is nothing by "Yes." The response is in their soul and essence. The whole process of creation is a single timeless moment. It begins and ends in a single point, the divine Essence, which is outside the spatio-temporal framework and beyond our limited perception.

That heavenly voice said to Umar, "Set Our servant free from want. He is Our highly esteemed favorite, pure, worthy and blessed. Hasten and draw full seven hundred dinars from the public treasury and carry them on foot to the graveyard for him."

Awed by that voice, Umar sprang up, and, with the purse under his arm, hurried towards the graveyard in quest of His choice servant. He ran long around the graveyard and was exhausted, but saw none there, except the broken old minstrel. "How should such a one be His elect? Surely, this is not my quest," he said to himself. He went round again, but saw no one else. After much wandering, when he was certain that no one other was there, he said, "Many an illumined heart is to be found in darkness," and came and sat down beside him with the utmost reverence. A sneeze seized him. The old harper started up. Seeing Umar, he stood perplexed and decided to leave. He began to quiver with fear. He said within himself, "Help. O God! The Inspector has fallen upon this broken old man."

Seeing the harper pallid with fear, Umar said to him, "Fear not! Do not flee hence. For I have glad tidings from God. He has praised your disposition so often that I was moved to love your face. Sit by me, and listen, so that I may breathe His secret message into your ear. He sends you greetings and inquired how you are faring in your deep affliction. Here are some dinars to pay for silk. He asks you to excuse their inadequacy. Spend them, and, then, come here again."

Hearing this, the old minstrel began shaking all over. He gnawed at his hand, melting with shame, rending his garment, and crying, "O peerless Lord!" When he had wept long and his sorrow exceeded all bounds, he dashed his harp on the ground, and broke it to pieces, saying, "O you that have barred me from God and for seventy years, have sucked my blood, because of you I am disgraced before His Perfection. Have mercy, O Lord, on this life spent in iniquity."

He cursed the harp, as the Prophet had banned stringed musical instruments, and the professional musicians those days were generally of a disreputable character, so that the harp was a symbol of the animal soul.

THE PLACE OF MUSIC

A part from the chanting of the call to prescribed prayer and the Koran, music has no place in Islamic ritual. Many Muslims and Sufis consider it detestable, even unlawful. Others hold different views.[1] In Rumi, the *sama* (lit. audition, but here includes music, chanting and whirling) has a spiritual significance. He introduced it into the religious service. The dead were carried to the burial place to the accompaniment of joyous hymn-singing, as the human spirit's journey home was an occasion for "rejoicings, thanks and whirling." The *sama* to him is to recall the sound of "Yes," affirming the Lordship of God at the primal covenant. It is to sunder oneself from oneself. It is to experience the doubly rapturous ecstasy of dying to self and savoring everlasting life in utter self-extinction. He also speaks of "the music of the spheres," the creative "*Be!*," so that the entire creation is the speech of God and our "earth is but an echo of the spheres."

Rumi was fond of playing the rebeck. He said that it called the inner self to love and knowledge of God, while the formal, prescribed prayer only called the external self to serve God. Because of the peculiar gyrations performed by Rumi's followers, they came to be known in the West as the whirling dervishes.

THE PENITENCE OF THE HARPER

Continuing his penitential supplication, the harper said, "You gave me life the worth of every day of which none knows except You. And I, time's fool, have breathed it all away in treble and bass. Minding the modes and notes of music, I grew mindless of the bitter moment of separation from this life. My heart withered spiritually and died. Now, help, O God. Save me from this iniquitous self. I seek help against none else but this wronger, this false self, which appears as one wronged when thwarted by age or otherwise, and so, is seeking help and justice. I turn to You, as I will receive justice from none except You who are closer to me than hands and feet, closer to me than myself. For every moment this I-hood comes to me from You. It is Your gift. When it comes no more and my craft is gone, I see none but You. One must regard not oneself, not the gift, but the Giver, the One who moment by moment renews and replenishes one's existence."

Umar said to him, "This wailing of yours is a sign of your sobriety, your self-consciousness and self-consciousness is a sin, as it involves duality—God and self. The way of self-negation is different. Self-consciousness arises from thoughts of the past.

Past and future both are veils that hide God from us. The true seeker of God, the Sufi, is "the son of the moment," "the son of the time," living in an eternal now, absorbed in contemplation of God, with whom is neither past not future. He is above all-relations of time and space. As man is a pattern of mind-and-sense data, and he becomes what his thought is, unless he leaves aside all thought, even the highest, and there is no wandering from unity, his existence, according to the eminent Sufi Junayd (d. 910 CE), "Is a sin with which no other sin can be compared."

INTOXICATION AND SOBRIETY

Rumi, like the eminent Bayazid Bastami (d. 874 CE), places spiritual intoxication above sobriety, while Junayd and some other Sufis place sobriety above intoxication. Intoxication is ecstasy involving the loss of reason and self-consciousness, the passing away of the human attributes in the divine attributes, the rapturous longing for God, while the state of sobriety involves the return of the negated senses to normal consciousness, to the world of attributes, so that nearness to God has to be sought anew. The second sobriety, far more difficult to attain, involves their return to supernormal consciousness in which the essence is revealed as the attributes and intoxication is lost in sobriety. One is no more superior to the other or even distinct from it. Like all other dualities, this duality also is transcended and harmonized as a single unity.

"Set fire to yesterday and the morrow," continued Umar. One should set fire to every thought, high or low, even to the quest for God. For when you are going about searching for God, you are absorbed in your search, not in God. It is said in the Song of Solomon, "By night on my bed I sought him whom my soul loves. I sought him but I found him not. I will rise now and go about the city in the streets, and in the broadways I will seek him whom my soul loves. I sought him but I found him not." God is not to be found if one seeks him in private prayer and meditation at night or in places of public worship. Seeking is not finding.

To continue with Umar, "Remembering or seeking," you are still with your dark self, not self-negated, not with Him. "Twixt light and darkness what commerce? O you, whose knowledge lacks knowledge of the knowledge giver, your repentance means circling round yourself and is worse than your sin. When will you repent of such repentance? At one time, you turn to the sound of music. At another, you are in love with weeping and wailing, both of which are self-conscious acts. As unconsciousness of sin is repentance (Junayd), forget your past sin and repent of forgetting God."

In the case of a novice, of course, the remembrance of a past sin may be of value. It may keep him from its repetition. But the harper was no more a novice.

When Umar became a reflector of mysteries, the old minstrel was awakened from within. His individual soul died and the universal soul was born. Lord of sense and self, he was beyond weeping and laughing which are bodily acts. A mystical bewilderment invaded his soul. He scaled past the ramparts of heaven, searching and questing beyond all words and feelings, super-sensible, beyond intellectual comprehension, utterly ineffable. He was sunk in the beauty of the Lord of majesty, where none knew him except the divine ocean and whence there was no deliverance or return. The "journey to God" had ended. With it, all questing. The infinite "journey in [the attributes of] God" had begun.

6 THE COUNTRYMAN AND THE TOWNSMAN

There was a townsman who was the friend of a countryman. Whenever the countryman came to town, he would be his guest for two or three months. He would stay in his pavilion and enjoy his sumptuous hospitality. The townsman would provide free of cost whatever his friend wanted during his stay with him.

Once the countryman said to the khwaja, the townsman, "Are you ever coming to the country for a change Come, for it is not spring. Roses and anemones are in bloom and the sown fields wear a delightful look. Or come in summer in the fruit season. Bring your retinue and your children and kinsfolk along and stay in the country for three and four months."

Once the countryman would renew his invitation every year. The townsman would put him off with some excuse or other and a promise to visit him next year if he could escape from the pressing affairs that kept him at home.

On his last visit, having enjoyed his lavish hospitality for three months, the countryman again said to the townsman, "How long will you cheat me with false promises?"

The townsman said, "I am longing to visit you, but every change depends on the divine decree. The human being is like a ship and has to wait until the Lord sends the favorable breeze."

The countryman took his hand three times in covenant, saying, "Come soon with your children and see the beauty of the countryside. Please make a special effort. My family is eagerly expecting your children."

After ten years and each year with similar entreaties and promises, the khwaja's children said to him, "Father, the moon, the cloud, the shadows, all make their journeys. You have taken great pains for his sake and have placed him under so much debt that naturally he wishes to repay some part of it by having you and us as his guests. He also told us in secret many times that we should coax you to come."

The khwaja said, "One should always beware of the ill-will of those whom one has shown favor. Friendship shows its true self only at the last. While those is a friendship, as with genuine people, which produces noble thoughts and deeds which are recompensed hereafter, there is a friendship, as with religious impostors, which destroys all nobleness and eventually turns into estrangement. The Prophet said that prudence consists in "thinking evil," so that one may know that at every step there is a snare, and knowing it, he may avoid it and be quit of evil. One must not advance boldly. If he has eyes, he should not walk like a blind man. If he does not have eyes, he should walk warily, using the staff of prudence and judgment. If he lacks this staff also, he should use the seer's eye as his guide so that he does not fall into the pit of delusion or become the victim of the carnal soul as has been the fate of countless worldlings in the past.

At length, the countryman's persistent cajolery prevailed over the Shaykh's prudence. In approval of his invitation, the children were chanting, "Let us frolic and play." But, as in the case of Joseph whom the words "frolic and play" [12:12] parted from the protection of his father, Prophet Jacob and brought him much suffering, in this case also, as will be seen, leaving the comforts of home for the fancied joys of the countryside was going to be no "play," but a deadly game, contrived deceit and fraud.

We must not let anything, no amount of worldly treasure sever us from God or from a prophet or saint. The saint may be poor, but he has all the treasures of divine knowledge and wisdom in his keeping. It may be recalled how severely God rebuked the Companions of the Prophet, when, in a year of famine, on hearing the sound of the drum announcing the coming of a caravan with imported merchandise, they abandoned and made void the Friday congregation and hurried towards the caravan so that others might not forestall them and buy the imported goods cheap. They left the Prophet standing alone in prescribed prayer with two or three dervishes who were firm of faith. God said to his Companions, "In greed of wheat you forsook that man of God, the Prophet. Companionship with him is better than frolic and riches. Was it not certain to your greed that I [God] am the best Provider?" How should He who gives nourishment from Himself to the wheat let your acts of trust in Him go to waste? For the sake of wheat, you have been sundered from its sender from Heaven.

The khawja, his children and kinsfolk made preparations for the journey. They set off for the country saying to themselves, "Our destination is a sweet pasturage. The friend who has invited us is kind and charming. He will leave his whole orchard to us and let us take back to town the store of the countryside which will last us all through the winter. Let us hasten and get this abundance."

But reason was entering a caveat from within, saying, "*Exult not, lo, my Lord loves not the exultant*" [28:76]. Rejoice but moderately "*on account of whatever He causes to come to you*" [57:23]. Rejoice in Him for He is the resuscitating spring. All else, howsoever grand, even scepter and crown, will only make you oblivious of Him and lead you to perdition.

"Rejoice in sorrow, for it is a treasure, a means of attainment to nearness to Him. In this way, one ascends downward— through humility and self-abasement. How should children, those spiritually raw, be impressed by this treasure? They are beguiled by the name of "play," and run after it, not knowing that deadly snares and pitfalls are concealed in this way, nor that in the clay of the body, there is no opening for spiritual advancement.

One should turn towards the heart, the spirit, and journey on. The heart is the home of security. It abounds in flowing spiritual fountains and rose-gardens. One should not go to the country. The country makes a fool even of a wise man. "To dwell in the country is the grave of the intellect," said the Prophet. If one stays in the country even a month, ignorance and spiritual blindness will be his portion for a long time. The country is a symbol for the shaykh who only pretends to have attained to mystical nearness to God, but in fact is given to conventionality and disputation and is a slave of sense and self. The town, on the other hand, is universal reason, the logos.

Let us, however, adhere to the outer form of the story for it will lead us to the inner meaning at the end. The first stage of every the human being is form, the spirit. The beauty of disposition comes after it. First comes the body and then the spirit within it. First the form of every fruit and then its sweet savor.

The party rode afield, singing of the benefits of travel. For only by travel does the crescent become the full moon and the pawn in chess a noble queen. From the imagined delight of the country, even the rough road seemed like paradise. For the bad, if associated with something good, also appears good. From sweet-lipped ones, bitterness becomes sweet. From the rose-garden, even thorns become charming. A merchant sits in his shop until nightfall. The trader fares over sea and land. The carpenter works on wood—each for the sake of his waiting beloved.

GOD THE REAL OBJECT OF LOVE

But all things fair and our love for them decay and die. Even love of one's father and mother, of the milk and nipple does not endure. Our friendship with any existent thing, for anything other than God, is like the radiance of the sun. On whatever object it falls, we love the thing. But when the radiance returns to the sun, we love it no more. Whatever we love is gilded with divine qualities. When the goldenness has returned to its source, we proceed to discard it. Its beauty was borrowed. Under its comeliness is the base substance that is not comely. As the gold from the face of the false coin returns into the mine, why should we not go towards the mine? As the sun's radiance on the wall returns to the sun, why not go towards the sun?

The shaykh was deceived by form and mistook flattery for sincerity, cupidity for munificence. He and his kinsman had left the mine of universal reason for the country of delusion, entoiled in the fancy that gold already lay packed for them. They went along laughing, kissing joyfully anyone who came from the country, saying that as he had seen the face of their dear friend, he was to them as the eye. They behaved like Majnun who would kiss and fondle Layla's dog which was the guardian of her abode. When an idler accused him of madness, he said, "Do not go by external form. Look at its high aspiration. Consider where it has made its abode. It is my close-bosomed companion, the sharer of my sorrow and joy." The dog, of course, was spiritual, while the countryman was tombed in self.

As the shaykh and party did not know the way to the countryman's village and had no guide, they kept going from one village to another, suffering much fatigue and tribulation in the quest. Whether it is traveling to the Kabah or earning a living, one needs a guide or teacher, unless one is a Muhammad, so that God Himself teaches him the Koran and gives him all knowledge, or is an Adam so that He teaches him the Names. For those attached to the body, He has made the pen the source of acquisition of knowledge. To learn the skill of penmanship, one needs a human teacher. Guideless, with no help from any quarter, the townsman's party became sick of the country and the honeyed words of the hypocritical countryman about whom and whose like, God has said, *"We will drag him by the forelock"* [96:15].

It took the party a whole month to reach their dream village. They arrived provisionless and with no fodder for their beasts. When they found the countryman's house, they hastened like kinsfolk to its door. But the people in the house bolted it from inside. The shaykh was made with rage, but to no avail. They remained at his door for five days, bearing the heat of the sun and the cold of night from necessity, as they lacked the means to move on. Necessity often binds the good to the wicked. The townsman would see the countryman and salute him, saying who he was, and how often he had treated him to viands at his table, and on which particular day, he bought him this or that merchandise. His munificence to him was no secret in the town.

It is customary to show respect and gratitude to one's benefactor. But the countryman pretended that he did not recognize him, saying to the shaykh, "I neither know your name, nor your dwelling place, nor whether you are a fair fellow or foul."

The shaykh said that this moment was like the day of resurrection, since "*a man flees from his brother*" [80:34]. It is best not to behold such a malicious, hypocritical face as that of the countryman. Ungratefulness is a most heinous sin.

On the fifth night, thick racing clouds began to shroud the sky, threatening dreadful rain. The shaykh and his company had reached the end of their forbearance. He knocked at the door shouting, "Call the master." After repeated entreaties, the master came to the door and said, "Why, what is it, dear sir?"

The shaykh said, "I renounce my claim to your gratitude and hospitality and to all else I was fancying. I have suffered five days of burning heat. These days have been like five years of pain. A single injustice from a friend is as thousands of injustices from others, since the sufferer was accustomed to his kindness and did not anticipate cruelty and injustice from him. Tribulation or grief is nothing but the result of something that is contrary to habit. I acquit you on all counts. But on this awful night, give us some shelter, so that for this good deed you may receive a reward at the resurrection."

"There is a nook," the countryman said, "which belongs to

the keeper of the vineyard. Bow and arrow in hand, he keeps watch there against the wolf, ready to shoot him if he should come. If you are prepared to do that service, that nook is yours. If not, please seek another place."

The shaykh said, "I will do this service and a hundred others, only give me a place and let me have the bow and arrow." The nook was cleared. They went in and had to crowd together, one on top of the other like locusts, as it was a narrow nook, with no room to turn. All through the night, they cried, "O God, this serves us right."

They realized that this was the price of consorting with the vile, of showing worthiness to the unworthy. It is better to be the slave of an illumined soul than to be a favorite of earthly kings from whom all that one can get is the empty sound of a drum. Compared with the perfect human being, who is the spirit of humanity, even the townsmen—here symbolizing theologians—are brigands. They ambush the spiritual wayfarer and hinder his Godward ascent. Who then is the countryman? A plain fool void of spiritual gifts. He who, lacking rational foresight, chose to follow the serpent-souled Iblis is accursed. A death-bed repentance will not save him.

The shaykh kept watching for the wolf outside, unaware of the wolf within, the animal soul which imagines this deluding world to be the origin of all delightful things. He had left the universal reality behind and set off for the country of delusion. Gnats and fleas were stinging them in the wilderness, but they did not have the time to drive them away because of the fear of a sudden attack by the wolf. If he should come and inflict some damage, he (the shaykh) would have to face the devilish wrath of the countryman.

About midnight, all of a sudden a deserted wolf-like figure raised its head from a hill top. The khwaja immediately released the arrow and it hit the animal. It fell to the ground.

The countryman uttered a wail, crying that it was his asscolt that had been shot down.

The shaykh said, "No, it is the wolf. The features of wolfishness are apparent in its form. Night causes many a thing to appear wrong. Examine more carefully."

"O no," said the countryman. "I know for certain it was my colt. You have killed it. May you never be delivered from trouble!"

Losing patience, the shaykh sprang up and seized the countryman by his collar and said, "You fool and impostor, in the darkness of night, worsened by clouds and rain, you know your colt, but you do not know me, your own ten years' comrade."

THE BOGUS SAINT

"You pretend to be drunk with God, a great gnostic, saying 'I am a gnostic unaware of myself. I cannot tell heaven from earth. I cannot even recall what I ate yesterday. My heart is full of God and has no room for aught else. I am in such bewilderment that I should be held fully excused for anything I say or do. The divine Law absolves the drunkard and the opium-eater. The scent of the peerless king is more intoxicating than a hundred vats of grape wine. How then should the obligations of the Law apply to one like me who is God-intoxicated?' God has said, 'It is no sin in the blind,' and I am blind in regard to myself. I see by the light of God. I am exempt from all obligations.

"You are bragging of your dervishhood. You pretend as if you were an eminent Sufi like Junayd or Bastami, or one like the martyr-saint Hallaj. But you are no saint or Sufi, no man of God, but a plain hypocrite, a fraud, a windbag of selfhood. A lover of God is dead to sense and self, dead to this world, drenched in Him. Even the trumpet blast of the Resurrection cannot shake him into self-consciousness. But you are a lover of this visioned show of pairs and opposites, a slave of the flesh and the devil. What you said about your colt is full of affirmation of your self, clear proof of your self-existence. Thus does God expose the hypocrisy of your like and prevent the egoist from escaping from the snare of His omnipotence. There is a testing of every vile person in this world. None escapes detection.

"You are a devil's friend who only turns away his associates from the way of God. You are not divinely inspired as you claim. You have ruined our honor and spiritual life. You have drunk, not the wine of God, but the phantom cup of naught, and are conceiving a false opinion of your nearness to Him because of His imminence. Know that nearness or affinity is of more than one kind. One is the attribute of nearness of a saint which has a hundred miracles and powers. It consists of the inspiration of divine love. Distinct from it is the essential nearness, which is in respect of His creating and sustaining us. Both sappy and dry boughs are near in essence to the sun, but while the former's attribute of nearness gives us mellow fruit, the latter's lack of it makes the bough to wither sooner. Do not be one who is drunk with the wine of egoism and sensuality and feels sorry when he returns to his wits. Be an inebriate of the spiritual kind at whose sight even the carnal spirits regret they are not similarly intoxicated. Only he who is dead to self abides in God and is conscious of the divine realities. Such prizes do not come before dying for with God naught avails but dying."

7 Daquqi:
his Visions and Miracles

Daquqi was a spiritual lord of goodly bearing, who loved God and possessed miraculous gifts. Afraid of becoming attached to any place or person, he would make his abode for no more than a day. He constantly moved saying that even a stay of two days in one house kindled love of it in his heart. He traveled in the daytime. At night he prayed and was in constant contemplation of God.

He was severed from God's creatures in a sense, but not because he was ill-natured or because he regarded them as other than God. Nor because he was a religious ascetic who believed that salvation must be sought in jungles and deserts away from the haunts of men. He was compassionate to them and was a kindly intercessor whose prayers on their behalf were answered. For the good and the bad alike, he was a sure refuge. He was better than a mother, dearer than a father. His isolation was different in kind.

The Prophet said, "O sirs, to you I am compassionate and kind like a father, as you all are parts of me." Likewise, in so far as Daquqi was sunk in contemplation of the divine unity, he was isolated from men, but, as the created form of the universal spirit, he was the whole of which they were the parts or individualization. Why should the part be torn from the whole? A limb severed from the body becomes carrion. Until it is rejoined, it is useless. A Sufi also, if severed from the communion of saints, is spiritually dead, even though he may still be fulfilling the formal religious obligations and observing the exoteric practices of the Path. He is regenerated only on rejoining the communion. The terms whole and part, union and separation have only a figurative application to the relations that exist between Reality and Its countless phenomenal forms of manifestation. The divine Light is joined with all and yet apart from all.

Even though in giving legal judgment, Daquqi was the leader, in piety and religiousness all-surpassing and the cosmic journey of his perfect soul was never-ending, yet he was ever seeking the saints of God. In travel, they were his main object. He would be praying to Him to make him a companion of those whom his heart knew and whom he was prepared to serve and make those whom he was debarred from knowing kindly disposed to him.

The Lord would say, "What unquenchable passion is this? When you have My love, why seek another's love? When you have Me, why seek a human being?"

Daquqi would reply, "O All-knowing Lord, although I abide in You, I would like to commune with the elect and hear what each could tell me of divine knowledge revealed to him."

"Greed for Your love is grand and glorious," while that for another is shameful and ruinous. But the sea of divine knowledge is fathomless. Who can measure the immeasurable? Even Moses, despite his perfection as a prophet, quested for the mystic sage and guide Khidr, as God had not given him the same intimacy with the divine consciousness, the same illumination of divine knowledge as to Khidr, lest it should interfere with the discharge of his exoteric prophetic mission. Mystically, Moses was Khidr's disciple. One must not regard this spiritual greed to be less than the sensual greed for worldly possessions. Only the former leads to spiritual advancement and the latter to spiritual decay and death.

Discontent is divine. We must not tarry at any spiritual station in the way, but keep going greedily onward. For the journey is infinite. Above the visible blue firmament are innumerable firmaments, bluer, lovelier, to scale, and, at last, the Lord's sort is reached, which is the boundless plane. As the mystic's attention is only in measure with his internal purity, which is but grossness before the divine purity, the true seat of honor is not any spiritual state or station attained, no matter how lofty, but the journey itself—the "journey to God" and then the "journey through God." His highest attainment is an infinite aspiration transcending every attainment. Daquqi was spiritually dropsical, ever unsatiated, for the object of his love was infinite. He said that he had traveled a long time between the spiritual and material worlds, unconscious of the way, absorbed in God. But how can one reach the shoreless shore?

When asked why he walked barefoot over thorns and stones, he said that he was bewildered and crazed. One must not consider these feet that walk on the earth, for a lover of God does not walk on his feet. He walks on his heart. How should the intoxicated heart know aught of road, stage, or short or long distance? Long and short are bodily attributes. The cosmic journey of the spirit is outside the category of space and time. The body learned from the spirit how to travel. The journey is how, though seemingly in the form of howness. It is spiritual ascent while still in this earthly body and it knows no end.

THE APPARITION OF THE SEVEN CANDLES

Continuing, Daquqi said that one day he was going along, yearning to see in man the divine radiance, a sun enfolded in a speck, a perfect human being. He reached a certain shore. It was evening time. Of a sudden, from afar, he saw what seemed to be seven candles. He hastened in their direction. The light of each candle was soaring aloft to heaven. He was bewildered as to what kind of candles were these that God had lighted.

They were the seven substitutes (*abdal*) of the saintly hierarchy who preside over the seven climes or the seven principal divine Names or they symbolized Adam-born people of the unseen" who have vanished from this world. In Hujwiri's *Kashf al-mahjub* (*The Revelation of the Veiled*), a famous mystical treatise, the saintly hierarchy is said to consist of three hundred good (*akhyar*), forty substitutes (*abdal*), seven pious (*abrar*), four pegs or supports (*awtad*), three overseers or leaders (*nuqba*), with the axis (*qutb*) at the top. But neither this hierarchic order nor the number under each head is fixed. Some limit the number of substitutes to seven and rank them next to the axis.

The seven substitutes or high-ranking saints outshone the splendor of the moon, and yet, were invisible to the gaze of ordinary men. The latter's eyes were banged by the divine destiny. As is said in the Koran, "*No one knows the hosts of the Lord save Him. Whom He wills He sends astray, and whom He wills He guides*" [74:31].

Daquqi then saw the seven candles become one and again, that one became seven. His bewilderment only increased. This vision of the candles was a revelation of the truth that all prophets and saints are one in reality. Only as forms of the One Essence do they outwardly differ. The connections between objects and the spiritual world are countless and mysterious. They can be known only by immediate perception or mystic sight, not by speech and hearing. Description is not vision, just as vision is not experience.

THE WORLD OF ARCHETYPAL IMAGES

Daquqi's vision of the saints was in the world of similitudes or archetypal images (*alam-i-mithal*) which is the second of the three stages in which the descent of the absolute into manifestation may be described. The first is the spacious world of pure, abstract ideas, called the world of non-existence because of its utter abstractness or inwardness. It is the world of barest potentially. This world feeds another world, narrower in extent, the said world of images where ideas are dressed in fantasies of light and know no actualization or materialization. This intermediate world, which is neither purely spiritual, nor purely corporeal "where spirits are corporealized with celestial etheric matter and bodies spiritualized," feeds our still narrower world of external existence, both spiritual and sensible, the sensible being the familiar world of flower and color, narrower than the spiritual.

The concept of the world of visions occurs in most ancient faiths and thought-systems. Thus, the ancient Zoroastrians had their paradise of Yima in Eran-Vej which secretes its own light and was inhabited by beings of light. It was the threshold to the dimension beyond. In Suhrawardi (d. 1191 CE), who is known as the shaykh of the theosophy of illumination, it is called the paradisical earth of Hurqalya, with its self-lit emerald cities lying atop the Emerald Rock—the cosmic pole, above the all-encircling Mount Qaf, situated at the boundary of the ninth celestial sphere. This is the approach to what the illuminationists call the orient, not the geographic, but the esoteric orient.

In all accounts of the intermediate world of which everything in this sensible world is a copy, a materialized image,[1] the symbolic psycho-cosmic mountain has to be scaled. The spiritual seeker regresses from the outer world of space into the inner world of light. His soul climbs up step by step to the zenith of consciousness, symbolized by the Emerald Rock, which is the beginning of the orient, and, then, above this summit, to super-consciousness, which is the greater orient, the pleroma of pure lights or intelligences. The spiritual climb is limitless, as its object is unlimited.

Daquqi could see the seven substitutes as his senses were transmuted into supra-senses and his sensory perception into super-sensory because he was born into the world of symbols so that he could see the visionary or archetypal images in concrete or sensible form. His spiritual eye was open.

THE CANDLES APPEAR AS SEVEN MEN

As Daquqi advanced further towards the candles, he fell unconscious and lay in a state of spiritual intoxication for a while. When he returned to sobriety, he rose up. The candles now appeared to him as seven men, that is, in the form in which the substitutes appear in the sensible world. Their light was mounting to heaven, obliterating by their brilliance the daylight and every other light. This vision was in the world of sense.

THE SEVEN MEN APPEAR AS TREES

Each of the seven men now took the appearance of a green tree—an individualization of the symbolic tree of life and knowledge. It was like the tree of Moses made radiant by divine illumination. Its boughs were shooting up above the highest paradise, reaching beyond the void, while its roots had gone down lower than the bottom of the earth. From its fruit shot forth flashes of light, revealing the divine Essence and attributes to the elect.

More simply, each saint is like a life tree, whose boughs are saintly qualities. He leaves his outward actions and fruit blessings of divine grace emanating from him. His spiritual influence works directly and indirectly in the disciple's heart bestowing on him spiritual life and knowledge.

The Koran speaks of, *"A goodly Word as a goodly tree, its root set firm, its branches rising into heaven, giving its fruit at every season, by permission of its Lord"* [14:24, 25]. The reference is to the word of God revealed to His elect, the logos, which is "the tree of the divine attributes where of the root is fixed in eternity and its boughs in the heaven of everlastingness. It is watered by the seas of divine favor and gives its fruit, revelation of the Essence and attributes, to the spirits of those who love and know God and realize His unity."

It is also said in the Koran that the Beneficent has created the human being and taught him the explanation [55:1-4]. God's teachings are interpreted in Sufism as a pre-eternal mystical revelation of the Koranic essence.

The human spirit is ever asking the same questions and finding similar answers. The tree symbolism also, like so many other symbols, is ancient and universal. The divine Names, these saints, the trees, which brought this world into manifestation provide all creatures with material and spiritual sustenance as well as shelter. "How was it then," wondered Daquqi, "that thousands of people who were prepared to risk their lives for the sake of shade and shelter from the wrath of God, should go past the trees, the saints, not seeing them and their shade."

God has sealed their hearing, sight and hearts [2:7]. They sought only worldly wealth and exoteric knowledge which was no protection against His wrath. They did not know that the Lord in His munificence pardons the believers, makes them of the honored, and says to them, *"Enter paradise"* [36:26, 27]. The saint brings to them tidings of such forgiveness and rich recompense, but the incredulous ones deny him. Should anyone counsel them to go and seek felicity from him, they all would say that by divine destiny, through prolonged melancholy and practice of austerity, the witless wretch had become mad. Even the intelligent and the discerning say the same. Each tree is calling these wretches towards it, but in vain. To every tree was coming the cry from God, "We have bandaged their eyes. Alas! No refuge" [75:2]. The misguided caravans are provisionless although the loaded boughs are stretching down and dropping their fruit of esoteric wisdom beside them.

"I have faith in the trees," said Daquqi to himself, "I go up and eat their fruit. But when I see these thousands of people, including the so-called knowledgeable, laying waste their lives in the painful pursuit of the false joys of their animal soul and fleeing from the trees and their spiritual fruit, I wonder whether I am without sense or entoiled in some fantasy?"

Daquqi was troubled by doubt. Why did God not establish the saints in the esteem of the people? The answer is given in the Koran where the prophets thought that their hope of receiving the promised divine aid, which would justify them in the pubic eye, had been falsified by the continued disbelief of the wicked. It was only after this doubting on their part that the divine aid came to them and whom He would was saved [12:110]. "In God's work, all's love, yet all's law." Hence, a prophet or saint need not despair, but climb up the tree of the spirit, eat of the fruit of divine knowledge and distribute it to others according to their allotted portion and receptive capacity.

The unbelievers, of course, have no portion of such fruit. A well-known example is Abu Lahab, an enemy of the Prophet, who was astonished by the doctrine of divine unity preached by the Prophet, and said, *"Does he make the gods one God? Lo, this is an amazing thing"* [38:6]. He could see neither the tree nor the fruit.

As Daquqi went ahead, all the seven trees became one. Every moment they were becoming both seven and one. He as in the unitive state contemplating the unity of the one and the many, the single Essence manifesting itself in multifarious forms, two mirrors, one mirroring the other. They were drawn up behind a tree, like a regular Muslim congregation behind a leader and without knee or waist, standing, kneeling and bowing in the ritual prayer, bringing to Daquqi's mind what God says of the trees, *"They bow down"* [55:6].

This was no idle fantasy. The trees, representing the divine Names and Attributes, are individualization of the divine Essence, and possess life and soul. God has made every created thing His glorifier. Each object glorifies Him by displaying some of His attributes. The glorification of God by the trees—in angelic green—was a part of this universal glorifying process.

THE SEVEN TREES BECOME SEVEN MEN

After a long while, the seven trees became seven men all seated in contemplation of God. Daquqi wondered who they were and what the had of this world. They appeared to be men of the unseen world, a class that has vanished from this earth. Coming closer to them, Daquqi greeted them. They returned his greeting, saying, "O Daquqi, the pride and crown of the noble!" As they had never eyed him before, Daquqi wondered how they had recognized him?

Immediately reading his unspoken thought, they said, "Is this still hidden from you? How should any mystery of this spatial world be hidden from a heart which is in the valley of bewilderment with God? If a name disappears from the consciousness of a saint, it is the result not of his ignorance, but of his total absorption in God at that moment. It is because, in spiritual ecstasy, he is conscious of nothing but His unity."

DAQUQI LEADS THEM IN PRESCRIBED PRAYER

They said that they would like to follow his leadership in prayer. Daquqi agreed, but asked for time, so that by spending a while in their holy companionship, he may throw off time's shackles, and negating himself, his human attributes steeped in the universal attributes, achieve their spiritual freedom and become worthy to lead them. They nodded their assent.

When Daquqi had participated with them in meditation for a while and was separated from himself, his spirit was freed from time and its limitations. It is a mystical experience of timelessness unknown to those who believe in the reality of time or who are bound by it and, hence, cannot progress towards spiritual timelessness to which the only way is mystic bewilderment. The hours are simply unacquainted with hourlessness. As all change arises from time, he became free from change also, and, with liberation from time and change, no howness or relation remained. He became familiar with howlessness.

But we all are not Daquqi. In this world of time, God has appointed keepers or guardians [82:10-12] representing in the present context the unseen powers of divine destiny—angels and satans—that operate for good and evil in each one of us. They keep us to our appointed stations and control all our movements. The sinner or sensualist pursues his fancies and lusts and is their slave. He denies the action of his keepers, denies the invisible divine destiny, saying that it is his carnal self, not they, that is deterring him from taking to the path of mystical poverty by threatening him with the loss of mundane riches and delights. Let him behold his choice and perceive that it is not free. All thoughts, words and deeds are pre-ordained.

According to the divine Law, a leader with a clear sight,

even if he be a fool, is better than a blind leader howsoever learned. For the latter is unable to see and avoid dirt and filth and cannot fulfill one of the preliminary conditions prescribed for the performance of the prescribed prayer which is outward purification from filth. But while one physically blind is in outward or material filthiness, one spiritually blind is in inward filthiness. He alone is unclean. God has called the infidel filth. That filthiness is not on his outward self, but is inward. It is infinitely worse. It is in his disposition and religion. Outward filthiness can be removed by water, but not inward filthiness, which can only be washed by penitent tears. As the leader must always be, Daquqi was clear-visioned, both outwardly and inwardly.

The Koran says, *"Do not let the idolaters, the unbelievers, come near the holy place of worship"* [9:28] although they may be outwardly clean. Tell the believers to lower their eyes and be modest, as that is purer for them [24:30]. The body has five external senses, which are the means of sense-perception. They must be used to righteous ends and kept pure. Their idle or evil use will only drain away one's understanding and spiritual energy. If the interior is not to be reduced to a barren desert, that loss must be made up by infusions of divine grace or by filling the jug of the body with the wine of love drawn from the jar of the perfect shaykh who is full of God. Thus replenished, one can concentrate in full on the remembrance of the Lord and on contemplation of the divine unity and fit himself for admission to the many-mansioned house of the Lord.

People praise different prophets, but the object of the praise is in essence not more than one, none other than the Nameless of the hundred Names, so that from this point of view, all religions are but one religion. Individuals, even saints and prophets, are praised for attributes thought to be theirs, but which belong to the light of God and are only on loan to the created forms or are reflected in them so that in praising them, we are really praising His light which alone has the right to be praised. Similarly, when the infidels praise the moon's reflection of light upon a wall or in the well, the praise belongs to the moon, not to its reflection. When the light withdraws itself, the reflection returns to its source. The moon was above, while the infidel fancied in his ignorance that it was below. His praise of the reflection is infidelity. The wall and the well are only a focus for the light, not its creator.

People indulge their thirst and lust of things and repent afterwards as their indulgence was only with a passing phantom. They are left remoter from Reality. Human love is like a wing that bears the soul upward to divine love provided it purifies the soul. But when one merely indulges a lust, that wing drops off, the beloved's spiritual image vanishes from the heart, and he is grounded, cheated by sense. He was led astray by preordained perdition. But the phantom the true lover loves is no illusion, for he sees through the veil of outward things, seeking the Reality behind each veil and phantom. We should follow in his footsteps, and not tear out the wing, but save it, so that it may fly us to paradise.

THE REAL ESSENCE OF THE PRESCRIBED PRAYER

Daquqi went forward to perform the prescribed prayer, which consists of four postures: standing, bowing, prostration and the confession of faith and repeated pronouncements of the words "God is greater" (*takbir*). Following his leadership, the seven saints drew up in a row behind him, who, as a perfect human being, mirroring actively all the divine attributes was superior to any rank or number of angels. When they pronounced the words, "God is greater'—which the Law requires should be pronounced at the time of slaughtering the victim— they had slaughtered the carnal soul and uttered the funeral prayer over it. This is the real meaning of the pronouncement. The spirit had pronounced these words over the body which was not merely killed, as it is by lusts, but had become a pure sacrifice to God. The essence of the *takbir* is self-mortification.

Allegorically interpreted, the standing up posture represents the human being, erect with pride and insolence. The bowing posture represents the animal state, as all animals bend or stoop. The self-abasing posture represents the plant state, as all plants bow themselves. This last posture may also be said to represent the rock or mineral state, involving humble submission on the lowly earth, which holds rock and mineral in its embrace. The confession of faith—originally made before God at the primal covenant—signifies the soul's entry into this world, and, after self-sacrifice, its return to the other world [7:172].

According to Ibn al-Arabi, the mineral is the highest form of creation, as lacking external sensibility and consciousness, it implicitly acknowledges and glorifies God. The plants which are sensible to music and may even have a memory come next, as their glorification is less implicit. Next come the animals which live and move and are instinctual. They are grateful for any kindness received from the human being. And for one creature to be grateful to another is to be grateful to God. The human being, veiled as he is from God by his self-consciousness, his egoism, reason, intellect, even religion, comes last. By words and actions, he has to fulfill his covenant with God. The standing, bowing and prostrating postures are thus progressive degrees of humility, the sincere practice of which will wean the soul from self and carry it towards the footstool of God.

As the form of the prayer signifies not only the human being's entrance into this world, but also his return to the other world, the seven saints, while performing the prescribed prayer, were standing in God's presence, engaged in self-examination, shedding tears like one who has risen erect from the dead on the day of resurrection.

The prescribed prayer, as Rumi interprets here, is an enactment of the resurrection scene. On that day, God will say, "How have you expended your hands and feet, your senses, intellect and the divine nature which I gave you for righteous works? They did not come to you on their own, nor did you buy them from the earth. They were gifts from My bounty. What were

7 Daquqi: His Visions and Miracles

your thanks for them? What have you produced for Me during your earthly life?"

In the standing posture, hundreds of such painful messages come to the worshipper from the Lord. From shame, the strength to remain standing goes and he bends double in the genuflexion and on bowed knees recites a litany of praise. Then comes the divine command to raise his head and answer His questions. The shame-faced one lifts up his head. One whose earthly life has been imperfect and impure falls on his face. Then comes the divine command to him to lift his head from the prostration and detail his deeds. Once again, he lifts his head and again falls flat on his face. As his soul is awe-struck by His stern words, he has no strength to stand up and so, sits down in deadly dread of examination by God. At the end of the prescribed prayer, he turns for help and intercession towards the spirits of prophets and saints stationed at the right of the divine throne. They tell him that the day for remedy is past. He had his chance of repentance and good works on earth, but he neglected it. He then turns to his family and relatives on the left, and they tell him, "Who are we to help? Answer for yourself to God." All hope lost, he raises his hand in prescribed prayer and throws himself on the mercy of the Lord, who is the First and the Last, the Hidden and the Manifest.

One should behold these signs in the prescribed prayer and know for certain that all this will come to pass at the Resurrection. The believer also performs the prescribed prayer, but his prayer is of the spirit. He is not bound by prayer five times a day as prescribed, but is continually at prayer.

A SHIP IN DISTRESS

When Daquqi began to perform the prescribed prayer on the shore, with the goodly seven standing behind him, of a sudden he heard cries of "Help! Help!" coming from the direction of the sea. He turned towards it and saw a ship in its fateful hour, tempest-tossed, wave-lashed on left and right, on a night that was thick with darkness and dark clouds. The people in the ship were trembling with terror and uttering cries of woe, with no help in sight, all expedients dead, and death almost hovering overhead. There are no kindred like calamity's kin. Reprobate and ascetic alike had become God-fearing and sincere in their devotion to God. Those who had never prayed before saw a hundred benefits in the prayer.

But as is his wont, the devil sought to deter the penitent from the way of salvation, crying, "O infidels and impostors, death and woe will be your portion in the end. Once you are delivered from the present calamity, you will only be too glad to relapse into sin after repentance, outdevilling the devil himself in the pursuit of phantoms and lusts. You will show ingratitude to God, forgetting that in the hour of crisis, He took your hand and saved you from your decree. Your last plight will be worse than the first.

But only a good ear can hear such words from the devil, not every ear. The majority are ignorant. They are inwardly deaf and blind. The Prophet has said that what the wise person sees from the beginning the ignorant see only in the end, when it becomes manifest to the wise and the ignorant alike. The wise person thinks and does what will be to his good after death. The ignoramus indulges his lusts, and, from fear of poverty is preoccupied with worldly business. He does not know that because of this fear, he is in the mouth of greed which is never full-greed which alone is the essence of poverty. He should fear the creator of poverty. Spiritual treasures will be his on earth. Even if he is unsure of salvation, he should be prudent enough to repent before it is too late. Also, he should remember the words of the Prophet who said that prudence is to "think ill of the world," and expect a sudden calamity at any moment, so that when destiny brings it, he is not wholly unprepared or overwhelmed by surprise."

DAQUQI INTERCEDES FOR THE SHIP'S DELIVERANCE

When Daquqi saw the tragic plight of the voyagers, pity welled up in his heart, and tears streamed from his eyes. He said, "O Lord, do not look at their action! Take their hands and bring them safe ashore. O gracious and merciful one, overlook the wickedness of the plotters of evil. You have given a hundred eyes and ears, intellect and understanding free of cost, before any merit was existent, and have suffered ingratitude and sin from us. We have burnt ourselves from greed. Pardon our transgressions, without exposing them. Even this invocation we have learned from You. In reverence for Your teaching us to invoke You, we beseech You."

Thus was invocation issuing from Daquqi like the tender words of faithful mothers, the shaykhs that feed the spiritual children with the milk of knowledge and the tears kept rolling down his cheeks. Through his invocation, the ship was saved. But it was no normal invocation. It was not from him, not from his own mercifulness, but was spoken by the All-merciful God. For Daquqi was dead to self. His body and spirit had no awareness of making that supplication. The supplication as well as the answer was from Him.

The saints are the purveyors of divine grace. They can save us from all kinds of vengeance, as through Daquqi's prayer, God saved the ship. But the voyagers thought that their own efforts had saved them, thus denying credit to their real savior.

We in this world seek pomp and power in order to impress our superiority over others and gain their adulation, unaware that we are only in thrall to our animal nature. We are falsely proud. We have not cured our own vices and seek to cure the ones we see in others. The physician must heal himself first before setting out to minister to others.

THE TRUE HEART

As a part of the healing process, one has to renounce all worldly interests, all guile and contrivance, and, giving up seeking manna where none is, devote his heart to the king of the hearts, the saint. God bestows favor on the heart when, like a part, it goes to its whole. The lover of a part does not love the whole. The part he loves will eventually return to its whole, its home and origin, leaving its lover disillusioned. If one loves a sun-lit wall, when the sunbeams return to their whole, the sun, and the wall loses its goldeness and becomes dark, will he not be disenchanted?

God says that he has bestowed regard on the heart, but He has not bestowed it on the external form. He has bestowed it on the true heart. We say that we also have a heart. But it is not a real heart. The real heart is cleansed of earth and is pure. It transcends the physical universe and is higher than the highest heaven while our heart is below and is earth-defiled. We must not say of our heart that this is a heart.

The sea of mercy, the saint, is calling us. The water, the spirit, in the earthen body desires to return to the sea. But the earth is drawing it back. The spirit that is intoxicated by the wine of egoism and sensuality cannot leave the earth of the body and unite with the saint or attain to union with God. One should abandon life's toys and trifles and seek the shaykh.

But we are so carried away by our flying fancy that we say that our heart is pure, and so, we need no help from a saint or shaykh. Do we think it possible that our heart which is in love with milk and honey is untainted? Living in this world we may partake of the objects of lust in measure with our necessity, but we must not let them become our master. Our master is the saint, the deified perfect human being. We should know that all good and beautiful objects derive their attributes from the secondary reflection of goodness and beauty that are first reflected in the heart of the saint.

The saint's heart is the sea of light. It is the theatre for the vision of God, the eye through which He sees the universe. It is the substance and the world is the accident, the shadow or reflection. How should the heart be in love with its shadow, this black earth and water? How should the shadow consider itself independent of its source?

Infinite in its real nature, externally non-existent, the heart is the universal spiritual essence of the human being that comprehends in its indivisible unity all the diverse forms of individualization in which it manifests itself. The saint pours blessings of hope and fortune from the divine blessedness—the source of all purifying power—on those who are pure of heart, who supplicate and are inwardly present with God and are deserving of the largesse.

THE DISAPPEARANCE OF THE SAINTS

The saving of the ship coincided with the finishing of the prescribed prayer. Standing behind Daquqi, unespied by him, the saints were softly murmuring among themselves as to which of them had invoked God, outwardly or inwardly. Each one said he had not. It appeared, said one of them, that moved by pity for the voyagers, Daquqi had meddled with the working of God and offered an orison on their behalf. Another one said that to him also, it seemed the same.

Hearing these murmurings, Daquqi turned around to see what was going on. He was surprised to find that the saints had vanished, leaving no trace behind. He wondered where they had gone? Had they entered the tents of God where, as the tradition goes, the friends of God secretly abide? He remained amazed how God had caused the saints to be concealed from him.

It is said that the ship symbolizes the body of Daquqi, the ship's crew his bodily senses and faculties. These are saved from drowning by his return to normal consciousness at the end of the prayer, for during the prescribed prayer he was lost in contemplation of the divine unity.[1] The vision of the saints also vanishes with the return to normality.

THE TWO CLASSES OF SAINTS

The seven saints were perfect quietists (*ahl-i-rida al-taslim*) who deemed any prayer as an unwarranted, if not unlawful, interference with the divine decree. They regarded Daquqi, whose invocation had saved the voyagers, as acting like one of the class of saints who believe in the efficacy of prayer. But he had not acted as one of that class. As stated earlier, he had lost all consciousness. Both the prayer and the answer were from God. But as he did pray, the two classes of saints are not rigidly apart.

THE CONTINUAL QUEST FOR SAINTS

For many long years, Daquqi kept grieving for the loss of the saints. For many life-times, he shed longing tears for them. One may wonder how a man of God should think of human beings beside God? The problem is that we tend to regard the saints as flesh. The saints are not human beings, not clay or flesh, but spirit. Even their body is all spirit. Why must we regard the external forms as satan did, who went by Adam's exterior and said that he was superior to him, as he was made of fire and Adam was of clay, and fire was superior to clay [7:11-12]? A spiritual aspirant should seal his satanic eye and seek the saints with tears of longing, without losing hope, knowing that searching is finding and is the pillar of fortune, a painful toil is the pre-requisite of every success. Detached from mundane entanglements, let him keep uttering, "Where? Where, O where?" pondering well, solaced by the merciful words of the Lord, *'Pray unto Me and I shall hear your prayer'* [40: 60].

8 THE LAWYER OF BUKHARA

The lawyer of the ruler of Bukhara, who loved his master, came under suspicion. In fear of his life, he fled the city, and for ten years wandered distractedly now in the mountain, now in the desert. He had been glad to escape from the wrath of his master, but now through longing for him, he had become unable to suffer separation any longer.

How should patient suffering allay the state of the abandoned lover? From separation from water, the soil becomes barren. From separation from the embrace of spring, the loveliest garden becomes leafless and decays. Separation is like sparks of fire. It burns. Hell burns from separation from divine mercy. Old age has become frail from separation from the robustness of youth. One can keep talking of separation until the resurrection without covering even a fraction of a vast whole.

Nearness is the root of every separation. When we love anything phenomenal, we should also think at that time of our parting from it. What delights us has delighted others also, but it escaped them at the last. Why then set our hearts on what is passing? Why not flee from it before it flees from us? Why not renounce desire although renunciation is difficult and heartbreaking?

The king's shattered lover said to himself, "If I have become an infidel, I shall become a believer and return to the ruler and say, 'I throw myself before you. Revive me or slay me. To be slain and dead before you is better than to be king elsewhere. I have tested it many times. My life has no sweetness without you. Every moment, I am being roasted in the flames of separation.' Come what may, I am going to Bukhara, the city of my king."

To the lover, the fairest city is where his sweetheart is. Wherever a moon-faced Joseph is, it is paradise, even if it be the bottom of a well. In the lover's eyes, this is the meaning of love of one's native land.

A good friend of his sought to dissuade him from returning to Bukhara, saying, "How can you go back? You are crazy, only fit for chains and prison. In his anger, the king is sharpening the knife for you. Do not burn yourself like a moth. After your escape, God has given you the open road. If you had ten kinds of custodians over you, intelligence would have been needed to escape from them. But you are not ruled by a single custodian. Why are the past and the future sealed to you? You know what you did and what retribution to expect."

Secret love had made the man of Bukhara captive of the king's anger. It was striking its captive, its myrmidon, without compunction. But his well-meaning friend was unable to see that hidden custodian.

We all have hidden custodians within, representing the unseen powers of divine destiny, spiritual and sensual faculties, that control all our movements, and keep us bound to our appointed stations [6:61]. If the wicked were aware of their hidden custodians, they would go before the king of kings, crying out in distress and seeking security from the devil. But no evil passions dominated our lover. In any case, it is not the evil doer, but his ruling passions that are hateworthy.

The lover said, "How long will you advise me? My bonds are grievous. Your learned doctor, your teacher, was not acquainted with the pain of love and gave no instruction about its cure. Instead of being afraid of dying, I am dying in desire of death. The lover experiences diverse sorts of mystical states and dies to them in succession, until he attains nearness to God. For each life he thus sheds, he receives tenfold its like [6:160]. Self-existence is spiritual death. Release from it is life. As the martyr-saint Hallaj said, 'Kill me, kill me, O trustee friend. Lo, in my being killed is life on life.'"

The repentant lover was a transformed man. He had renounced everything save the real object of his love. His soul was bound for Bukhara. But his purpose was not to attend lectures or learn from any teacher. For lovers, the only teacher is the beauty of the beloved. His face is their only book and lecture. Their only lesson is enthusiasm and the God-intoxicated dance of the whirling dervishes, symbolizing the ecstatic experience of dying to self and attaining to life everlasting. It is not the niceties of jurisprudence. Of the ineffable mystery of love, the best jurisprudent is painfully unaware.

In Bukhara one can attain to perfection in external sciences. Such knowledge is by no means to be despised. Words and expressions, even tales of divorce, signify qualities, and as the mystic knows, the essence of every quality is God. Hence, when he speaks or thinks, he is aware of experiencing some particular spiritual effect of His nature. But if one turns to self-abasement, one is freed from the vexation of external knowledge, and finds 'spiritual candy' in Bukhara. Our lover was not after exoteric knowledge, but was set on the vision of the Beloved. One thus set or who in solitude has attained to the vision beatific will not seek power by means of such knowledge, but will only have disgust of traditional learning, of logic and jurisprudence. For vision is superior to knowledge. It is for this reason that in the eyes of the worldings, the present world which they see is superior to the other world which is invisible to them.

His heart throbbing, his eyes streaming blood-stained tears, his wits gone, the lover set out at top speed and felt the rough journey smooth as silk. To him, as to any spiritual seeker, this Bukhara is not merely the center of exoteric learning, but is the heart of the king, the shaykh, the spiritual director, and is the fountain-head of spiritual knowledge. In his presence, one is in Bukhara and possessing that knowledge. One is a native of

Bukhara. Not exoteric knowledge, but self-abasement is the means of entrance into it. "I am seeking the full moon," the perfect human being," he said. "I am seeking the ruler of the world."

But he was not fully cooked. Hence, when Bukhara dawned on his vision from afar, a mystic illumination appeared in the darkness of his grief. He fell and lay senseless and outstretched for a while. Love had cut him off from himself. In vain did people sprinkle rose water on his head and face. Encumbered by intellect, but congealed in spirit, they were unaware of the rose water of his love. He had seen a hidden rose-garden.

Coming to himself, he entered Bukhara like one drunk with love, imagining that the moon was calling him into its embrace. Everyone who met him said, "Flee hence before you are seen! The king is seeking you in great anger, and may wreak vengeance on your life. Do not rely on your clever words and wiles. You were his constable and trusted noble who managed his affairs. You acted treacherously and with a hundred guiles managed to flee and escape punishment. What has brought you back—folly or your fate? O you who humble Mercury, the celestial intelligence, the source of worldly wisdom, remember that destiny makes a fool of intellect and the intelligent. It has countless more wiles than you. As the Prophet said, 'When destiny comes, the spacious field is straitened.' Ways and places of refuge abound on all sides, but are barred by destiny."

The lover replied to his well-wishing warners, "I am dropsical, and none so afflicted will flee from the water, though he knows that like dropsy, the water will kill him. My inward state is such that I wish the sea were flowing within me and its water would burst my belly. If I lose consciousness in the sea of the perfect human being, with my attributes sunk in his, such death of self-hood would be most welcome. A lover is a blood-drinker like the earth and the embryo. He is ever engaged in the trade of blood-drinking, of self-mortification. I repent the devices I set to flee from him and escape the punishment that his anger desired to inflict. Let him restrain himself no more.

He is the feast of the sacrifice. Deem me, his lover, as the buffalo that is nurtured for the feast and the slaughter. I eat drink and sleep like others, but not for my own sake. I have no object in life save self-sacrifice. One must slaughter his carnal soul, must die to self, so that his dead spirit may be resuscitated and endowed with life eternal.

"Without death, there can be no new life. From non-existence, I was brought into the mineral state. Dying to mineral, I became plant. Dying to plant, I became animal. Dying to animal, I became human—as I am today. Dying to my humanness, I shall become an angel. To the angel also, I must die and become that which transcends the imagination. *"Everything perishs except His Presence"* [28:88]. Ultimately, I shall become non-existence, which is proclaiming to me, *"Verily, unto Him we shall return,"* to Him who is the First and the Last.

In the death of self alone is real life. "The water of life is hidden in the land of darkness." To quote Hafiz,

> Yesternight, at dawn, they delivered me from sorrow,
>   and in that darkness of night,
>   they gave me the water of life. (*Diwan*)

The journey to the Emerald Rock, also begins in the darkness of night, and the midnight sun bursts into flame to the approach to the summit. The light is dark, as it is spatially or outwardly non-existent.

The ruler's lover had negated himself. His attributes had passed away in the beloved's attributes. Only his essence remained. There was no risk of retrogression for him. He said, "I have crucified myself in excuse for having fled from my Beloved."

Prostrating himself on face and head, the lover went towards the ruler. People were waiting to see whether he would be burnt or hanged. They said, "Like a moth, this utter simpleton deemed the candle flame to be the light and is burning himself to death." They were unaware that the candle of love is not a burner. Its flame although seemingly fire is light and sweetness. It consumes carnality and illumines the heart at the moment of nearness.

The lover was burning in the flame of love. His sighs were mounting heavenward. Kindness came into the heart of the ruler. He was commuting with himself at dawn. Speaking through him, God said, "The lover sinned and we saw the sin, but he was not well-acquainted with Our mercy. The sinner's heart becomes afraid of Us, but hopes abound in his fear. I frighten the unafraid by My knowledge of their sin and by telling them of its consequences. I do not frighten the afraid. I remove their fear by My clemency. My disposition, kind or severe, is to everyone in perfect measure with the requirement of his essential character."

LOVE IS UNIVERSAL
—RUMI'S DOCTRINE OF MONOTHEISM

The lover's yearning for the ruler was reflected in the latter's heart. Forgiveness of the sin was surging in him. This forgiving feeling was only natural because there is a window between heart and heart. The hearts are two, but not separate or apart like two bodies. They are like two lamps which are not joined, but whose light blends in its passage. How should the beloved remain indifferent when the lover aspires to nearness to him. In truth, no lover seeks nearness to his beloved without his beloved's seeking him.

In the words of Hafiz, "Love is born first in the heart of the beloved." The lover, the man of Bukhara, had returned home because of the ruler's desire for him. The human being needs God and God needs the human being. The thirsty person's thirst for water is the attraction exerted by the water. The attraction of the lover and the beloved, of the seeker and the sought, is mutual, but differently manifested. Whilst the love of the beloved irradiates his face and makes his body comely, the love of the lover consumes his soul and withers his body. The poor intellect is bewildered as to whether the attraction comes from this side or that side, whether it came from the side of the ruler or his loving servant.

God's fore-ordainment and wisdom have paired all the particles of the world as mates. They are mutually linked by the original unity from which they come and to which they seek to return. Duality divides and love makes one out of two. Each mate is in love with its mate. In the sight of the intellect, heaven is man and the earth woman. Whatever heaven casts forth, the earth nurtures. In astrology, the twelve signs of the zodiac are divided into four groups, each group connected with an element. The sign of earth replenishes the dust of the earth. The sign of water breathes freshness into it. The sign of air wafts the clouds towards it so that they sweep away the congregated pestilential vapors. And the sign of fire supplies heat. When the earth has no heat or moisture left, heaven supplies the deficiency. Without the earth, how should the flowers or corn grow? What purpose would the water and heat of heaven serve? Earth and heaven act intelligently, and, evidently, possess intelligence.

God planted desire in man and woman for each other so that by their union children may be born and the world kept going. Similarly, night and day, although enemies in appearance, cooperate to a common purpose. If night did not provide sleep and rest to a person, how should he or she have energy to perform the tasks of the day? The entire creation is based on well-balanced contraries, by strife and love. Their universal correlation serves God's desire for Self-manifestation. Divine love pervades and governs the cosmos.

THE LOVER OF GOD

To return to our story, when the king arrived and his loving slave beheld his face, the latter fell unconscious and grew cold from head to foot. Incense and rose water were applied, but to no avail. When the king saw his pallid face, he dismounted from his steed, went towards him and said, "You are a lover of God and He is such that at one look of His, hundreds like you disappear. I think you are in love with self-negation. You are a shadow and in love with the sun. The sun comes and the shadow is instantly negated."

The king from kindness was slowly and caressingly bringing the senseless lover back to his senses, saying, "I have come to protect you. You have suffered much separation from me. Come to yourself from selflessness and return to normal consciousness." But that stage was not yet.

At the primal covenant with God, as we are told in the Koran, the human being, the only creature capable of perfect justice and knowledge whom pre-eminence in love had made overweening and disdainful of self's limitations, pledged himself to bear the burden of divine love and gnosis. He is *"very unjust and very ignorant"* [33:72]. He is unjust to himself and to his soul, as he has to kill his empirical self in order to realize the mystery of the divine unity and do justice to God. Self-existence is polytheism. And he is very ignorant, as he does not know that the human intellect cannot attain divine knowledge, for nothing human, but only the divine, can live in the divine. All else dies upon the threshold. It is only when a person fulfills the pledge by ceasing to regard himself as existing and acting, by leaving his self behind and becoming mystically one with Him, that injustice and ignorance are expelled from him and he is admitted into His embrace. His injustice to self gives the lead to all justices. His ignorance is the instructor to all knowledges. They enable him to fulfill the ultimate purpose of creation which is to return to God. Our lover, however, had yet only attained to the state to self-abnegation.

Acting through the ruler, God took the lover's hand, saying, "As his body will come to life only if I breathe the spiritual breath into him, it will be My spirit that will turn its face towards Me. The spirit that is not thus favored cannot experience My bounty or see My face. This privilege is reserved for the perfect human being who is the object of My love by eternal pre-election."

Turning to the lover, God said, "O spirit that has departed

from anguish, We have opened the door to union with Us. Welcome! O you whose selflessness and intoxication are caused by Our Self and whose being is constantly derived from Our Being. I tell you the old mystery afresh, the mystery of *"God does what He will"* [3:35]. But it cannot be uttered by mortal lips or apprehended by mortal ears. I will commune with you in silence. You open the ear of earlessness, your spiritual ear in order to hear it."

When the lover began to hear the call to union, little by little, he started to move. This was no wonder, for it is self-extinction that brings everlasting life to the lover of God. He is not less than the earth which, at the caresses of the breeze, puts on a green garment and uplifts its head from wintry death. Is not the substance of non-existence itself, which is God's Workshop, continually bringing to birth a whole universe? How should He not, in manifestation of His grace and omnipotence, bring forth the living from the dead, the divinely illumined heart from the soul that has died to its carnality [30:19] also the heart that is living in sin. The lover sprang up, quivered, and after a couple of joyous dance-whirls fell to worship.

In praise and thanksgiving, he turned his face towards the beloved, the ruler, and said, "O perfect human being of God, O Seraphiel who brings the souls of the dead into their bodies, I offer thanks that you have mercifully returned to this handful of dust from the divine realm where your spirit dwells and beg you to listen to me as you used to in days of yore. Countless times, I grew witless in nostalgic longing for you ear and your life-quickening smiles, for that harkening of yours to my matters great and small, and to the beguilements of my evil-thoughted soul. How, though knowing the truth, you accepted my false speech as true only because of my impudent importunity! All clemencies are but a speck of dust before your clemency. Now hear! In leaving your service, I lost everything—both this world and the next. I sought long, but found no second to you. It is as if I have been guilty of polytheism. I just lost my wits, my discernment and all. My eyes have shed tears of blood in separation from you. Behold, even now, heart's blood is falling from my eye."

Ecstatic cries were breaking from his heart. He did not know whether he should speak or weep for if he spoke, his weeping, which irrigates and freshens the soul, would be lost. If he wept, he could not give thanks and praise to the Lord. Torn by doubt, he was speaking, weeping and laughing simultaneously. So crazily so that the people of Bukhara were simply bewildered as to what was love and what was ecstasy. Which was more wonderful—separation from Him or nearness to Him when nearness also, like separation, was accompanied by tears of blood, commonly signs of grief, not of ecstatic joy as in lovers?

Love is a stranger to the two worlds. In it are seventy-two madnesses. Islam has seventy-two sects. It is wholly hidden. Only its bewilderment, its effects are manifest. Like the fire in the wool and cotton, they cannot be hidden. The religion of love is apart from all religions, from all faiths. For lovers, the only religion and creed is God.[1] At the time of the *sama*, love's minstrel strikes up the strain—servitude is fetters and lordship is headache.

Love is the sea of non-existence, a sea in which the intellect cannot swim. Servitude and sovereignty, the respective attributes of lover and beloved, are known, but they are veils that conceal loverhood. Any attempt to describe it verbally, only adds another veil. Speech and self-existence or the intellectual quest are the bane of spiritual perception. The unitive state of the mystic transcends the duality of servility and lordship. It cannot be comprehended by minds which think in terms of the logical correlation of opposites. What unites lover and beloved is the non-existent 'Essence and Reality' known in mysticism as 'love'.

THE DOCTRINE OF RESERVE

The real cause of every effect is non-existent. The effects of love, itself hidden, are manifest and can be seen in His frenzied lovers. But when any lover of God, drunken, distraught and loose-tongued, begins to talk about His love and coquetry, about the essential unity of love, to any other than a trustworthy adept, the heavenly host prays to God to refrain him from divulging the mystery of love. This mystery is not meant to be proclaimed openly as the fleshly ear cannot comprehend it and also there is the danger that the misunderstood announcing lover may be taken for a liar or a lunatic and may even be imprisoned or hanged. "Cast not pearls before swine," said Jesus.

While Rumi upholds this 'doctrine of reserve', his interlocutor, speaking for the God-intoxicated saints, says that the essential unity of love must be declared to the adept, who can be trusted to keep it hidden. The saints, as we know, are His very elect. They are filled with the wine of love and are always with Him. He causes them to illumine this dark phenomenal world during their earthly sojourn. When they die and their shadow is lifted from this earth, He takes them back, saying that He never ceases pouring Himself into them. They abide eternally with Him. Death is dead for them.

The drinker of earthly grape-wine is never sated with it. Hence, the Arabs gave wine the name of *mudam*, that is, continual. How should the drinker of the wondrous wine that is distilled from paradisical grapes ever know satiety? There is no final attainment or end for him, only an ever-beginning aspiration, for his object is infinite. Who can climb up the ever-climbing wave?

With anyone disturbed there is a Disturber. It is God who causes the wine of realization to bubble and dance in the soul and acts as the cup-bearer to the true lover. When anyone seeks the reality with the wine of His good help, the essence of the spirit is the wine and the body the flagon. When He increases the wine of help or favor, the wine's increased potency bursts the flagon, shattering his bodily nature. The body is all transfigured, it becomes all spirit. The spirit becomes both the Cup-bearer and the drunken lover. No duality remains. This is the state of the life eternal after self-negation, a state in which the lover may proclaim with Bayazid, the 'Pole of the Gnostics', "I am the wine and the wine-drinker and the cup-bearer."[2]

9 THE STORY OF AYAZ
THE RAGGED APPAREL

Ayaz, a favorite slave of the great conqueror and champion of Islam, Sultan Mahmud of Ghazna (d. 1030 CE), would hang up his old rustic shoes and ragged sheepskin jacket in a private chamber and humble himself by wearing them on the quiet every day. They were a daily reminder of his lowly origin from seed. Looking at his shoes, he would say to himself, "These are your shoes. Do not regard your present eminence at court."

His rivals, ignorant of his real nature, were envious of his favored position with the King. They said to his majesty that Ayaz had a strong-doored private chamber where he kept hidden much gold and silver.

The King wondered what Ayaz had that was concealed from him. He had shown him numerous kindnesses and favors. Would he be so disloyal or mean as to hide silver and gold from him? Surely, such a charge was sheer nonsense, utterly incredible.

Accordingly, at midnight, the Amir, with thirty of his trusted officers, all carrying torches, set forth jubilantly for the chamber of Ayaz. One of them said, "Let us raid the room and each of us appropriate a purse of gold."

"Why gold?" asked another. "Speak rather of cornelians, rubies and emeralds. Speak of pearls! What should even these be worth to Ayaz, who is the most privileged custodian of the king's treasury, and also his beloved, his very life?"

Although the king knew that Ayaz was free from all manner of deceit, his heart, like any lover's heart, was not unshaken by fear howsoever baseless that in case the accusation against him proved true, his feelings would be hurt and he would be overcome by shame.

Ayaz was one of the Lord's favorites about whom He says, "By Me he hears and by Me he sees." (Tradition) How could he do anything wrong? Acting as His mouthpiece, the king said to himself, "Even if Ayaz has done what he is alleged to have done, it is right. He is free to do anything he likes for he is my beloved. Whatever he may do, it is I who have done it. For 'I am he' and 'he is I'."

THE PERFECT HUMAN BEING

God made the human being in His own image and the creation in the image of the human being. All the phenomena, both worlds, temporal and spiritual, are the secondary reflection of His light first mirrored in his heart, so that he is the origin and cause of creation, which God created for the manifestation of the treasure that He was. The human being is the consummation of the divine plan, creation's crown.

Ayaz, a type of perfect human being, was a fathomless ocean, as the king said of him. The entire existence was but a driblet of its waves. All purities came from it. Every drop of it was alchemical, spiritually regenerative. He was the king of kings, the king-maker rather for he actively reflected all the divine attributes and Essence, and was the medium of God's Self-manifestation to Himself, which was the purpose of creation. He was named Ayaz and was formally a slave only to keep away the evil eye, including the good eyes of the elect which were evil to him, as his transcendent beauty was an object of jealousy to them. Lacking his perfect vision of Reality, they undervalued the revelation of the divine beauty in his heart.

THE SHOES AND THE SHEEPSKIN JACKET

The old shoes and the tattered jacket are the clay, semen and embryonic flesh which God keeps before us so that we may not forget our lowly origin [86:5-7].[1] From being symbols of self-effacement in the way of love, the jacket and the shoes had become the prayer-niche of Ayaz. Not that it was necessary for him to devote himself to these symbols. He had become pure and there was no danger of his backsliding into sin and self. Nevertheless, everyday he would look at them so that by shutting out any possibility of pride and arrogance, which are barriers in the way of self-effacement, they would ensure his enjoyment of the life and vitality of non-existence.

The lovers of the flesh, purpled by sin, are heedless of their maker. If at all they pray to Him it is only for false self-satisfaction, social conformity or ostentation. Their life is one long reign of sin. At last, when the death agony comes, they utter cries of lamentation and remember their tattered shoes and jacket, and may say, as Adam said, *"O Lord we have done wrong"* [7:23]. But a death-bed repentance or prayer is of no avail. The balance sheet of life is already cast up. The debits are heavy and will have to be cleared. None can help them. Even the devil will abandon them to their fate when they are in despair.

Ayaz was not their kind. A perfect saint, his spirit in origin before the creation of his body, was akin to the King's spirit. His gaze was fixed on the place where the body and all things were first sown in the field of non-existence.[2] He knew the beginning and the end of things. He knew that the old shoes and the jacket were the right ship for the spiritual journey in trackless seas to shoreless ends, the journey to God. Hence, he would look at them and wear them in secret every day. Their public display might have been misunderstood. He might have been taken for mad or a hypocrite.

The example was first set by Adam who would keep in view the old shoes and the jacket, saying, "I am of clay." But his contrary iblis was crammed with egoism and pride. He disobeyed the Lord's command to bow to Adam, saying that he was superior to him, as he was made of fire, and Adam was made of clay [38:76]. Fire was superior to clay. Also he was the prince of believers and a favorite of God, when Adam was not even existent.

"The son is the marrow of his father," said the Prophet. The egoist often cites this saying in order to support claims similar to satan's.

But why adduce a cause? Why speak of satan's pride or of the envy and covetousness of Ayaz's rivals? It was God's compelling decree in operation. His action is causeless and is inscribed from eternity on the tablet of destiny. In the Prophet's saying, the marrow or real nature of his father refers to God's work. His creative energy is our father. His work is the kernel. The skin—the shell—is the formal physical father. The nut-like body should know that love, the divine Beloved, is its friend. The Beloved's soul will draw the human soul into its embrace, and batter the skin, the shell, to pieces. But he whose skin is his friend and mistakes it for the kernel, nurses it with power and riches, its fat and flesh, for the sake of pride and arrogance which are the product of the skin. As hell-fire has no other fuel than the skin, God's vengeance tears it off that pride and the skin is ready for burning. God has said about the disbelievers, "We shall expose them to the fire. As often as their skins are consumed, we shall exchange them for other skins," [4:56] so that they may continue to sustain punishment. Similarly, He renews the sensual faculties of the skin lovers, of the wicked in general, thus providing them with means of self-indulgence.

Rumi compares worldliness to a bath-stove fuelled with dung. Power and riches are the dung. Piety and purity are like the bath. The devout and the pious are the hot bath and are clean and pure. The proud rich, devotees of satan, are like the carriers of dung for the servant to use as fuel to heat up the water in the stove. To abandon the stove is the essence of the bath. Not to abandon it and remain in the stove is to act as a servant to him who uses the bath. Why be a servant to another?

We are friends of the skin, as we have not seen the kernel, the spiritual principle, leave alone the kernel of the kernel. We have forgotten the divine beloved. When we overcome this forgetfulness, our eyes will be opened to the Reality. We shall no more be attracted to this world or its false delights, but desire God, and naught else.

But no stone can turn into pure ruby until—as went the belief those days—the sun takes away its stoniness and fills it with sunniness. If, then, the ruby loves itself, it is love of the sun. If it loves the sun, it is love of itself. There is no difference between these two loves. These two aspects are like the rosy sunrise and its radiance. But not until the stone becomes the ruby is it a single 'I' because the stone is dark and impervious to light. Two contraries, dark and light, two 'I's', are there. It is only when the stone is self-negated that it becomes a ruby and has the right to say 'I' as it is no more dark and blind to light. Pharaoh never became a ruby. He remained a dark stone, an enemy to light. Hallaj was a true carnelian, a passionate lover of the light. When he said, "I am the Truth," he was in mystical nearness to Him.

The lesson is that not until we cease to be spiritually insensible and become lowly and self-negated, can we lose our false 'I' and attain real 'I-ness'. Not without reason would Adam bring into view his rustic shoes and sheepskin jacket. They reminded him of his humble origin. He would say, "I am of clay." Ayaz would visit his shoes and ragged jacket and wear them every day, lest his eminence at court intoxicate him with pride. They were perfect human beings, completely self-negated and non-existent, God's very elect.

We should know that the creator of existence works through non-existence. Non-existence is the workshop where He uses His creative energy. Or rather, it is His working material from which this multitudinous creation is created. In our mundane life also, nobody writes on a page already written over, but seeks a blank page. Nobody plants a sapling on a sown plot, but seeks an unsown plot, as were the hearts of Adam and Ayaz and other perfect human beings, so that God, the super-craftsman, may inscribe or sow therein the mystery of divine love and gnosis. Nothing can display His perfection so well as the pure, virginal heart of the perfect mystic. Not-being the best mirror of Being.

But the journey to the divine darkness of self-negation, the 'luminous night' from whose midst the light breaks forth—the midnight sun—is an interior journey, arduous, endless, demanding our all. The spiritual wayfarer needs a guide who is familiar with the twists of the wayless Way. We must not be deceived by the false dawn, an exoteric teacher personifying this world of good and evil. He can only lead us into darkness and destruction. Nor must we mistake the true dawn for the false dawn, a man of God like Ayaz for a false guide. Such a mistake is not uncommon, as the evil-doer, who is suspicious and imputes his own vices to others, sees his own evil interior in others. Of this class were the mean-minded Amirs who falsely conceived that Ayaz kept a rich treasure buried in his private chamber. They were only seeing their own wicked love for worldly riches in the taintless heart of Ayaz. They could not discern between saint and sinner.

THE ONENESS OF LOVER AND BELOVED

The king had told the Amirs to go and raid Ayaz's chamber, but he was distressed by the thought of how Ayaz would feel if he heard that it was the king himself who had given this iniquitous command. But then he would say to himself, "Ayaz is too constant in his devotion to me to be offended by my accusation," or, "With his ability to contemplate the ultimate consequences or ends of things, he is too constant in his devotion to be ignorant either of my real purpose, which was to know his inmost thoughts, or of the fate of his accusers and rivals. Even if for the sake of trial I struck him a hundred blows with my sword, his nearness to me would not suffer. For he would know that I was only striking myself with the sword, as, in reality, I am he and he is I. We are mystically one, not two. Nothing can divide us. In any case, real being belongs to God alone, so that none else has the right to say, 'I am.'"

A mirror is an illustration of the real meaning of the oneness of the lover and the beloved. It is formless. It reflects nothing when nothing is before it. It is the opposite of form. And, yet, when a form is before it, the formless mirror reflects that form. The form is thus reflected in the formlessness of the mirror.

As every nearness is the death of selfhood, the death of all 'otherness', of sex, rank or creed, and is essentially spiritual, the sameness of the sex of Sultan Mahmud and Ayaz is irrelevant in this context. Of similar irrelevance was the difference in the sex of Layla and Majnun in the popular love romance of the same name *Layla and Majnun*. To Majnun, all was Layla. She was the cup out of which he drank wine, contemplated her real essence, and had no eyes for the beaker. He envisioned divine beauty in her and had no use for its reflection in her flesh and blood which would only interrupt that celestial vision. But he was of this earth. Suffering the anguish of long separation from her, he became ill. His blood boiled up and symptoms of quinsy developed in him. As the physician who came to treat him said that there was no other remedy than blood-letting, the cupper came to bleed him. He bandaged his arm and was about to use the lancet for the operation, when Majnun cried, "Stop! Take your fee and go. If I die, let my blood return to dust."

"But why?" asked the cupper. "Why are you afraid of the lancet when you are not afraid of wild animals like lions and wolves and bears, who (as the story goes) roam with you by day, and gather round you and guard you at night?"

Even wild animals know what love is. Because of the abundance of love and ecstasy in the heart of Majnun, they did not smell the human in him. They smelt love, and so, did not attack him. How should one, the selfish worldlings, who has not smelt the heart in his own kind, smell the heart in animal kind? How should he know that love secretly inter-links all in a universal harmony?

Majnun refused to be bled, not because he was afraid of the lancet, but because he was a lover. He loved the pain of love. As his whole being was full of Layla, he was afraid that if the cupper let his blood, his lancet might of a sudden wound Layla. He and Layla were one in spirit and the spirit is the ruler of the flesh.

In the case of eminent Sufi Bayazid Bastami, God said to him, "Go forth with My attributes to My creatures. Whoso shall see thee shall see Me and whoso shall take himself to you shall betake himself to Me." When on another occasion He said to Bayazid that His creatures desired to behold him, his answer was prompt, "Adorn me with Your unity. Clothe me in Your I-ness. Raise me to Your oneness, so that You may be there, not I." God had raised Bayazid to unity and oneness with Himself. Like an ounce of vinegar dropped in an ocean of honey, his attribute of separateness was lost, although his essence was inviolate and everlasting.

The Prophet said, "Whosoever belongs to God, God shall belong to him." Our infirm, temporary personality came from the permanent personality of God. When it passes away, it is sunk in Him and becomes everlasting.[3] In other words, our personality or selfhood is a temporary reflection, a finite mode of the infinite, all-pervading selfhood. Only by dying to self can we find the universal self, which is the source and essence of our being.

LIBERATION BY STAGES

The aspirant should not seek to scale the ramparts of eternity at one bound because such direct penetration is most difficult for the embodied. Rumi exhorts us to dig earth like a well-digger, so that we may reach down to some living water. He elaborates this in the story of "The Thirsty Man"[4] not included in this collection. Seated on a high wall that stood on the bank of the stream and separated him from the water, that man kept tearing bricks from the wall and hurling them into the stream. The noise of the splash was as music to his ears, as it meant he was getting closer to running water. The tearing of the bricks and turfs is like prostration in prayer. It is self-abasement which takes us near to God. So long as the wall of the earthly body is lofty and proud and not razed to the ground we cannot perform prostration in prescribed prayer on the water of life and attain nearness to Him.

The correlative terms like the one and the many, lord and slave, lover and beloved, are only names for different aspects of a single Reality, each aspect necessitating the other aspect and being interchangeable with it. As God loves His lovers, He empties them of themselves and unites them with Himself so that He is both lover and beloved in Himself. The perfect human being may also be said to be God Himself in the likeness of a reflection. All the divine attributes are reflected in his unbounded heart or spirit. In the unitive state, the divine and human aspects are interchangeable.

Not that the supreme lover of God becomes God in the unitive state. This state has two aspects, negative and positive. The negative aspect involves the death of selfhood or negation of self. The positive aspect involves the affirmation of the real self. If one passes through oneself, and, having left his self behind, has become entirely void of self, what remains but being, the one eternal. Hallaj, who was executed for his blasphemous utterances, but later came to be venerated as a martyr saint, exclaimed, "I am the Truth," which according to Rumi, emanated from a feeling of oneness with the Light of God. This, however, does not appear to be quite in keeping with the spirit of Hallaj's mystical utterance. He applied the term *hulul* to his doctrine of mystical union, but not in its technical, theological sense. The fact is that in the deep drunkenness of love of God, utterly dead to sense, to all consciousness, to any distinction between affirmation and negation, the mystic is entirely irresponsible for his utterance. He may exclaim "I am the Truth" or "I am nothing." Bayazid would exclaim in moments of ecstasy,"There is no God except I, so worship me," but himself could not remember on return to sobriety what he had said in the drunkeness of love.

AYAZ'S CHAMBER RAIDED

The evil-minded amir, the originator of the plot, went at midnight with his officers to the chamber of Ayaz. They found it locked with intricate bolts. They unlocked the door with great difficulty. Ayaz had put on this lock, not because he was guarding any treasure in the chamber against any possible theft, but because he did not want common people to sneak in, and, seeing his shoes and jacket, think him to be a hypocrite who was showing this rough and worn-out apparel the sheepskin jacket as a blind, and had kept his treasure hidden elsewhere in the chamber. A man of high aspiration guards his soul's secrets more securely than gold or rubies are guarded in the mine.

Urged by greed of gold, ignoring the wise counsel of reason, the Amir and his officers opened the chamber and, jostling each other in the doorway, moved in and looked in all directions. All they saw was torn shoes and a sheepskin jacket. Almost certain that the treasure was kept buried in some part of the room, they brought picks and dug holes and cavities every here and there, but found nothing. Their disappointment was great. They had chased a mirage. They were ashamed of their baseless suspicion of Ayaz and besought God's help. It is only when one's vain conceit is broken and he is deluded that the rebuking soul, his conscience, upbraids him and he listens to its reproaches [75:2]. But it was too late to undo what they had done.

They filled the holes and cavities with care, but the wall could not possibly be repaired. How could they hide their evil thought regarding Ayaz and pretend innocence? The walls and the floors bore strong testimony against them. Pale-faced, covered with shame and confusion, they returned to the King.

God says in the Koran that on the day of resurrection, *"We seal their mouths, and their hands speak out and their feet bear witness to that which they had earned"* [36:64]. Not only there, but here also, when our hands and feet do harm, they bear witness to our conscience. The lofty boughs and leaves proclaim the nature of the hidden root.

Seeing their fallen faces, the king knew at once that the amir and his officers had failed of their evil purpose. He asked them how it was that their arms were empty of gold, and if they had concealed their precious find, where was the radiance of joy on their countenance?

Pallid with fear, trembling, excusing themselves, the officers threw themselves on his mercy. They said that it would be perfectly just and lawful if he shed their blood, but if he forgave their crime, it would be an act of mercy and bounty in accord with his character, as their black deeds were in accord with theirs.

The king replied that he would neither give this punishment, nor show this mercy to them. The right to punish or forgive belonged to Ayaz against whose person and honor the offense had been committed—for though he and Ayaz were spiritually one, they were formally two, and his own formal self had remained unaffected

THE ORIGIN OF SIN

The problem of sin is as old as the human being himself. It is from the Lord's forbearance that it first arises. Otherwise none would dare sin. He is aware of actions, but His forbearance prevents their exposure. As in the divine Law, the blood-wit for man-slaughter falls on the murderer's kin on the father's side, so, because of the nature of the eternal spiritual relation between God and the human being, the payment of the blood-price for the crime of the evil soul falls on God's forbearance. What happens is that His forbearance intoxicates our soul. While it is intoxicated, the devil sneaks in and leads it astray. God had taught Adam the Names. Adam was the teacher of knowledge to the angels [2:31-33]. And yet the wine of the Lord's forbearance, that potent opiate, confused him and made him yield to satan's temptation. His reason could only seek refuge with His forbearance, saying, "You have been my intoxicating the cup-bearer so help me now."

The king said that in the case of the amir and his officers, it would be equally right if Ayaz punished them or accepted their repentance and forgave them. Each course had its advantages. The slayer is constrained to slay, not by his own independent will, but by divine fore-ordainment. At the same time, "Within justice a thousand mercies are enclosed." God has said, *"And for you in retaliation there is a life."* [2:175]. He who considers retribution detestable is only taking into account the life of the murderer, and ignoring the numerous lives that will be kept safe by fear of punishment. Punishment must not only be retributive, but also preventive or deterrent. It must seek to bring to the criminal the consciousness of his guilt and reform him. That is, it must be reformative.

The king praised Ayaz's incorruptibility. He said that if he tested him a hundred times he would never find him wanting. While people were ashamed of tests, all tests were ashamed of being applied to him. His knowledge and his forbearance were profound. Neither was creaturely.

Ayaz replied that all this was the king's gift. He himself was nothing but those shoes and the sheepskin jacket. The Prophet has said, "Whoso knows himself knows God," meaning that he who knows himself to be lowly and of no account knows the Lord to be omnipotent. The seed from which one is conceived is just one's old shoes and one's blood, the sheepskin jacket. All else—organs and faculties—is his gift. He has given it to us so that we may seek more and not think that this was all that He had to give. All treasuries are with Him. It is like the gardener who shows us a few apples by way of samples in order to give us an idea of the yield of the trees and the orchard.

The king told Ayaz to proceed and dispense justice. The sinners were deserving of execution, but hoping for pardon, they were waiting to see whether mercy prevailed or wrath, the pure water of the fountain of abundance or the flames of hell.

Forbearance and wrath exist from the primal covenant of

"Am I not your Lord" until now for the purpose of carrying us aloft to God. They are eternally involved in one another like affirmation and negation in the words which God addressed to the human souls in pre-existence, meaning, *"Am I not your Lord (alastu bi rabbikum)?"* to which the soul replied, "Yes [7:172]." *Alastu* is an affirmative question, meaning "I am," proclaiming His Lordship, but it has also the negation *laysa*, "is not," in it. These two divine attributes, wrath and mercy, which like the other attributes, appear indivisibly as one in the divine Essence, have been let down from above into this material world, so that, as determinants of all human destinies, wrath may draw to itself the proud and the wicked and mercy the self-effaced and the righteous. Each part is drawn to its whole, to its ultimate abode. Good qualities and actions accompany good men. Evil qualities and actions accompany vile men. In the words of the Koran, *"The good women come to the good men and, to the wicked men, the wicked women* [24:26]." The sight of a friend arouses mercy in us and that of a foe violence.

The king urged Ayaz to decide their fate expeditiously, for suspense is a kind of vengeance, a kind of death rather. Justice delayed is justice denied.

Ayaz said to the king, "The command is entirely yours. When the sun is present, the star is negated in its radiance. Who is Venus or Mercury to shine in the sun's presence? If I had ignored the shoes and the sheepskin jacket, I would not have given cause for suspicion and slander. Also, it was futile to put a lock on the door of the chamber amid an envious multitude given to foul suspicion and vain imagination. They attribute iniquity and disloyalty to me. They cannot see things as they really are. But I do not entirely blame them. Destiny is the ultimate determinant of all our experience. Nevertheless, it was absurd on their part to try to find a fault in me."

Without breaking one's egotistical self, one cannot become a kernel or hear the voiceless voice of the kernel. The walnuts have voices in their shells. The kernel and the oil have no audible voice, but they are not voiceless. If the kernel was not sweet-voiced, who would listen to a rattling walnut shell? One endures that rattling for the sake of the kernel. But the worldings hear the rattle of the shell and think that there is nothing more. We worldings hear the rattle of the shell and think that there is nothing more. We may speak in verse or prose, but the reality behind the speech is beyond their perception. It is best to keep external silence and speak the wordless language of the mystic. Since that also is above them, it will at least obviate unnecessary argument.

The king said to Ayaz, "Why have you mingled your soul's love with your old shoes and tattered jacket? You have hung these lifeless things in your chamber and hold long and loving conversation with them regularly, telling them your joys and sorrows. What Asaf (King Solomon's minister), what wisdom, dwells in your shoes? And your jacket one would think was the shirt of Joseph whose wondrous perfume cured his father Jacob of his blindness." The king asked these questions just to get Ayaz talking.

THE SORCERY OF LOVE

Love and imagination are great sorcerers. They weave a hundred forms as beautiful as Joseph. They create a form of fantasy in memory of one's beloved. Attracted by that fantasy, that form, one is brought into conversation with it. He breathes out his woes, joys and a hundred secrets in its imaginary presence. It is like one friend communing with another friend. No material form is there and yet, from it comes a hundred utterances of the words, "Am I not your beloved?" From you a hundred, "Yeas"—as at the primal covenant.

That which is the object of love is not material form, which decays and dies and is forgotten, but something spiritual. Love can even be for something drawn from fantasy. It is like a grief-crazed mother who, beside the grave of a newly dead child, moans forth fond and tearful words as if the lifeless corpse were still alive, and the earth in the grave had hearing, vision and intelligence. She fully believes that the earth is listening and throbbing in sympathy with her pain. Lovingly and tearfully, she lays her face on the fresh earth in a manner in which she had not laid it on her son while he was alive.

But love for the dead is not lasting. When God takes away the enchantment, it dies. When the fire is out, what remains but ash? The mother mourns for the dead child for a few days and her love becomes a portion of the past. Nothing now comes from the earth except cold indifference and forgetfulness. One should set one's love on the Living One that increases spiritual life, not on these passing forms.

THE SHAYKH

As the perfect shaykh's spirit existed in the divine Mind before the creation of form, as every soul existed potentially there as an idea and as every idea is related to a particular object, the shaykh has intuitively beheld every entity in non-entity, every conditioned being as unconditioned, and has foreknowledge of the entire creation.[5] Inspired by divine love. He beholds nothing anywhere but the divine beauty of which all phenomenal forms are but reflections. He is our true love, whether young or old—not necessarily old, for many such are dark-hearted. It is not palsied age, but oldness in wisdom that counts. The shaykh brings help to his disciples, to despairing thousands.

In separation, the beloved weaves many forms of fantasy, but in nearness, He comes forth saying, "I am the origin of mystical intoxication and sobriety. All phenomenal beauty is my reflection. I have lifted the veils at the moment and raised my beauty into direct view. Because you have been engrossed with My reflection, you have become capable of contemplating My Essence, stripped of the veiling forms."

The old shoes and the jacket, though phenomenal, have an intermediate spiritual value. They serve as a symbol of self-abasement which is a means of Godward ascent. When His pull comes, one grows unconscious of any intermediary between him and God, unconscious of the shoes and jacket, whose symbolic task is done. Even the shaykh is needed no more.

True moral goodness consists in the abandonment of anger, lust and greed. Such renunciation of sensuality is the way to paradise. Its indulgence the way to hell. As the Tradition goes, "Paradise is encompassed with things disliked," disliked sensually, and "hell-fire is encompassed with sensual desire." Ayaz was a knight of God. His moral goodness was true moral goodness. It was that of reason, not that of animality. He had the strength and intelligence of prophets and angels.

The king commanded him repeatedly to explain the reason for his showing so much humility before his old shoes and jacket because he wanted others to benefit by knowledge of their inmost mystery. For as the Prophet said, "Religion consists of giving sincere advice." Ayaz had set an example for them. As the king said to him, "You have lent life and luster to slavery. Your splendor has shot up from lowliness to the sky. The true believer is one whose belief amid life's ups and downs makes even the infidel regret that he is not a slave.[6]

10 THE BREAKING OF THE PEARL

One day, the king went to the assembly chamber, and found all his courtiers assembled there. He took out a pearl and put it into the hand of the minister and asked him what it was worth? "More than a hundred ass-loads of gold," he said. "Break it," said the king. "How should I break it?" asked the minister. "I am a well-wisher to your treasury and wealth. How should I deem it proper that such a priceless pearl should be broken? "Good," said the generous king and presented him with a robe of honor. He also gave him the garments he wore and took the pearl back.

The king conversed with the courtiers on sundry subjects for a while and thereafter, placed the pearl in the palm of a chamberlain. He asked him what its value was to a possible buyer? "Half a kingdom," he replied. "Break it," ordered the king. "It would be a great pity to break it," he said. "Leave alone its material value, behold its splendor and brilliance before which even the bright daylight blushes with shame. How should my hand move to break it? How should I be an enemy to the royal treasury?" The king presented him also with a robe of honor, increased his salary and praised his intelligence.

After a while, he made trial of the minister of justice, and, one after the other, of some fifty or more amirs. They all said that what the minister had said or something similar and were similarly rewarded.

The honors that the King bestowed on these amirs—symbolizing the money-loving worldlings—flattered their vanity and were sweet to their sensual souls, but they were superficial, delusive. They betokened his displeasure, his abandonment of them to their fate and relegation from the way of salvation to the depths of perdition.

Imitation is doubtless the pillar of the world. Even originality is, in a sense, imitation from a great many, not easy enough to differentiate and identify. Hence, in imitating the minister, the amirs were only following the way of the world. But when imitation is put to the spiritual test, it disgraces the imitator. What one needs on the spiritual path is personal verification and guidance by one's inner light, the light of the conscience or spirit, not any alien light.

Passing from hand to hand, the pearl, an emblem of worldly riches and distinction, came at last into the sagacious hand of Ayaz. The king asked him what it was worth? "More than I can say," he replied. "Break it," ordered the king.

Ayaz's reaction was different from that of the amirs. He was not beguiled by the king's gifts to robes of honor, riches and salary increases or by his commendation of the intelligence of those money lovers. He was not an imitator. For the imitator, although a Muslim, ought not to be regarded as a real Muslim, as it is rare that he holds fast to the faith and emerges safe and unsullied from the trials of this probationary existence. He lacks the spiritual eye of the seers and is deluded by appearance. The truth is one. Its contrary is deceptive, although very like it in appearance. As the imitator does not know the contrary so as to distinguish it from the truth—contrary can only be known by contrary—how should he know the truth? Mistaking the fires of lust for the sunlight of life, indulging what is forbidden, crimsoned by sin, early or late, he becomes void of the faith, turns an infidel, and pays the wages of sin, except in the rarest of cases, where despite such ignorance, the Lord's favor preserves one, when no harm comes to him from that ignorance.

10 The Breaking of the Pearl 153

Ayaz had come with two stones in his sleeve, fully prepared to do what he intuitively knew to be right. Hence, the moment the king asked him to break the fabulous pearl, he broke it to bits with the two stones.

The loss of one's horse and bishop, the supposed means of triumph in the chess-game of life, means little to a gnostic. For he needs no phenomenal means to carry him to his goal. He knows he is the winner by divine favor. He is amongst the foremost in the race who will be brought to the Throne in gardens of delight [56:10-12]. He fears no defeat, no painful war, certain that God will checkmate his adversary.

Assailed by hope and fear, the ascetic worries about his plight on the day of resurrection. Formerly, the gnostic also was assailed by similar feelings. But as he and his like were acquainted with the material form of every existent being before the universal soul was fettered by materiality, they know by intuitive thought the mystery of the divine decree. They know the beginning and the end of things. They know that they will reap what they had sown. They are exempt from the ascetic's feeling of fear and anxiety regarding the end. They know who in this world is for paradise and who for hell. [1] Hence when Ayaz the perfect gnostic broke the pearl, he acted rightly, as he had attained to knowledge of the eternally pre-ordained destiny and was only fulfilling the divine decree.

When the pearl was broken, a hundred outcries arose from the amirs. They exclaimed, "What recklessness, what sacrilege is this? The breaker of this pearl is surely an infidel." They reviled Ayaz.

Ayaz said, "O nobles of renown, your eye is set on the material pearl, not on the king. Tell me, which is superior—the king's command or the material pearl, this tinsel? I will never look away from the king. Never, like the polytheist, will I turn my face towards a stone. The soul that prefers a colored stone, and puts my king behind, is void of the spiritual pearl, of faith and knowledge of God. Turn away from these worldly baubles, and lose your reason in the bestower of color. Enter the river of

Reality. Break the pitcher of form. Set fire to mere color and perfume which only mislead the soul."

The nobles hung down their head in shame, begging forgiveness for their sinful forgetfulness of the spiritual pearl. From each heart burning sighs were curling up to heaven.

The king, symbolizing God, signalled to the old executioner —the angel of divine punishment—as if to say, "Remove these men wretches, these wrong-doers from my presence. For the sake of a colored stone, they broke the command, treating it cheap and inconsequential."

AYAZ'S INTERCESSION AND SUPPLICATION

It was like the day of judgment. When the amirs were about to be killed, Ayaz, interceding on behalf of the sinners—as the perfect human being will intercede on that day—rushed into the king's presence. Prostrating before him, he said with bated breath, "O noble and gracious king, if anyone disregards your command, he certainly deserves the gallows. To whom should he turn for support except to your pardon? It is from the fullness of your grace and clemency that the heedlessness and irreverence of these sinners arise. When you called yourself forgiving, you let them fall into sin. If you had said that sin would not be forgiven, none would have dared sin. Heedlessness arises from irreverence and irreverence from spiritual blindness. Reverence alone gives clarity of vision, burns up irreverence and the consequential heedlessness. For how should one with awe of God, with reverence for Him, be heedless of Him and flout His command when he can see inwardly that the ultimate consequence of such heedlessness will be spiritual perdition."

It is said in the Koran, *"Punish (us) not if we forget or commit a fault"* [2:286]. This is proof enough that forgetfulness is a sin. For one who was forgetful did not attain to reverence. True, his forgetfulness was fore-ordained, and, therefore, inevitable, but the sinner was a free actor in choosing to be remiss in his feelings of reverence, and chose the very means by which forgetfulness is born. He cannot plead innocence. It is like the case of a drunken man who commits a sin and seeks to absolve himself of responsibility for its commission on the ground that he was unconscious at that time. He should know that senselessness, that loss of power to choose to remain sensible, did not come on its own. It came by his invitation. The sin was committed because he drove away his power of right choice.

But one who is intoxicated by God is not responsible for any sin he may commit or for any irresponsible utterance. He is overpowered by the spiritual cup-bearer, drunken with Him, without exertion on his part. His freewill is lost in His freewill. Hence God is his support and intercessor. His sin, his loss of consciousness, is better than the sobriety and obedience of others, and is worthy of devotion.

Continuing his supplication to God, although nominally addressing Sultan Mahmud, Ayaz said, "All forgivenesses sing the praise of your peerless forgiveness, of which they are but the reflection. Grant the amirs their lives. Do not banish them from your presence. Myriads of bitter death cannot compare with the anguish of separation from you. Have mercy on him who formerly enjoyed your favor. In hope of nearness to you, even the infidel says amid hell-fire, "If God were to look on me with favor, what pain would remain?" That look sweetens all pains. It is the blood-price paid to Pharaoh's magicians for amputating their hands and feet, which prompted them to say, *'It is no hurt, for unto our Lord we shall return'* [26:50]. They had realized that this world, this life, as the Prophet said, is, 'The sleeper's dream.' It is no harm if the body is amputated in dreams.'

Ayaz had passed away in union with the light of God. "How should I," he said, "beg for mercy from you who are in anger, or indicate the path of clemency to you who are all-knowing? Nothing is that you do not remember or can possibly forget. Who am I, non-existent as I am, to say 'Forgive,' O you who are all-forgiving, whose mercy precedes all precedents of mercy, and who is the quintessence of the creative utterance 'Be'? I deserve thousands of cuffs for this insolence."

In mystical nearness, there can be no consciousness of anything other than God, no room even for an apostle, an angel or the spirit, no intercession on behalf of another, as intercession implies duality. Hence, pardon for it and also, for begging his pardon, he deemed himself guilty, for this also implies duality, the seeker and the giver of pardon. He was God-fearing. Such fear arises from knowledge of His attributes and actions, knowledge of His wrath and majesty. He is most feared by prophets and saints. The Prophet, the seal of the prophets, is reported to have said, "I know God better than you and fear Him more than you." None fears Him, as God has said, except those of His servants that are possessed of knowledge [35:25]. Hence Ayaz's fear of God and self-abasement.

Continuing, Ayaz said, "O you who have made this nobody somebody, pray listen to my supplication. As you have emptied me of self and my attributes are absorbed in your attributes, it was really you, not I, that made the intercession to yourself. You made the prayer to issue from me. As you were its original inspirer, be gracious enough to be the hope for its acceptance, so that I may boast that you have forgiven the sinners for the sake of this slave, although he is only the instrument of your action. Previously, before I died to self, I was self-seeking. My selfhood was an agonizing affliction both to me and others. Now you have made me a divine physician, a knower of existent beings from pre-existence, and so, a remedy for the spiritually sick. I was a hell full of grief and woe. Your gracious hand made me a fountain of abundance. I cause anyone's faculties which the hell of sensuality has consumed, to grow anew."

This hell is the burner. It is like death. That fountain of abundance is the perfect human being. Like the spring, he is a life restorer. Like the trumpet blast of Resurrection, a spirit awakener. As interpreted by the venerable Sufi Najm al-Din Kubra (d. 1221 CE), it is "the wine of gnosis in the cup of love." It is Ayaz in the present context.

"Your kindness, O Lord, draws towards the fountain of abundance all of them whose bodies are burnt by hell. Your mercy has said, "I created the creatures in order that they might profit by Me, not that I might profit by them" (Tradition).

By this utterance of munificence, all wrongs are righted. All defects made whole. Pardon these flesh-worshippers, these sinful slaves. Pardon from You who are an ocean of pardon is more worthy than creaturely pardon which is like a torrent or river that runs to its parent ocean. Every night, not only these creaturely pardons, these qualities of mercy and clemency from individual souls, but all good and evil thoughts, all actions, whatever stirs this mortal frame, return to their eternal home in the divine Essence and attributes. Every dawn, You send them back into the cage of the bodies, until it is night once more when again they fly back in order to sever their bonds with the body and find bliss in Your loving embrace. Flapping their wings in the spiritual air, with no fear of fall, hopefully they come before You crying, *"Lo, unto Him we are returning."*

To the pure-hearted Sufis—not to the infidels or wrongdoers, whom God does not love [3:57]—the call comes from Him, "Come! After returning to Me, desire or anxiety will afflict you no more. As exiles and strangers in the phenomenal world, you have suffered much. As a result of suffering you have learned to value Me. Now come under My shade and protection and rest evermore on the bosoms of the houries, that is, of the souls of prophets and saints." They receive them with love and affection, saying amorously, "Sufis who had fallen for long in the dust-pit of the world have returned, stainless and unsullied, like the sunlight of the orient that returns to the sun."

"This group of sinners, O mighty king," continued Ayaz, "has been overcome by penitence. They have come to recognize their error and crime, though earlier, they had been beguiled by the shifts and devices of divine destiny. No experience is self-willed. Each spirit is like a die in Your hand. You play with it as You like, determining all its diverse experiences, following or changing what You have decreed. Now these sinners have turned their faces towards You, uttering grievous sights. O You whose mercy is opening the way to sinners, quickly grant the amirs entrance into the Euphrates of Your pardon, and into the cool fountain of Job where they could wash and purify themselves of the prolonged sin [38:42-43]. In this way might they join in prayer the innumerable ranks of the angels. *'There is not one of them but has his known position,'* as says the revealing angel [37:164].

"Although they broke Your command and are deserving of punishment, those who are intoxicated with You are different. Their drunkenness is caused, not by self-will as in the former case, but by Your wine. At the time of *Alastu*—*'Am I not Your Lord'* [7:172]?—while the affirmation of the infidels and sinners came with reluctance and only for fear of damnation, and that of the orthodox Muslims was based on faith and they sought the delights of paradise, the affirmation of Your elect, of saints and Sufis, came from their inmost souls. They sought only You and nothing but You. Their spirit saw Your face on that day, and that was also the day when 'You taught the Names,' revealing the knowledge of all that is to happen unto everlasting. The savior of the day of *Alastu*, that vision and knowledge, will stay in their hearts till the day of resurrection. The delight of their pre-election for felicity at the primal covenant does what a hundred jars of grape-wine cannot do.

"As You have overpowered me, I stand excused. The overpowered one is like the non-existent, with no freewill of his own. As one drunk incurs no penalty until he returns to sobriety, and You have made me drunk with You, punish me when I become sober. But whoever drank of Your cup is permanently delivered from his senses. His intoxication consists in abiding everlastingly in a state of unconsciousness. He that dies to self in love never returns to himself."

Nay, the God-intoxicated lover is not intoxicated by the wine of divine love, but is the wine himself. Human attributes have departed from him. He is the very essence of the divine love that throws him into intoxication. That soul of the soul, the perfect human being—like Ayaz—acting as God's viceroy can re-unite with himself those who are severed from him by sin and infidelity, like the Amirs, and inspire them with his own love of God. The fires of hell, that is, carnal attributes, hold no terror for him, as they are but shadows cast by the fire of divine love which consumes them. Heaven itself is of little worth to them, as it is only a derivative of the divine beauty that abides in their hearts.[2]

11 COMPULSION AND FREEWILL

The human being tends to deem his own little as much and another's much as little and envies his well-merited reward. The amirs were no exception. When they boiled with envy over Ayaz because of the special favors shown to him by the King, they taunted the king, saying that surely Ayaz did not possess thirty intellects. How should he draw the salary of thirty amirs?

The king along with the amirs went out hunting in the desert and in the mountains. He saw a caravan in the distance, and said to an amir to go and ask the caravan from what city they were coming.

The amir went and returned with the reply that they were coming from Rayy. "What was their destination, the king asked?" The Amir had no answer.

The king then said to another amir to go and ascertain the caravan's destination.

The amir went and said on return, "It is Yemen." The king asked him what goods were they carrying? The amir was puzzled and remained silent.

The king then sent another amir to inquire what their merchandise was? He went and returned with the answer that it was of every kind, but largely consisted of cups made in Rayy. "When had they set out from Rayy, the king asked?" The amir was speechless.

This way, thirty or more Amirs were tested, but typifying discursive reason, weak of judgment and mental powers, they were simply unable to tackle a problem in all its relevant aspects.

The king said to the amirs that one day he tested Ayaz separately, saying, "Go and inquire from where the caravan has come?" He went and asked all these questions wholly on his own and ascertained everything about the caravan. What they discovered in thirty visits he discovered in a single visit.

As unlike the amirs, Ayaz was a type of universal reason, nothing relevant escaped his attention. It was this difference that accounted for his superiority to them in rank and favor.

NECESSITY AND FREEWILL

Trying to rebut the king's argument, the amirs said that surely this was a species of the divine favors to Ayaz. It had no connection to personal exertion. The beautiful face of the moon is given to it by God and the sweet scent of the rose is fortune's gift to it.

The amirs were necessitarians. They attributed Ayaz's superiority to providence. This doctrine of necessitarianism, especially if carried to its extremes, however, can be dangerous. It can lead to a complete abdication of exertion and responsibility, of all sense of ethics and morality, reducing this world to some kind of lotus land where men live and lie idle, and this life to a shadow, not even walking but static.

God differentiated particular souls in pre-existence as objects of His knowledge, imprinting each soul with its essential characteristics. It is from these characteristics that all our pains and joys arise in this world. We cannot escape from our pre-dispositions. We cannot act differently from what the pen of iron has inscribed on the rock of destiny. Teleologically, what we deem as the effect of our action is also its final cause. The human being's retributions and rewards are pre-fixed in eternity. His actions here are designed to lead towards the realization of their pre-fixed ends. What we call causation is really correlation.

But his does not mean that the human being is helpless as

a fabric before the needle. God has honored the human being [17:70]. He has honored him by placing in his hand the reins of freewill. He created him in His own image, reflecting all His attributes in him, so that his personal will reflects in some measure the attributes of His freewill. His universal power of choice brings into existence the individual's power of choice which he is free to exercise in subordination to the divine will. He tells us to strive in His ways, to manifest and fulfill His eternal will and decree. He Himself is never idle. Everyday He exercises universal power [55:29]. Every moment He renews the universe although we are not aware of it as the renewal is of like by like and is too swift for our perception.

The Koran lays down prohibitions and commands holding out promise of reward and threats of punishment. If we are not free to choose to be holy or wicked, how should we be justly rewarded with paradise or condemned to hell? Compulsory praise of God earns no wages.

In our day-to-day life we see the working of both compulsion and freewill. Take the simple instance of the movement of the hand. One man volitionally shakes his hand. Another, suffering from palsy, also shakes his hand, but under compulsion. In both cases, the movement is created by God, but the two movements are not identical in the mind of the mover. The normal person has cause to feel ashamed of the impropriety of his act because it is volitional, while the other person has no cause to feel ashamed, as his act is involuntary.[1]

God not only creates our power of choice, but also gives to each action a form in the unseen world corresponding to its nature. Thus, until not very long ago, a gallows was the form given in retribution for robbery. Property was considered a prolongation of one's personality and its theft a kind of murder. Hence this was the form which the ministers of law and justice followed in this world.

His will may change this form with time and clime, and these ministers will follow the changed form.

God in His wisdom has not given us knowledge of our destiny. For if He had made known to us the evil consequences of a particular action, would we have not recoiled from it? In that case, this world would have ceased to be a world of probation and that world the world of recompense. It would be as at the resurrection, with none committing sin.

To return to the amirs, their argument was one-sided. It covered their mental slackness. The king corrected them saying, "No, all our actions result from or personal merits and deficiencies. Otherwise, how should have Adam said to God, *'O Lord, we have wronged ourselves,'* [7:23] when he and Eve had tasted the forbidden fruit? On the contrary, he would have said that this sin was from fate, from destiny, against which no precaution or expediency can prevail. He would have followed the argument of iblis who also had disobeyed the Lord's command to do homage to Adam, and said, "You have led me astray" [7:16]. Unlike Adam, like most of us, he hid his own role in the act.

Nay, divine destiny is a fact. The human being's exertion also is a fact. They are two facets of the truth, but this duality of compulsion and freewill operates only in this multifarious world and not in the spiritual world of unity where all is foreknown, but which itself is free from all distinction of necessity and freewill, from all duality and pairs of contraries. God creates the actions which issue from us, along with our freedom to act or not to act. Let us not look only at one facet of the truth. We vacillate between two alternative acts both of which are in our power to perform—like going to Teheran or Isfahan, or wielding the pen or the spade. Vacillation is necessarily connected with freewill, with the power to act or abstain from it. Without freewill, it can have no meaning.

God is *"the most Just of Judges"* [11:45]. Retribution is in precise measure with the quality of one's action. They say that the sword shall perish by the sword. When one commits a sin, he should look into himself and admit that he has committed it and lay the blame upon himself. Let him make peace with His retribution and justice. Let him repent and turn into the right road, and not be deluded by the wiles of the flesh. Nothing can be hidden from the All-knowing Lord. Just as the material specks of dust are manifest in the beams of the material sun, the specks consisting of thoughts and ideas are manifest in the beams of the central spiritual sun. *"Whoso does an atom's weight of good or evil will see it at the resurrection"* [99:7,8].[2]

12 Shaykh Muhammad Sarrazi of Ghazna

There was in Ghazna an ascetic eminent for his knowledge of theology. His name was Shaykh Muhammad and title *sar-razi*. Every evening he would eat vine-tendrils (*sar-i-raz*), and fasted the rest of the time. For seven years, he was incessantly engaged in questing for the vision beatific. He experienced numerous marvels from God, but not that vision which was the sole object of his quest. Sick of himself, he went to a mountain top, and said to Him, "Manifest or I will throw myself down."

God said to him, "The time for that munificence is not yet. Even if you fall down, you will not die. I will not kill you."

The shaykh probably had the case of the Prophet in mind. Whenever the latter was overwhelmed by the sense of separation from God, he would be about to throw himself down from Mt. Hira, when Gabriel would appear to him, saying, "Do not cast yourself down, for great fortune is coming to you from God's creative utterance, '*Be*.'" He continued in this fashion until the veil was lifted and his heart's desire was fulfilled.

As if what God told him was not enough, the shaykh threw himself down and fell into the depths of a stretch of water. Finding himself still not dead, he lamented over himself for having been separated from death. He was begging death from the unseen, crying like Hallaj, "Verily, in my death is my life." He loved death as others love life. To him, as to the caliph Ali, the sword and dagger were his 'sweet basil', his heart's delight, and the 'narcissus' life's sensual pleasures, his soul's enemies.

A wondrous voice from beyond the occult and the visible came to him, "Go from this desert to the city, and, there, for the sake of self-abasement, became an ideal beggar. Beg money from the rich and give it to the lowly poor."

"To hear is to obey," he said. Much conversation passed between the Lord and him.

In obedience to the divine command, the shaykh went to Ghazna. A vast crowd came out to welcome him. The nobles and grandees got their palaces ready for his reception. But the shaykh hastily but quietly stole into the city. He said, "I do not come for self-publicity. Talking or discoursing is not my intention. I come in utter humility. The Lord's command is that I should only be a beggar. I am devoted to His command. I will go begging from door to door. I will not use choice expressions but vile ones, as the ideal beggars do, so that I may hear abusive words from all and sundry and be utterly abased. As self-abasement is the very law of love, humble and base is he that covets God. As He command is my very life. From now on, beggary and abasement are my very soul. I will out beggar any beggar."

The shaykh was in such intimate nearness to God that his prayer and the Lord's response were each other's essence. Yet, his external business was to go about crying, "Give something, sir, for God's sake, if He prompt you to be generous."

The prophets also, every one of them, practiced beggary, persisting in their exhortation to the really poor people to whom they were sent. *"Lend to God, lend to God a goodly loan,"* [73:20] free of interest or any selfish thought. *"Whatsoever good you send before you for your souls, you will find it with God, better and greater in recompense"* [47:2]. *"Help God! If you help Him, He will help you and strengthen your foothold"*[47:7].

Although all help comes from God, this is how we are tested in this probationary existence. If we give the life of the animal soul, He gives a manifold spiritual regeneration. If we empty this body of worldly taint, He fills it with pearls of purity.

As the shaykh was practicing beggary for the sake of the Lord, not for the sake of his gullet, his eating bread, honey and drinking milk was better than the religious retreat and fasting of a hundred dervishes. God has said, *"Be not immoderate"* [7:29], but follow the middle path. He has said this in the context of eating bread, not in the context of eating light. The doctrine of the golden mean has no application here. It applies to the sensualist whose gullet is on probation, but not to one like the shaykh who does not eat out of greed or cupidity, but who only follows the divine command. When a saint demands complete obedience from his disciple, he is not motivated by any selfish thought, but by his desire to transmute his base metal into pure gold which, without such obedience, is not possible. The perfect human being eats light, so to speak, feeding on material food and producing spiritual illumination like a flame that consumes wax in a candle and produces increased light. The mean belongs to the realm of the finite. This light is infinite, with no beginning or end, and hence, no middle. In relation to it, any thought of excess or moderation is irrelevant.

God had offered the shaykh all earthly treasures, but as he was a lover, he said, "To seek anyone but You would be impious. If I serve You in hope of the eight paradises or in fear of hell, I would not be a lover of God's love, but only a common believer, a mere wage-earner, seeking salvation, for both hope and fear are concerned with the body." A hundred bodies are nothing to the lover who has been nourished by God's love. In truth, the body of the perfect human being should not be called a body. It is permeated by the divine light, transfigured by the radiance of eternity, and is pure as absolute spirit. In the words of Hafiz,

> From head to foot you will become the light of God,
> When in the way of the majestic one, you become without
> > head and foot.

Not only to a lover of God like the shaykh, but also to a romantic lover like Majnun, who was crazed by love of Layla, the kingdom of the earth was worth nothing. Earth and gold were the same in his eyes. Life itself was valueless. Wild animals like lions and wolves would gather round him like his own kin. They know what love is. The smell of his humanness did not come to them from him because of the fullness of love and ecstasy in his heart and the utter absence of animality. The spiritual influence which emanates from the sage or lover kills everything carnal or worldly. Love devours all except love. The two worlds are but a single grain in its beak. How should a grain devour the bird?

God loves those who by means of devotional works ascend to knowledge and love of Him. When they become His friends, they become His consciousness, so that by Him they hear and by Him they see. They are dead to this world and live through Him.

In this world of duality, the slave desires freedom from his master, as these two, master and slave, are separate and contrary. He is ever seeking a robe of honor and worldly riches, so that he may gain superiority over others. But in the spiritual world of unity, the lover seeks only freedom from his servitude. All his robe of honor, all his delight is his vision of the Beloved. Lord and slave are correlates. God is the ultimate truth. God is the only lover and the only beloved. There is no otherness or duality. Love is a fathomless ocean into which it is futile to sink the string of thought.

Following the command of the wondrous voice from the unseen, one day the shaykh went four times to an amir's palace with a basket in his hand, crying, "Something for God's sake, if you have a divine prompting to give. The creator of the soul is seeking a slice of bread," which fattens the body but wastes away the soul. That is, give something of the leafage of the body which is leaflessness or provisionlessness of the soul. Alms-giving is one of the basic duties prescribed in the Koran. Esoterically, it is self-giving. It is giving one's whole self for the sake of the Lord.

This is certainly a topsy turvy world. Even universal reason is dumb-founded that the spiritually rich saints should beg from those who are rich in worldly possessions, but spiritually poor. The practice keeps the saints self-abased. It helps the worldly rich against the ills of the flesh. Nothing is without a purpose, baffling though it be.

Angered by his obduracy, the amir said to him, "What insolence, what disgusting importunity is this that you come in here four times in one day? You are a disgrace to all beggars."

The shaykh said, "I am a slave to the Lord's command. Be not in such a rage. Keep silence. During the seven years in the desert I ate nothing but vine leaves. If I had found in me any greed for bread, I would have ripped my belly apart. You just do not know how my inside is burning with love of God."

One must not wound or revile God's lovers. The astronomers may study astronomy in great depth and see a star in the daytime. The sorcerer and the magician may learn as much of their sciences as is humanly possible. But hidden from the intellect of these acute persons is the mystery of love which is more manifest to the mystic than is the sun to us on a clear day. We should view God's lovers with the eye of love and apprehend their real state. But as the true and the false are mixed in this world, we should always be cautious and not be carried away by the enthusiastic utterances of seeming saints, many of whom are wretched quacks. We must not wholly discard prudence which the Prophet defined as thinking ill. If one's genuineness is at all in doubt, especially today when religious quacks abound, one should take the middle course and suspend judgment.

What miracles are not wrought by love? It can affect even inanimate objects, leave alone the animate, the humans. The loving sincerity of Moses turned the rod into snake, made Mt. Sinai dance and crumble into fragments, and the sea to clear a passage for the Israelites. The sincerity of God's beloved Muhammad impressed the moon, rending it in two [54:1], a portent of reason, and, it is said, on one occasion, it made the sun turn back after sundown in order to enable him to perform the afternoon prescribed prayer which he had missed as he had fallen asleep at the prayer time.

In our story, moved by his own words, the shaykh broke into

ecstatic cries. Tears were streaming down his cheeks. Touched by his sincerity, the amir also fell to weeping.

After the two had wept bitterly for a while, the amir who had shown him irreverence, said to him, "Rise! choose whatever you like from the treasury. The entire treasure-house is yours, though even the two worlds mean nothing to you."

The shaykh said that God had not given him permission to pick out anything with his own hand. To choose of his own accord would be rank impertinence. Making this excuse, he took leave and departed.

He had declined the offer, as it was not sincere. In any case, sincerity of the ordinary kind had no esteem in his eyes. He said that God had commanded him to go as a beggar and seek bread.

The shaykh begged for two years. Now another command came to him from the creator, "O shaykh, for two years now, you have begged and given by Our command. Henceforth, give, but do not take. We have made you a mat like the wallet of Abu Hurayra—the reputed Traditionist and Companion of the Prophet who lived in poverty, but whose food bag never failed him. Whatever you desire will be found under the mat. We have bestowed on you this power that you may continue to give to anyone whosoever he be, regardless of what or how much is involved. Have no anxiety. Give from the unlimited treasure of Our mercy. In your hand earth will turn into gold. Our bounty is boundless, knows no reduction or diminution, and suffers no regret for such generosity. But in order to disguise from the avid eye the fact that money comes from the other world, first fill your fist from under the mat and then give the money to the beggar who is broken by poverty and to the debtor for his relief from the debt. *Save those who believe and do good deeds, for theirs is a wage unfailing*" [84:25]. The Koran says, *"The Hand of God is above their hands"* [48:10]. Be like that Hand and give ungrudgingly and without minding the cost." That Hand is the perfect human being, the saint, who is like a six-faced mirror through which God looks upon this six-directional world. He looks upon none except through him. It is only from his palm

12 Shaykh Muhammad Sarrazi of Ghazna

that He bestows bounty on those deserving of His mercy. The unseen voice thus urged the shaykh to act like a saint and be the medium through which His gifts may be dispensed.

The object of the miracle was that the people may know for certain that there is a world beyond this world, though not easy to describe. To follow Rumi: In that world, a handful of earth will turn to gold in your hand. If a dead man enters it, he will become living. The most inauspicious will become the most auspicious. Infidelity will become faith. Poison will become an antidote. That world is neither within this world nor without. It is neither beneath it nor above, neither joined with it nor apart from it. It is whyless and howless transcending attribute and relation. Every moment, it manifests myriads of sighs and effects in this world. Its relation to this world is like that of manual craft to the form of the hand, of the glances of the eye to the form of the eye, of the eloquence of the tongue to the form of the tongue.

During the third year, the shaykh's work was to give gold from the purse of the All-judging Lord. The earth would turn into gold in his hand. He knew the secret thoughts of the beggars who came to him and the amounts the debtors owed without their telling him how much they were. This was a sign that he was following the Lord's command, "Go forth with My attributes to My creatures." What could remain hidden from one blessed with His attributes?

When asked how he could read the unspoken thought of the beggar of the debtor, he said, "My heart is empty, and like paradise, wanting nothing. It has no occupation except love of God, no inhabitant except the thought of nearness to God. I have cleansed it of good and evil. It is full of love of the stainless One. When I see anything in it other than God, I know it is nothing of mine, but reflected from the beggar who has come. It is like some form seen in clear water which cannot but be from without, not from within."

We pollute our heart with love of meat and raiment, with love of visible things. It is only when it is purified of all sensuous and material affections, all false imaginings and vain fantasies, that like the heart of the shaykh, it can become a true reflector of the hidden aspects of visible things.[1]

13 THE STORY OF BILAL

There was an Abyssinian slave named Bilal, whose master used to flog him with a thorny branch for disbelieving in his religion and celebrating Muhammad instead. At each blow, the blood spurted from his body. From love of the Prophet, he cried involuntarily and vauntingly, "One! One!" thus uttering the mystery of the divine unity. He was so full of love's passion that there was no room for the entrance of any thought of relieving the pain of the thorns.

The Koran speaks of two seas, one of sweet water and the other of bitter water, whose waters meet but do not mingle. There is a barrier between them which they do not overpass [55:19, 20]. They symbolize the righteous and the wicked who meet in this world, but are kept spiritually apart by their predetermined character. Bilal was the heart, rich with divine jewels of faith, gnosis, and unification. His master was the carnal soul which was the abode of vice. What commerce was possible betwixt the two?

Bilal's experience was similar to that of numerous martyrs, of the magicians of Pharaoh, for example, whose hands and feet were amputated by him for their reject religion and declaring their faith in the Lord of Moses and Aaron [26:44-49]. As they had attained to eternal I-hood, and this life, as the Prophet said, is but sleepers' dream, the amputation was no pain to them in this dream-life. Similarly, the pain of the thorns was no pain to Bilal, who was full of God.

At last, one day, Abu Bakr happened to be passing that way. He heard that cry and from it caught the fragrance of a lover of God. Tears filled his eyes and his heart was troubled. Afterwards, he saw him in private, and said, "Keep you faith hidden from the enemies of the faith. All actions that emanate from us are the effects of the pre-dispositions He has implanted in us. He is the Knower of all secrets. Conceal your desire."

Bilal repented before him as if to promise that he would follow his counsel.

The next morning when Abu Bakr was going in that area on some business, he again heard the sound of blows and cries of "One! One! His heart burnt with grief. Again he admonished Bilal. Again, Bilal repented before him. But again love came and devoured his repentance.

After much repenting of this kind, Bilal outcast repentance from his heart and proclaimed his faith in Muhammad. He devoted his body to suffering, crying, "O Muhammad, my heart is so full of you that it has no room for repentance."

"How should I repent of the life everlasting that can come to me only through Muhammad?" he asked.

"Love is all-conquering, and it has conquered me. The lover rocks not of the gross bodily nature, as distinct from the spiritual essence. I am but a straw before the fierce wind of love, which whirls me about and will drop me where it chooses. I follow God without questioning Him. I follow Him blindly as the shade follows the sun. To offer to settle with the divine destiny is self-mockery. Love's agitation gives me no peace or rest."

The lovers of God have no option but to resign themselves to God's ordinance. They are like the millstone continually moving and moaning according to the command of the Lord. He is ever at work. His action keeps the heavens in continual revolution. They have no rest whatever. How should the lover's heart then seek rest? One may cling to secondary causes and means in the hope that they will save him from being carried by the river of divine action, by the action, by the action of the divine beloved.

But what surety is there that the hidden hand will not frustrate his hope. This world is in perpetual flux.

One who sees not the hand in the writing thinks that the act of writing proceeds from the pen. Let him look around and see the evidences of the divine action. Not only is He continually busy, He is the sole agent of action. At His command, the giddy wind howls. The sun and moon go round keeping an eye over the world. Now it is day, now night. Now the world is like spring and summer, delicious as honey and milk. Now like winter, biting with piercing cold. Universals are like balls prostrating themselves before His bat. The divine action keeps the entire creation ever on the move. How should Bilal or any lover of God who is one of the myriad particulars, not be in restless movement at His decree, not be moaning and moist-eyed incessantly like the water-wheel, so that green herbs may grow from the courtyard of the soul? Running tears always attract the divine mercy.

The creative utterance, *"Be,"* gives order and pattern to the creation. "The heavens themselves, the planets and the center observe degree, priority and place in all line of order." As part of the creation, we should also be at the Lord's disposal. If He tries us to a peg, we should remain pegged. if He unpegs us, we should leap and rejoice. We see that when the sun deviates from its fixed course, it is divinely punished with an eclipse for the deviation. Our reason is not superior to a sun. Let it not lead us crookedly so that we may not suffer disgrace like the eclipsed sun. When the sun is less, only a part of the sun is eclipsed. God says, "My justice is adapted to the sin, making equal retribution for every wrong done. I overhear and oversee all things, good or evil, manifest or occult."

Bilal suffered thorny blows from his cruel master. It was anguish yet anguish that was rapture and ecstasy. Identifying himself with Bilal, the poet describes the rapturous state thus:

NEW YEAR'S DAY IS COME

> The Creator has sweetened the mouths of the creatures with spiritual sweets.

> The Water of Life has returned into our street.
> Fortune is prancing and dragging its skirt along
> > and striking the drum as a signal to break the
> > vows of repentance.
> Once again has the flood-water carried repentance away,
> > the opportunity has come, the watchman is over
> > taken by sleep.
> Every wine-bibber has drunk the wine and is drunk,
> > all our possessions we shall pawn tonight.
> From that life-lengthening spirit's ruby wine.
> > We are ruby within ruby, ruby all through.
> Again has the assembly become joyous and heart-
> > illuminating,
> Arise, burn rue-seed to keep the evil eye away.
> The cries of the jubilant drunken lovers
> > are coming to me,
> O Love, I would love this state to continue to everlasting.
> Behold a new moon has become a friend of a Bilal,
> > the blows of the thorny whip have become to him
> > delightsome as roses and pomegranate flowers.

Bilal said. "If my body has become a many-holed sieve from the blows, my soul and body have become a garden of felicity. My spirit is intoxicated and ravished by loving One and the fragrance of a beloved soul and loving friend, the Prophet, is coming to me." The Prophet is said to have declared that during his Night Journey he heard the sound of Bilal's sandals in paradise. Upon his return to earth, he blessed Bilal, saying "How dear to me you are, how dear."

Hearing this ecstatic speech of Bilal, Abu Bakr abandoned talking of repentance. Afterwards, he narrated his plight to the Prophet and said, "That God-loving man is at the moment in love with you and is your captive. He is a royal falcon who has fallen among the owls, the fanatical foes of the faith. They are tearing out his plumes in anger. His only crime is that he is a falcon, a perfect human being, as the only crime of the prophet Joseph was that he had beauty. They falsely imagine this tinsel

Eden, this world, to be paradise and the falcon a deadly danger to all they cherish in life not knowing that what they cherish will only lead them to perdition. They are crucifying him, flogging his bare body with a scourge of thorns, saying to him. "You are always making mention of the spiritual world Yonder, of the King and of abiding nearness to Him. You call our paradisal village an owlery. You are misleading us with false fanciful ideas, sowing dissension amongst us, and seeking to wean us from our faith. By your hypocrisy and nonsense, you want to become the king and leader of us simple people.

"Blood is spurting from his body, and, yet, resigned to the divine destiny, he is uttering 'One'! I advised him to hide his faith from the accursed infidels, but he is a lover to whom the spiritual resurrection has come, so that the door of repentance is shut to him".

How should loverhood and repentance go together? Repentance is an attribute of the human being and love an attribute of God. Repentance involves the consciousness of sin, its abandonment and a resolve never to return to it. Literally, it means a return, a return from what God has forbidden to what He has commanded. Love, on the contrary, is divine. It alters not, nor bends. It is an ever-fixed mark that looks on tempests and is never shaken. It is all-exclusive, all-devouring. Love for anything but God is unreal. Love is for beauty, and the divine beauty alone is real. All else is but its reflection, a gilded beauty, whose exterior is shining light, but interior like black smoke, an unreal object of desire. That beauty returns to its source, leaving the object shamelessly exposed. Thus, the moon-lit wall looks lovely, but the moonlight returns to the moon, and the moonless wall is no pleasure to the eye. Similarly, when the gold leaves a base coin, the exposed copper loses its glitter and its worth. Early or late, the lover of false beauty is deluded, and his unreal love dies. The divine love is the sun of perfection. The divine creative utterance, "*Be,*" (*kun*) is its light. The creatures are its shadows. "Heaven's light for ever shines, Earth's shadows fly".

Bilal was no pursuer of flying shadows. His love was set not on any gilded beauty, but on the gold mine of Reality, which transcends space and admits of no base sharer in aureity, and waxes day by day.

Muhammad was intensely delighted to hear this story, and asked Abu Bakr what was the remedy?

He said that he was going to buy him at any price his owner might ask, as he was God's captive on the earth and had become the victory of His enemy.

The Prophet said, "The infidels will certainly haggle hard and overcharge you. Be my agent in this noble enterprise. Buy a half share in him on my account. Take half the purchase-price from me."

Abu Bakr said that he would serve him in every way. Having said this, he set off for the house of Bilal's heartless owner. He thought to himself, "Pearls can be bought very cheap from children, these foolish infidels. The devil buys their reason and faith in exchange for the kingdom of the world, for the pleasures of the flesh. He decks out the carcase so fair that it can buy him two hundred rose-gardens from them. The prophets held the candle of the true faith before them, but, by his sorcery, he made them appear ugly in their eyes and the light from the candle a burner of all that they cherished.

"The saintly Bilal is a precious pearl superior to both worlds. His ignorant owner is like an ass that knows no difference between a pebble and a pearl and disbelieves in the spiritual sea and its orientations. How should an animal be a seeker of pearls and ornaments? God has not planted love of them in his disposition. Has anyone seen asses with earrings? Their eye, ear and mind are set on the color and scent of the meadow. To them, "Good hay, sweet hay hath no fellow."

The infidel is essentially a devotee of the sensible world, of grass and pasture. A saint like Bilal is of negative worth to him. The Koran says, *"God has created the human being in the fairest stature,"* [95:4], created him in His own image. His spirit is perfection, the very soul of goodness in the perfect human being, knowing no fault or flaw. It excels the empyrean, transcends thought.

Abu Bakr went to the house of Bilal's master. When he

opened the door, Abu Bakr went in and sat down beside him, frenzied and furious. Bitter words leapt from his lips, "Why are you beating this man of God? What hatred is this, O enemy of the light? If you are true to your own faith, how is your heart allowing you to torture one who is true to his faith? View not things in the distorting mirror of your selfhood!"

Coming from beyond the blue infinities of space, copious fountains of wisdom were cascading from his mouth. It was like the blue crystalline water that outrushed from the rock when Moses smote it with his rod although the rock itself was waterless [2:60]. God made that rock a veil for Himself when opening out a way for the water. The white or retina of the eye has no light of its own, no relation with it, nor has the cavity of the ear any hearing, but He made then His veil when creating the light in the eye and hearing in the ear. He gives relationship to the unrelated and is the causer of causes. We speak of the one in the many, but in the ultimate, the many are in the one. He is the sea of origin. Our sight and hearing are related to His sight and hearing as the part to the whole. They are derivatives, utterly of no account in relation to their primary source. He is the real Seer, Speaker and Hearer whom the Sufi beholds unveiled. There is none but God in the two worlds. All things are full of Him.

Bilal's master told Abu Bakr that as he had so much pity for the black slave. He said that Abu Bakr could ransom him by giving him gold in exchange. Abu Bakr made an alternative offer. He said that he had a handsome slave with a white body, but a dark heart. He could give him in exchange for Bilal, who was black-bodied but had an illumined heart. He immediately sent a messenger to fetch the white slave.

Bilal's master was an idol-worshipper. When the white slave arrived, Bilal's master was struck by his comely form. His stony heart melted. But as he was sold to greed, he began to haggle, saying that in exchange for Bilal, he must have some money in addition to the slave. Abu Bakr offered him two hundred dirhams (current coins) of silver extra so as to satisfy his greed. Bilal's master guffawed in malice, imagining that he had swindled Abu Bakr. When asked, "Why this laughter?" he said that if he had not shown such keenness in the purchase of the black slave, he would not have haggled so hard, but sold him for a tenth of the purchase-amount. He was worth but little in his opinion.

Abu Bakr said, "O you simpleton, like a child you have given away a precious pearl very cheap. He is worth both the worlds. Of course, I am looking at his spirit and you at his complexion. The sensual eye that sees these seven bodily colors is veiled from perception of the spirit. If you had haggled harder, I would have given my entire property and riches, and, if necessary, borrowed gold in order to purchase him. You sold him cheap because you got him cheap. You went by his form and were ignorant of his intrinsic worth. You have thrown away your fortune and felicity. One day you will repent your folly and utter many a 'woe is me'. Now take this dark-hearted white slave. We both have profited. *"To you, your religion, to me mine."* [109:6].

Abu Bakr then took the hand of the sore-wounded Bilal and led him into the presence of the Prophet. When Bilal beheld his face, he fell down in a swoon. On return to consciousness after a long time, he began to weep tears for joy. The Prophet clasped him to his bosom. This was very heaven for Bilal. He was like copper that had touched the elixir. The Prophet addressed him words which were such that if they fell on the ears of night, it would become bright as day. We ourselves know what words the sun in the Aries which marks the advent of spring or the limpid water speaks to the herbs and the sapling. The work of God towards the particles of the world is like the spells recited by enchanters. Without lip movement or sound, His decree produces hundreds of effects and secondary causes. They are real, but beyond the conception of reason. It is only in union with Him that the working of His creative incantations can be understood, but the way to it reason does not know.

The Prophet reproached Abu Bakr, saying that when he had enjoined him to buy Bilal in partnership with him, why had he bought him for himself alone?

Abu Bakr said, "Bilal and I are your slaves. I freed him for your sake. Keep me as your slave and friend. I seek no freedom, as my freedom consists in being your slave. In my youth, my spirit would dream that the sun greeted me and raised me aloft to heaven. But I knew it was sheer hallucination. When I beheld you, I beheld and sunk myself in the goodly mirror of your heart, the universal mirror, and what was absurd became actual. By you I was filled with high aspiration. Love for the earthly sun fell in my esteem. The earthly garden looked despicable. I sought light and in you I saw the Light of light. I sought a handsome Joseph and in you I beheld a whole host of Josephs, a complete manifestation of the attributes of divine beauty. In your person, as the Prophet, the paradise of gnosis stood revealed to me. I know that while in relation to me, this is praise of you, in relation to you, it is but invective and satire. It is like God's praise uttered by the simple shepherd within the hearing of Moses. He said, 'I will sew Your shoes, comb Your hair, remove the lice, bring You milk, kiss Your little hand and massage Your little feet, wash Your clothes, and sweep Your room.'

"As this foolish prattle came from his heart, and any praise of God, who transcends all understanding and conception, is only an expression of one's subjective idea, necessarily inadequate, of His nature, God accepted the shepherd's blasphemous utterance as praise.[1] God values a pure heart, and not just a faultless tongue. It will be no marvel, O spirit of the world, if you also have mercy on our failure to comprehend you and your supreme perfection."

BILAL, THE PROPHET'S CALLER TO PRESCRIBED PRAYER

Bilal was the Prophet's first caller to prescribed prayer. Whenever the spirit of the Prophet felt weary through mingling with people, he would go to him and say, "Refresh us by chanting the call to prescribed prayer. Relieve us from worldly cares" (Tradition). "Raise your melodious voice which I—as the logos—breathed into your heart. You used to speak under your breath from fear of your old tyrannous master. Now go fearlessly into the minaret and cry aloud into every sorrowful ear. 'Arise, hasten to welfare'"—words which occur in the call to prescribed prayer.

Bilal could not pronounce *hayya* (throaty '*h*') correctly. He would mispronounce it as plain "*h*" (as in English). When people pointed this out to the Prophet and asked for another caller to prescribed prayer who could speak more correctly, the Prophet flew into a temper and said, "O wretches, to God Bilal's mispronounced *hayy* is better than a hundred *ha*'s and *kha*'s or any words and phrases. God prizes a pure heart not just a faultless tongue. He cares not of our prescribed prayer, howsoever well-worded or pronounced."

THE DOCTRINE OF RESERVE

Bilal suffered torture from his previous master for uttering the mystery of divine unity before one who was a heartless infidel. A perfect human being must follow the doctrine of reserve and meticulously observe the rule of silence. He may divulge this mystery to those who can understand, but should speak through silence as it transcends speech and words, his soul communing with soul. Why cast pearls before swine? Heedlessness of God only causes the petty worldlings to scorn the teachings of holy men, as Bilal's master despised Bilal, and blindly resisted the divine attraction that would draw them along the path of self-negation to everlasting bliss.

The real object of all seekers is God, even if they do not know it. Faiths differ because the forms of worship express different aspects of His nature. In essence, they are not different. He lays heavier tribulations on His favorites, as they make the soul stouter. This imposition is also a sign of His coquettishness, of His greater love for them. A pain throb here wins intensified bliss There. Sometimes He may deliver a blind man from blindness by giving him the knowledge that the kingdom of God is within him, not without, so that urged by that knowledge he gazes inward and pays reverence to Him. The Prophet has said,

"When God wills His servant good, He opens the eyes of his heart and lets him see the invisible world of Reality. He has only to say '*Be*', and it is."

Bilal was black-complexioned, but his heart was pure. Blackness is nothing to be ashamed of. It is dark-heartedness that is shameful. It is in the darkness of night, in the darkness of self-negation that the water of life, the holy grail, is found. The black pupil of the eye of the perfect human being, whose spiritual eye is opened, is a mirror of Light and organ of vision. It reflects all the divine attributes. The human being in essence is not body but vision, spiritual vision. Blackness has many virtues. In a sense, it is the parent of light.

BILAL'S DEATH

Like holy men, Bilal loved death. When he lay dying, his wife was beside him, her throat throbbing broken syllables of grief. She cried, "Oh sorrow! This is the parting. Tonight you will go to a strange country from which no traveler ever returned. You will become absent from us all. Where shall we behold your face?"

"Grieve not," said Bilal. "Say 'O joy! So far I have been in anguish from living. You do not know the delight and reality of death.'" As he was saying this, in testimony, his face was blooming with narcissi and rose petals. His eyes turned radiant with light. "My soul is going home from a strange country," he said. "This is not the parting, but union with God. You can behold me among His elected people, the blessed saints in paradise." Death is not the end, but the beginning of a wondrous new life.[2]

14 THE SUFI AND THE JUDGE

A sick man went to a physician. He asked the physician to feel his pulse. By feeling it, he wanted the physician to diagnose the state of his heart for the hand-vein is linked with the heart. The outer hangs from the inner.

The heart is invisible, and so, its symbol has to be sought from a physician who is in immediate connection with the heart. This is true of all invisible things. They can only be known or seen through the veil of an appropriate symbol. Thus the wind is invisible, but the floating dust and the dancing leaves will tell us that the wind is blowing and also from which direction it is blowing. Divine love is hidden, but its signs are evident in the languorous eyes of the lovers of God. The mark of their bowing and falling in worship before Him, the trace of prostration, is on their foreheads [48:29]. Divine Essence is invisible, but its description can be recognized in the prophet and his miracles.

THE MIRACLES OF PROPHETS AND SAINTS

All miracles, whether performed by prophets or saints, bestow spiritual life and knowledge on those who possess the capacity for conversion. Such capacity or receptivity, however, is not a personal acquisition, but comes through divine grace.

There is a distinction between the miracles of prophets and

the secret miracles and grace (*karamat*) of saints. A miracle that produces an effect on an inanimate object is like the rod of Moses. It involves a breach of the natural order. If it immediately affects the soul of the beholder, it is because through a hidden link, his soul is brought into connection with the producer of the miracle. The effects produced on the inanimate object are only accessory. They are for the sake of the invisible spirit so that by their means, the heart may be psychologically affected.

The miracles and grace that proceed from the spirit of the saints and Sufi spiritual guides work secretly and directly upon the heart of the disciple. They are spiritually resuscitating. They are a gift of divine grace. As faith and gnosis are the product of immediate or direct spiritual experience, their production by any external or evidentiary, secondary means cannot but be inferior in degree or less wonderful. How exquisite is the table spread unstintingly with food sent down from heaven in answer to the prayer of Jesus [5:112-15]?

Saints are divine physicians, reflecting the attributes of God. The disciple who has devoted himself to a saint is fortunate in losing himself in the saint. He has lost his attributes in the attributes of God and become His companion. If the uninitiated one who remains unaffected by the miracle desires to sit with God, he should seek the company of saints, sit with them like a faithful disciple so that by seeing and imitating them, he may become a pure searcher.

Except for the prophetic mission of the Messenger, which makes him superior to the saint, there is hardly any difference between the two. Saintship is the interior aspect of prophecy, so that every prophet is a saint, although no saint is a prophet. Esoterically, however, a prophet may be endowed with less perfect knowledge than a saint lest more knowledge should interfere with the performance of his prophetic mission. Thus, the mystic sage and guide Khidr was superior to the prophet Moses in this respect. But every saint is not Khidr. Some Sufis believe that the saints and their miracles are the means by which the proof of the Prophet continues to manifest itself, their miracles being derived from him. The saints are the spiritual heirs to the Prophet.

In early Sufism, little attention was paid to miracles. The most eminent Sufis, Bastami and Junayd, for example, gave them no importance. The latter even considered them as obstructive veils in the spiritual path. The general public, however, demanded miracles as proofs of saintship. This demand had to be met if they were no be alienated from his fold. Also, the possibility that credence in the unnatural through miracles might lead one to overcome his incredulity in spiritual matters which transcend our limited perception and set him on the path of righteousness or religion may be said to lend some justification to miracles. According to Rumi they may even render then necessary.[1] Even today, despite our much-vaunted achievements in the scientific and other fields of exoteric learning, one finds some spiritual teachers who perform plain magical feats which are passed off and accepted as miracles—although some magicians may publicly repeat them with greater perfection. Life is doubtless based in some or great measure on illusion and self-deception.

Effects give information about their producer as they are manifest to the sense. The potency of a drug is hidden, but it is made manifest to us by its action and effects. Mystics intuitively recognize the saint when they see one, but others do not, as they go by appearances. The saints wear no special regalia. To them, he is made known by his holy speech and works. Recognition of his reality or identity may open one's eyes—not all eyes—and make him first an imitator of his external ways and later, a sincere seeker of the true knowledge that abides in his inmost center. It is the safest guide in this life.

What is strange is that although the effects reveal to us what is hidden and we become friends with certain things because of the particular effects they produce (with certain people on the basis of some fantasy), we do not become friends with God. It is God who is the producer of all effects and is the King of Creation. Our heedlessness and folly are incredible.

THE SICK MAN

To return to our story, the physician felt the pulse of the sick man and saw that it was absurd to expect his recovery. He said to him, "Do whatever your heart desires, so that this malady may leave your body. Withhold nothing for which you crave. Self-restraint and abstinence are injurious to your disease. It is in relation to a spiritually incurable case like this that God has said, *"Do what you will"* [41:40]—disregarding the punishment that is eternally predestined for him.

Following his desire, the sick man went for a walk along the river bank, hoping that it might do him good. In the course of his stroll, he found a Sufi sitting there, washing his hands and face. Seeing the nape of his neck, he felt like giving it a slap. Recalling the physician's words that self-restraint would aggravate his sickness, and also God's saying, *"Do not cast yourselves with your own hands into destruction,"* [2:191] and this abstinence was his destruction, he gave him a stinging blow on the neck. The Sufi cried, "O you scoundrel," and was about to give him a couple of hard blows, but restrained himself.

THE SICK WORLDLING

Human beings are like tubercular patients. They are incurable. They are given to slapping each other, injuring the innocent, backbiting, and other evils, fancying that indulgence of desire was their right cure and would bring them peace and happiness. But they are deluding themselves. They are vowed to self. They do not know that retribution, not bliss or glory, will follow their action. The one who prescribes this tempting cure is the same devil that led Adam to the forbidden tree saying that if he and Eve ate of its fruit, they would abide in paradise forever [7:19]. The devil caused Adam to swallow the bait thus giving him a slap on the neck. The slap returned and became a retribution for the devil, hurling him down to bottomless perdition. Not delight or eminence but chains and penal fire became his portion.

But Adam was saved. Even if he were filled with serpents of

sin, they could not have harmed him. He was a mine of the antidote to snake poison—the antidote of knowledge, love and faith. He admitted to God unasked that he had done wrong. God was his prop and helper and he was forgiven.

But we do not have an atom of that antidote, nor the divine grace like that bestowed on Moses so that we should find a dry passage through the sea [2:50]. If a blessed one fell from a minaret or a mountain top, he is saved. But we have done nothing to merit blessedness. We love our sins and have no mind to see and break the fleshly snare that binds us. Why are we then deluded by our hope of redemption, if we do wrong? Thousands like Ad [7:65] have fallen from affluence and high estate. If we are lacking in the art of rope-dancing and so cannot like Hallaj rope-dance to the death of self, we should be grateful for our feet and walk on the ground, striving steadfastly towards self-purification, knowing that we are all subject to the inexorable law of retribution.

Although the Sufi who had suffered a sharp slap on his nape was aflame with anger and dying to retaliate, he knew that this life was only a preparation for the life hereafter and foreseeing what the penal consequences of such retaliation would be, resisted the temptation. Such initial resistance can only be sustained with a clear vision of the consequences of yielding to it. Foresight comes only from the end-discerning eyes. It saves us from bodily actions that lead to perdition. The supreme case is that of Muhammad, who, from the vision of the end he had seen, saw even in this earthly life, hell in detail, the gardens of paradise, and the throne and footstool of God and woke mankind from its clumberous heedlessness of Him.

The wise, desiring security from harm, ignore the beginning and contemplate the end so that they may come to regard all non-entities, that is, all unseen eternal things, as really existent and all entities perceptible by the senses in this world of mutability and illusion as unreal. Do we not see that every human being of reason is questing night and day for the non-existent, for what is potential, not actual? In begging, he seeks a generosity that is currently non-existent. In the cornfields one seek a harvest, in the shops profit, in the colleges a knowledge, and in the monasteries, a morality, none of which—the harvest, the profit, the knowledge or the morality—is yet in existence.

Similarly, every craftsman in the workday world seeks relative non-existence for the exercise of his craft. The builder seeks a virgin site or a place in disrepair or in ruins. The water-carrier seeks a waterless pot. The carpenter seeks a doorless house. Deficiency exhibits the quality of their skill.

When seeking their objects, these good people turn their backs on what actually exists. They look towards the non-existent or invisible world of ends and final causes in quest of something non-existent. God's Workshop is Non-existence and the mine and treasury of His doing is non-existence in the process of being brought into manifestation. The real object of all seekers is God, whose treasure-house of non-existence contains the all by whose invisible action alone is their quest brought into existence and carried to its fixed end. And yet, unless one is a gnostic, he remains ignorant of God. He turns away from non-existence, from self-negation, that unites him with the essential source of all he craves for and that has fulfilled myriads of his desires. Why give the name of death to what is our spiritual provision when it is only the death of self-hood merely because it is non-existent, or sensually imperceptive? Behold the divine sorcery that exhibits provision as death to us. The magic of His working has sealed both our eyes so that the inclination for the pit, this shadowy world, has overpowered our soul, and made the immeasurable expanse above this pit teem in its fancy with venom and snakes. As a result of the soul's false idea of death, voluntary or compulsory, as something dreadful and hateful, it has made this narrow pit, this vale of tears, a refuge for itself.

When we follow any worldly ambition, we set our thoughts and hopes on an object that is only a potentiality, away from all we own. Why not set them on God who can give actuality to all the spiritual potentialities with which He has endowed us?

THE SUFI ABSTAINS FROM REVENGE

To return to the story, the Sufi thought that he should not take revenge for a single slap on his nape and expose himself to legal punishment. His resignation to the divine will had made it easier for him to suffer such blows. He also observed that his opponent was so terribly frail that one hard blow would kill him. Death was only seeking an excuse to carry off his fragile opponent. It would be a great pity if because of this virtually dead man, he himself should suffer retribution under the sword. As he dared not give him a blow, he decided to take him to the judge, who is a phenomenal manifestation of divine justice.

THE JUDGE

As God's scales and measures, the judge delivers one from the tricks and contrivance of the devil, settles disputes between the litigants and ends dissensions by his ruling. The fear of legal punishment makes the greedy adversary give up rebelliousness and become submissive. Punishment is not only retributive, but also preventive and reformative. Also, if there were no scales, would anyone with greed in his veins ever be satisfied even if he were given more than his due. The judge is God's mercy. He is a drop from the ocean of justice of the resurrection. Though the drop be insignificant, it shows up the purity of the water and that ocean. If one's eye is dust-free, he can see the Tigris in one drop of water. The parts give information about the state of their wholes. The after-glow of sunset [84:16] to the body of Muhammad in whom the sun of reality, the divine Essence, was immanent, making him an informer about the spiritual sun. He was the light of God. The human being would not dread the loss of his bodily existence, if from that single existence he had known of the existence of God, who is the formless Essence of all phenomenal forms. As a mystic said, "I never saw anything without seeing God therein."

One who commits unjust deeds may be glad at heart, but he

is heedless of the penalty he will have to pay for his misdeeds. Why forget that judge of judges? If he has been unjust to a lover of God, he should hasten to make full amends for it is here and now lest God's wrath should suddenly descend upon him and exact retribution too terrible to contemplate.

THE SUFI AND THE JUDGE

The Sufi was mad for redress of the wrong inflicted upon him. He went to the frail man who had slapped him, and laying hold of his skirt like a plaintiff, dragged him along and took him to the judge. He said to him, "Sire, mount this miscreant on an ass and parade him through the streets or punish him with lashings of the whip, as your justice may deem fit. For even if one dies under your punishment and flagellation, no responsibility will lie on you."

In such a case, the judge is exempt from responsibility, as he is God's trustee, the shadow of His justice, the mirror that reflects the real nature of the plaintiff and the defendant. He administers corrective justice, not for his own profit or honor or out of anger, but for the sake of the wronged party, for the sake of God and the day of judgment, and so, if he makes a mistake, the blood-price which, under the divine Law falls on the family of the killer on the father's side, will fall on God, not on His trustee.

Similarly, when a teacher chastises a child and the child dies as a result of the chastisement, no responsibility lies on the teacher, as he also is God's trustee. In punishing him, he was seeking the pupil's benefit, not any benefit for himself.

But if the father punishes his son and the son dies as a result, the father is guilty and liable to punishment, as the son is supposed to serve his father, so that his personal interest was involved when he punished his son. But the father enjoys immunity when he punishes the child for the sake of God, inflicting the penalty which the divine law prescribes in certain cases.

Laws may differ in different countries and also from time to time, as they are based on right as apprehended by common conviction. This concept may differ or change. Also, law is conservative. It is happiest in a static environment. Habits, customs and practices die hard.

The case of one who has negated himself is different from the ones just discussed in our legal digression which was only incidental to the purpose of our story. A selfless Sufi is a case of *"You did not throw when you threw,"* [8:17]—words which refer to the handful of gravel thrown by Muhammad in the battle of Badr which routed the enemy. The throwing was God's and Muhammad was the instrument through which He threw. In such cases, no responsibility falls on the Sufi or any self-negated lover of God. All claims against him are paid from the divine treasury.

To return from the digression into questions of law, which was only incidental to the purpose of the story, the judge said to the Sufi, "First prove the case before I give judgment. Where is the assailant? This man you have brought has been reduced to a phantom by his illness. Who would put a corpse in prison? The law is for the living, not for the occupants of the graveyard."

Those who are dead to self, who are mystically poor because they are dead to all phenomena, are a different class. They are a hundred times more negated than the physically dead. The dead man is negated only in the sense that his bodily life has ceased. Physical death is a single killing. The selfless Sufi, on the other hand, is dead in a hundred ways. Spiritual death is myriads of killings, with myriads of spiritual states, one following the other in succession. Although God kills His lovers repeatedly, each killing brings an incalculable blood-price. He lavishes vast stores of grace on them and brings them to life each time. The lover inwardly delights in being killed by the divine judge and rapturously cries for another deadly blow. Love for the existence which fosters the spirit is such that once killed, the killed one longs even more passionately to be killed again until all otherness is killed and the soul is in nearness to God.

The judge regarded the assailant as virtually dead, beyond his jurisdiction. He said, "I am the judge for the living, not for the dead. You have seen many a dead man in the grave. Now see the grave in a dead man, in one who is devoid of understanding, whose spiritual faculties are dead and entombed in the body. If bricks from the grave have fallen upon one, would he seek redress from the grave? You should not be angry with a dead man, nor hate him, but should thank your stars that a living one, a saint, did not strike you, for one rejected of a saint is rejected of God. The anger of the living ones is the anger and blows of God because those pure ones are living through Him. It is He Who has stripped them of all carnal attributes and taken them to Himself. His breath lends perpetuity to their spiritual life. It would not be right to mount your near-dead assailant on an ass and parade him. Who lays a mere picture of firewood upon an ass? His proper seat is not the back of an ass, but the back of a bier. In justice is nothing but to place a thing in an improper place. Anger and forbearance, sound counsel or wile, nothing that God created is vain. Nothing is absolutely good nor absolutely evil. Whether a thing is good or evil, useful or harmful, is relative to time and place. Hence discriminative knowledge is necessary which can only be attained through the practice of self-effacement."

The Sufi asked the judge if he thought it right for that rascal to strike and go scot free without suffering revenge or paying a price.

The judge gave no direct reply, but asked the Sufi how much money he had. He said, "Only six dirhams (coins) in the world." The judge said, "Spend three dirhams on yourself and give three to the defendant without further argument." The judge thought that the defendant was weak, ill and poor and would need three dirhams for vegetables and a loaf of bread.

The defendant's eye fell on the judge's nape. He found it more inviting than the Sufi's. Saying to himself that there had been no penalty, but gain in his slap on the Sufi's neck, he approached the judge's ear as though to whisper a secret. He gave him a stinging slap with his palm, saying, "O my two enemies, take all the six dirhams and I shall then be free from all care and trouble."

The judge was naturally incensed. The Sufi taunted him,

saying, "Your judgment was doubtless just. How can you, O shaykh, approve for me what you disapprove for yourself? Have you not read in the Traditions that whoso digs a pit for his brother will fall therein? For he has only made a snare for himself, as his iniquity will inevitably return on his own head. Divine justice has ordained worse punishment for worse sins. Practice what you have read. This one single decision has brought a blow to your neck. Consider what your other decisions will bring. You pity a wrong-doer from kindness and offer him three dirhams for food. You should cut off the wrong-doer's hand. There is no occasion to let him go unpunished and be free to do what he likes. O you to whom justice is alien, you are like the goat that gave her milk to the wolf-cub."

The judge said, "It is our duty to acquiesce in every blow or cruelty that the divine destiny may bring. Although my face has become bitter, since truth is bitter, I am inwardly happy with the divine destiny inscribed on the preserved tablet. This heart of mine is an orchard and my eye is like a cloud. The cloud weeps and the orchard laughs joyously. Tears shed in supplication are a promise of spiritual efflorescence. In a year of drought, the orchards suffered agony by the excessive laughing of the sun. The heat of hell-fire to which the infidels will be exposed is infinitely more intense than our sun's heat. The end of weeping is laughter, as wherever tears flow, the divine mercy is shown. The nurse of all nurses gives no milk without one's crying for it like a child. Why then keep grinning, lest in the round of vain delights? You will be the light of the house like the candle if like it you shed showers of tears. You have tasted the pleasure of laughter, O great laugher. Now taste the pleasure of weeping, which is a mighty mine of sugar. As the thought of hell brings weeping, it is of greater value as an object of mediation than paradise. This world is all topsy turvy. Laughter is veiled in tears, pleasure in pain, treasure in ruins.

THE NEED FOR A GUIDE

"The track to reality is confusing. It is easily lost.

Appearance is not reality. It is contrary to it. The water of life is found in the land of darkness, that is, spiritual luminosity is found in the divine darkness of self-negation. There alone must it be sought. Our fleshly eyes are unavailing. They can only follow the appearance which is deceptive. We must take counsel with the righteous. This was the Lord's command to the Prophet also, "Consult them." This way the possibility of error is reduced. The spiritual guide is our unfailing support and refuge. In any case, light invariably increases when the intellects are paired.

The saints also are the way, the truth, and the life. They are the Seraphiels of the present time from whom life and freshness come to the spiritually dead. It is the voice of God that comes from their throats. On hearing it, the dead souls entombed in the body rise in the shroud, spiritually resuscitated.

"We should follow the guide exoterically first, even imitating his external ways if we like, and then esoterically, following his footsteps first and then the musk gland, which symbolizes his intuitive knowledge.

SPEECH AND SILENCE

When one is in the company of Sufis, one should sit silent. The presence of a Sufi is a book, not composed of ink and letters, but a pure heart whence arise the moonbeams of divine Light and which is the opening of the doors of Reality for the gnostic.[2] When one is seeking the marks of the way, one should not make himself a mark for attention, a bezel in the ring of that goodly company. A careful look at the Friday service will show that the devout are one in thought, concentration, and in silence. The Prophet said, "In this sea of cares, know that my companions are as stars, as parts of the moon, as parts of me. They are perfect guides. On them, on the stars must we concentrate, not on our empirical self."

We must keep silence, as speech confuses the sight. Once we begin to talk glibly, we lose control over words. For talk is generally intertwined and draws from one topic into others. It is like tangled branches of which if one is pulled, others are drawn after it. Right words may draw wrong words after them. Dark falsehoods may follow on the heels of pure truth. Hence, only he should open his mouth who is free from all external attachments, and like a prophet, is pure and preserved by God, and speaks not from self-will, but from divine inspiration, and is guarded from error. The judge exhorts the Sufi to make himself one who speaks from ecstatic feeling, speaks from the roots of the soul.

THE SUFI'S QUESTIONS

The judge's emphasis on acquiescence to divine destiny prompted the Sufi to ask a number of questions. He said:
As the entire creation has come from a single Hand,
    why has this one come sober and that one drunk?
As all these rivers come from a single sea,
    why is this one honey and that one poison?
As all lights come from the everlasting sun,
    why do the true dawn and the false dawn rise?
As the blackness of every seer's eye is from a single
    collyrium, why do true vision and squint-eyed appear?
As God is the chief of the mint,
How is it that the good coins and the bad coins are minted?
As God called the Way "*My way*" [6:153]
Why is this one a guardian and that one a robber?
How is it that both the nobleman and the mean ignoramus
    come from a single womb, when it is certain that the
    son's father is the Lord's creative energy?
Whoever has seen unity in such countless numbers,
    or such myriads of motions from the essence of rest?[3]

THE JUDGE'S REPLY

In reply, the judge illustrates how the Essence as the sole ground and cause of existence is related to the outward forms in which its effects appear. He says to the Sufi, "Be not bewildered by this mystery. It is like the restlessness of lovers which results from the peace and quiet of their heart-ravisher. He is rock-firm in his disdain, while they are tremulous like aspen leaves. His laughter moves them to tears and his glory withers their glory. In the Essence and action of the sea of reality, the womb of all that is, there is no howness or whatness, no contrary or like, no conditionality. And yet by that sea alone, that sea of reality or non-existence, are all the varied contraries and likes robed in existence. Their forms may differ, but in essence they are one. If they were essentially other than God, they would either be like Him or unlike Him, and absurdity in either case. No contrary bestows existence on its contrary. On the contrary, when their natures are opposite, one flees from the other. Nor does a like create its own like, identical in essence, attributes and actions. If it did, how should one like, how should God, have more right than the other like to claim the title of Creator?

The numberless opposites and likes are no more than froth or foam tossing on the surface of the unconditioned, fathomless sea—a sea whose every drop is beyond the reach of intellect and spirit, even of universal reason. Take the soul. It is the least of its toys and trifles. Yet who can determine its quality and description? It is said in the Koran, *"The spirit is by command of the Lord, and of knowledge you have been given but little"* [17:85], less than little. Both the intellect and the spirit are more unaware of His Essence than the body is of the intellect and the spirit. How should then the concepts of quantity and quality contain that measureless sea? Even universal reason is ignorant of it and says that this sea of reality, the divine Essence, is "the abode of bewilderment," where common standards are reversed. Here the brilliant sun curtsies to the quivering note, the lion to the deer, the falcon to the partridge. And what is of immediate relevance, the master of exoteric learning, with his prideful airs of intellectual superiority is way behind the God-loving dervish, whose ignorance he despises. The dervish who has the knowledge of Reality and contemplates the diversity of forms in which the divine action manifests itself is sunk in God. He is drunk with Him. He is in ecstatic bewilderment. Here, even the Prophet seeks a blessing from the poor and lowly as he discerned that in their hearts, devoid of all phenomena, devoid of self, God has deposited the treasure of His attributes—a treasure hidden and buried in mystic, wonderful ruins. It was not his purpose to instruct his followers by setting an example before them. They were left in complete ignorance as to why he sought their blessings. The divine mystery is not for the masses.

Evil thoughts about the saint arise as his puny exterior belies his inward immensity, because only his shadow is with us, not his infinite spirit which is winging in the highest heaven and is with God. We see only his shadow which is no different from other shadows. The mystic recognizes him when he sees him for he sees him with his spiritual eye. It is only by the eye of spirit that the spirit can be seen.

The truth is buried in the Truth in endless layers. Hence, in Islam alone, seventy-two sects have arisen. Far more could have arisen. Reality in its outward aspect is the human being, a contingent being, and the human being in his essence is one with the inward, necessary aspect of Reality. The absolute inwardness of Reality is God. This is the secret doctrine of the unity of Being. He alone can recognize this truth who is unshackled from his illusive self and steeped in the One Eternal. He alone can feel His presence in every single object. Where ever he turns, there is the Face, the Presence of God, the eternal splendor is everywhere, but veiled by this transient garment, the world. A perfect human being is not a seeker of the treasure, but the treasure himself, not a seeker of the divine consciousness, but the divine consciousness himself. He is a personification of the logos. He is the Truth that other men seek in various ways. In the substance of love, how can the lover be distinct from the Beloved?

THE JUDGE'S ADMONITION

The Sufi's questions were like those of a novice. The judge's reply also is of the same type as the questions. He says, "This world is but a trifle, a shadow hung on the void infinite, but for every blow that comes to you from heaven, always expect an infinite reward thereafter. He is not the king to give you a blow and then not honor you with kingly gifts. Cast off these worldly chains and take the blows that come from God. Because of the blows that the prophets suffered on the nape, they could lift their spiritual heads above the highest heaven. Stock your heart with faith. Fix your mind on God. Be ever ready in yourself for His reception so that He finds you at home when He comes to you. Otherwise, finding none in, not your real self, waiting for Him, He will take back His gift of love and grace."

Pursuing his string of questions, the Sufi asked, "What would happen if mercy were uninterrupted and perpetual? If the world did not produce anguish by its continual changes? If night did not darken the day? If winter did not blight the orchard, no fever broke our health, no fear threatened our safety? How should His munificence and mercy suffer if His bounty were free from torment?"

THE JUDGE'S NEXT REPLY

The judge said, "You are an idle wanderer, empty of intelligence. Have you not heard of one sugar-lipped story teller who at nightfall would tell amusing stories of light-fingered tailors who, by their laughable jests and amusing tales diverted the attention of customers and while cutting their cloth, stole strips of it, unnoticed. He then narrated the story of how a master tailor told amusing stories to a Turk who had bragged that no tailor could take a coil of thread in his presence, how the jests so intoxicated the Turk that, lost in the guffaws, his reason gone, the boast went out of his head. The tailor flinched so much satin that he himself had to stop the Turk from further violent laughs lest the material would fall short of what was required for the garment he was making for him.

This is a parable that applies to most of us. This deluding, perfidious world is like the tailor. The lusts and women are the world's narration of amusing tales. Life is like a length of satin placed before this tailor to be made into a garment of eternity and an attire of piety. But because of our idle addiction to these jestful tales, the tailor, this world takes away, piece by piece, the satin cut by the scissors of time, leaving but little to serve the life's purpose. We must not blame God for tempting us with a whole host of pleasures, for He has endowed us with the freewill to choose between two alternatives, between what is sensual and what is spiritual, between this worldliness and the other worldliness.

Continuing, the judge said to the Sufi, "O Sufi, pay no heed to the happenings of time which descend from heaven and bring the fear of hunger, a pain and varied kinds of griefs and cares, nor bother about hoarding the daily bread for fear that it might run short. The Lord's bounty is boundless. The treasure of His mercy infinite and suffers no retrenchment or reduction. Only abandon carnality and become His devoted servant. Strangely enough, despite this world's anguish and bitterness, one is its reckless lover. One should regard the worldly kingdom as a divine vengeance, one's trial and tribulation as a mercy because it makes one turn to God for forgiveness and relief. Abraham allowed himself to be thrown into the fire by Nimrod, but he did not get burnt. The fire was all coolness and peace for him by command of the Lord, who cherished him in the fire and turned fear into security of spirit" [21:69]. Ibrahim ibn Adham renounced his worldly kingdom and honor and did not suffer. On the contrary, he became the supreme sovereign of justice. He was burnt in the fire of divine love. In the quest for God, the reality of things belies their exterior.

The Sufi, raising further questions, said, "God whose help we beseech can make our trading free from loss. He who turns the fire of Nimrod into roses and trees, can also render this world-fire innocuous. He who can bring forth roses from amid thorns can also turn this winter into spring, grief into joy. He makes every non-existent existent. What would He lose if He made it everlasting? He gives a soul to the body so that the body may live. What loss would He suffer if He did not cause it to die? What would it matter if that bountiful giver granted His servant his soul's desire without any toil or trouble on his part and kept away from poor mortals the waylaying cunning of the carnal soul and the temptation of the accursed devil? God is omnipotent, omni-competent. Nothing is beyond Him."

Opposite is made manifest by means of its opposite, happiness by means of sorrow, light by means of darkness. If God is hidden, it is because He has no like or opposite, because all likes and unlikes are in Him, because the many are in the One. They become different or contradictory only when manifested by Him in fulfillment of His desire to be known.

Hence, the judge said in reply, "If there were no stern commandment from God, no pebbles and pearls, no flesh, devil and ugly passions, no blows, battle and war, by what name and title would the Lord call His servants? How should there be brave ones without cowards, wise ones without fools, patient, sincere, spenders of alms, who keep with their Lord, and for whom are *'gardens underneath which rivers flow'* [3:15], without a brigand and Devil? Knowledge and wisdom exist for the purpose of discerning between the different kinds of men and between the right and the wrong paths. But if the individuals were identical and all paths were the right path, knowledge and wisdom would be without meaning. This world would then not be the world of probation and that world the world of recompense. Would you that both the worlds were ruined for the sake of sensual nature, negating His purpose in creating this creation?"

The judge knew the Sufi and his purpose in asking these questions, and said, "I know that you are not raw, but pure and enlightened. Your questions were asked not for your own sake, but for the enlightenment of the masses. Time's cruelty and all afflictions that exist are far easier to bear than farness from God and heedlessness of Him. For these afflictions will change and pass, but not that heedlessness. He alone who bears his spirit to God, awake and heedful of Him, is possessed of the wine of everlasting bliss."[4]

15 THE DERVISH AND THE HIDDEN TREASURE

There was a dervish whose wife asked him, "O you who have done with generosity altogether, why have you no care of me? How long shall I live in this misery?"

He said, "O my love, although I am destitute, I am exerting my utmost to earn money. As is my duty, I am providing you with cash and garments and they are not inadequate."

She showed him the sleeve of her coarse and dirty chemise and said that it was so rough that it had bruised her flesh. Did anyone get such a garment for anyone?

He said, "O wife of mine, I will ask you one question. I am poor. This is all that I am able to provide for you. I admit this chemise is rough and coarse. But think well as to which is rougher and worse for you—this chemise or divorce and separation?" Fighting the flesh and fasting are doubtless hard and rough, but they are better than being far from the Beloved.

THE DERVISH'S PRAYER

The wretched dervish suffered infinite agony from indigence. But he was a lover of God, and would beseech him in prayer, crying, "O Lord, the shepherd of all creation, You created me without any exertion on my part. You gave me these five external senses and five other occult senses. Your gifts transcend reckoning and computation. As You alone, without partner or associate made me, do now give me daily bread without any fatigue or toil on my part."

For years this slave of love kept uttering this prayer which is outwardly passive, but inwardly active in aspiration and quest. At last, his piteous petition was accepted. As the Prophet has said, "God loves them that are importunate in prayer." In truth, the actual asking of a thing is better for the petitioner than the thing besought of Him.

And yet while praying, the delay in the arrival of the reward would make the dervish skeptical at times. Then again, the Lord would cause him to feel sure that his prayer would soon be answered. Hope and fear alternated in his heart.

DUALITY THE BASIS OF THE UNIVERSE

The divine maker both abases and exalts. Without these two attributes of loftiness and lowness, no work is accomplished. How should the sky revolve if the earth was not low and the sky lofty? The lowness and loftiness of this earth are of another kind—half the year it is barren, half the year green and fresh. Of time, they are of still another kind—one half day, one half night. Of our blended bodily temperament, of still another kind—now radiant health, not painful sickness. Similar are the world's changing conditions—famine and drought, peace and war. By means of contraries of different kinds is this manifested world balanced and upheld, with one opposite manifesting and balancing the other opposite. By means of them are all souls always the abodes of fear and hope, the two complementary pillars of faith, so that the world may be always trembling between the loftiness of resurrection and the lowness of death. Ultimately, the spiritual world of unity and Reality may destroy the vale of this world of plurality, this visioned world of pairs and opposites, of varied original natures as made by God.

This earth, as can be seen, has many-colored, many-minded mankind. It makes then uni-colored in their graves. The grave is the salt-mine for the material bodies, whether of peasants or of kings. The salt-mine for supersensible things is different; it is spiritual and real. While the earthly newness has oldness as its opposite, the newness of the spiritual world is without oldness, without opposite, like or number, and is ever-enduring—from eternity to everlasting. The bodies that go into this spiritual salt do not become dust like the material bodies in the salt-mine of the grave, but are pure in essence, are absolute spirit, without any external trace, exempt from coloration.[1]

THE MYSTIC AND UNICOLOR

A perfect Sufi gnostic is often described as a fish. In the Talmud, the Messiah is often called *dag* or the fish. The gnostic is a fish that hates the myriad-colored dry land of materiality and is happy in the sea of gnosis, which is also the sea of love. He is never sated with the uni-colored waters of spirituality. The baptism of God is the name of that subtle color. It is like the vat of God wherein all piebald things become of one color. One who falls into this vat exclaims, "I am the vat."[2]

When the heart of a mystic is purified and illumined by the the light of Muhammad, which is the light of God, the true light which lights every human being that comes into this world he realizes that all faiths, Christian, Magian, or polytheistic, all forms of worship, are one in essence, and their object is God. He sees nothing without seeing God in it for all things are full of God. The atheist may deny God, but does he not know that thought is framed by God?

THE UNICOLOR AT THE RESURRECTION

But the unicolor that is all-pervading at the resurrection is revealed to the saint and sinner alike. The truth that is veiled and shadowed in this world will appear unobscured. For there, ideas are invested with form. Our visible shapes will reflect our moral and spiritual qualities. Our secret thoughts and intentions will be exposed and materialized in the form of books with good and evil actions recorded in each case which will serve as case-material for judgment by the most just of judges.

But during the present time, when people are many-minded, with different inward beliefs, different religious sects—Islam alone has seventy-two sects and disputations tongues, how should the one-colored world become unveiled? It is the reign of the wolf. He is eating into the spiritual vitals of man. Joseph, the divinity in us, is lying at the bottom of the well. The soul, which belongs essentially to the world of unity, has been created to reflect God's attributes of good and evil. As evil reigns, how should good unveil its face?

THE DAY OF SLAUGHTER

But in this world, there are some spiritual lions, some true believers also, who are not slaves of the world or the flesh, and are awaiting the Lord's command, "Come." When it is announced, they will depart from this world. They will have nothing to fear on the day of slaughter at the resurrection, which will be a day of destruction for the evil-doers. For His elect, it will be a day of festival. Their passage will be safe and easy at the last judgment. Their victory will be complete. Paradise as wide as the heavens and the earth will be theirs.

The day of slaughter is ordained so that they who perish may perish by clear proof of the sovereignty of the Lord, and they who are saved and know for certain that salvation or damnation depends on the divine providence may be saved by a similar proof of His kingship. That day will reveal and justify the divine decree which makes some falcons, that is, lovers of God, fit for the sultan's wrist and others crows, or the lovers of the flesh that are left to wallow in sensuality and end up in the graveyard.

The day of judgment is justice so that the spiritual aspirant may attain the object of his quest in full measure and the sensualist may go to perdition, everyone getting what is due and proper.

This world is the Creator's penitentiary. Let him who has chosen to take punishment suffer punishment. The wings and feet of the bird lying around the snare, mutely expound the nature of His retribution for its greed for grain. As is the divine purpose, the lover of the flesh enjoys his allotted portion of the world's counterfeits of bliss for his little life of a day and dies. His place is taken by a sepulchral vault. When he has lain long enough in the grave, even the vault vanishes.

God has planted particular dispositions in individuals, making this one God-intoxicated and that one bread-intoxicated. He sends provisions suited to each disposition. The provision of the holy ones is the wine of love and gnosis, that of the sensualists the deluding delights of eye and ear. Since one is happy with his disposition, why should one flee from that which is in accord with his pre-disposition? Why should the sensualist flee from worldly joy and pretend to be religious, a hater of the flesh and a devotee of the Lord? Why not be true to oneself?

THE TREASURE SCROLL

The dervish had been badly bruised by the bludgeoning of poverty. One night, in a wakeful vision, so familiar to the Sufis, he heard a voice from heaven saying that he should search for a certain scroll of a certain shape and color among the loose leaves of handwriting which the stationers sell as models. When located, take it, unespied by the stationer, and from to a secluded place and read it alone. Even if the secret became known, he should not worry, for none except him would gain any benefit from it. If the task proved time-consuming and wearisome, his constant litany should be, *'Despair not of the mercy of God who forgives all sins'* [39:53]. Go and endure this toil."

When the dervish regained consciousness, he could not contain his joy. He would have burst with excess of it but for the Lord's protection and favor. The cause of this rapture was that after piercing through 600 light-veils out of the 700, or according to some 70,000 veils, that are said to separate the soul from God, his ear had heard the answer to his prayer for Him. Each veil's exterior is of darkness and its interior is of light. In its downward ascent, the soul sheds one veil of light and puts on one veil of darkness. In its ascent, it sheds one veil of darkness and puts on one veil of light. As the soul has to perform seven series of purgations, rending an equal number of veils each time 100 or 10,000 before it can attain to the one Reality, the dervish was naturally delighted with his spiritual ascension. He uplifted his head and scaled past the heavens thinking joyfully that his sense of sight, following this auditory experience, might also penetrate the veil of the unsee. When both his senses had passed through the veil, his vision of the Lord and his hearing of His speech would be continuous.

Following the message from the unseen, he came to the stationer's shop, walked in and started looking round for the scroll among his models. All of a sudden a scroll bearing all the marks specified in the message caught his eye. He slipped it under his arm, unnoticed by the stationer, and said, "Farewell Khwaja! I shall be back soon."

He went into a lonely corner, read the scroll and was bewildered. He wondered how such a priceless treasure scroll had dropped and been left neglected among such papers. Again, the thought came into his mind that the Lord was the guardian for all. How could His circumspection let anyone carry off anything? If the desert were filled with gold and cash, not a farthing could be taken away without His approval. Or if one read a hundred volumes, he would remember nothing without His decree. The external knowledge gained from books or other sources only strikes the body and is concerned with the husk of reality. If, on the other hand. One serves God and does not read a single book. He will learn a hundred rare sciences from within himself. The kernel of reality resides in the inmost center of the human being. Hence, the hand of Moses could bring forth from his own bosom the radiant divine light whose entry the ignorant seek from without. As the mystic knows, the hand of God created universal reason first, and all else, including the two worlds, afterwards. Universal reason is the active essence of the perfect human being. He reflects all His attributes. But this did not enter the consciousness of the dervish.

On the scroll ran the inscription whose allegorical meaning was, "Go forth from the city of human nature, turn your back on the dome of carnal reason and the shrine of the animal soul. Face the *qibla* of unity. Shoot the arrow of inspiration from the bow of self-mortification in order that you may attain to contemplation."[3]

Following the literal meaning of the inscription, the dervish fetched a strong bow. He shot an arrow into space, and, bringing a pickaxe and mattock, began to dig up the place where the arrow had fallen. Both he and the implements were worn out, but not a trace of the hidden treasure was found. Every day, he shot arrows and digged for the treasure, but achieved nothing.

As he made this his daily exercise, it became the subject of whispered rumor among the people. A group of informers who had lain in ambush had come to know the reason for this practice of archery and earth-digging. They went and told the king in private that the dervish had found a treasure scroll.

Hearing that the king had come to know of his possessing the scroll, he saw no satisfactory alternative to resignation and acquiescence. Before he should be tortured on the rack on its account by order of the king, he went and laid the scroll before him saying that since he found this scroll, he had found no treasure, not even a mite, but only endless trouble. For a whole month, he had been in dire distress, evidently because any loss or gain was forbidden to him. It was possible that his fortune would disclose to him the mighty victor, this fabulous hidden treasure.

For six months or more the king shot arrows. His efforts were re-inforced by every great archer that could be found. Pits were dug in all directions in quest of the treasure, but the result was nothing but futilities and vexation of spirit.

Failing to find the treasure despite his strenuous and extensive efforts, the king threw the scroll before the dervish in anger and disgust. He said that he should keep it as he was its fittest owner because he had no work. Even if he did not find the treasure, he was stout-hearted enough never to cease or tire of seeking it—the quest in itself being valuable to a person like him. The king also gave him the right of possession if perchance he found the treasure.

The king gave up the search because he was ruled by discursive reason. Reason is not reckless. It shuns the way of despair and seeks something profitable. It is the disinterested lover who fights temptation down, bears anguish without complaining and seeks no reward. He has killed in himself all seeking of self-interest. God gave him existence, as to all, as a free gift, without cause. In his devotion, he gives it up again to Him without cause. Such pure self-sacrifice transcends every formal religion. For religion seeks divine favor or salvation while His lover gambles himself clean away with no thought of gain or loss seeking nothing but Him. He lives for His sake, not for riches. He dies for His sake, not from fear and pain. His faith is held for the sake of doing His will, not for the sake of paradise. Love is the hell-fire of his attributes and burns them up completely.

On receiving the scroll back from the king, the dervish felt safe from his rivals. He went and made sad thoughted love his friend because the lover has no friend in this material world, none to help him in his anguish. None is more mad than the lover. His madness is no ordinary madness. Love is the overwhelming grace of the divine beloved and the lover's madness is the effect. The science of medicine is of no avail here. Earthly knowledge is not intrinsic or real, nor is earthly beauty. They are but shadows of the real Beloved, just a veil of Him. The votary of love turns his face towards his own face, towards He who is His essential self, for he has no relatives except himself. Reality abides in fullness within. Nothing of it is without.

The dervish made a *qibla* of his heart and began to pray, "*The human being has nothing except that for which he makes effort*" [53:39]. He kept praying intently for many years. Although no heavenly voice or messenger came to him, his hope was always mutely saying, "Here I am," which was the response from the divine grace and was brushing away all weariness from his heart. For whoever moans bitterly, without thanksgiving for any favors received or complaint against their non-receipt and is already intoxicated with Him and utters one cry of, "O, my Lord," a hundred cries of, "Here I am," come from the Lord[4] and that is His invitation.

One devoted to a perfect human being will cling to him as if to God, for his spirit has grown up in him from his influence. Even if the perfect human being were to drive him away, his spirit would still hover round him as he is giving it life and sustenance. If for a moment it secretly disbelieves in thanksgiving to him for this favor, love, the vengeful magistrate, will expose it to the burning fire of separation saying, "Return! Abandon earthliness! Love, the king, is calling you." The perfect human being is every sick man's Jesus, his spiritual resuscitator. When the spiritual seeker has completely negated himself, he is sunk in the Beloved, his individual soul sunk in the world soul, and he has attained to the Essence of all life and energy.

THE METAPHOR OF THE REED

The *Mathnawi*, Rumi says, is inspired by his beloved disciple Husam, the radiance of God. It is his wailful utterance. It is a part revelation of the Truth. Ineffable mysteries remain entombed in his consciousness. We can speak but in part.

God has given us two vocal mouths like the reed. One mouth is hidden in the lips of the perfect human being, of God Himself, and is pouring forth such spiritual mysteries as can be poured forth. The other mouth is turned outward and is letting shrill notes fall on the air.

The metaphor of the reed finds repetition in the *Mathnawi*. Its very first verse is an exhortation to the reader to listen to the tale of the reed-flute which is a tale of the human soul, bemoaning its severance from the spiritual world—like the reed's from the reed-bed—and its painful longing to return to God, our origin and home.

Elsewhere, addressing the perfect human being, his disciples say:

We are as the harp,
    and you are playing on it with the plectrum;
Lamentation is not from us, but is your making.
We are the flute, and the music in us if from you;
We are as the mountain, and in us the echo is from you.[5]

Everyone who, like the reed, is empty of matter, empty of self, whose spiritual eye and ear are open, knows that the lamentation of his soul, the song of this reed, is from the lip, from the breaths of the perfect human being with which this reed is in communion. One parted from the lip, parted from God, clogged with matter, like a reed similarly clogged, can produce no music.

The contemplative gaze of the perfect human being of the shaykh is not limited to existential things. His spirit existed in the divine mind before creation. He sees things as they exist potentially in God, sees entity in non-entity, which no common mortal can see. He beholds the ideal and eternal beauty of which all phenomenal beauty is but a reflection. He can communicate such of the spiritual mysteries as can be communicated in particular circumstances. He acts as an unerring guide to the aspirant. The worth of such a guide depends not on his chill gray years, but on the hidden grey of his wisdom. His spirit abides with God and is eternal. Only his body is subject to the ravages of time.

THE SEA OF UNITY

The human being should go to the sea of divine Essence, which has given existence to all opposites and likes, to all individualized forms of being. They are its waves or a spray of it, just a flake of foam on its surface—"the multi-headed foam." One should not regard lowness as nobility and go towards the water and clay, towards the heedlessness of God. For God created him in His own image. He is the son of Adam. His versatility was an object of envy to the angels. He is the very crown of creation.

That sea, which is essentially his home and destination, has no like or contrary, no partner or consort, no conditionality, and is indescribable. It is the sea of unity. Outward and inward silence is the reality of unity of being because speech outward or inward necessarily involves duality, the speaker and the subject. But the squint-eyed worldings see double, ascribes a partner to it, talks duality, and, by this very means, this false seeing and false speech, is he driven away by the sea.

As we live among the double-seeing multitude, we may either assimilate and take duality like it, or be completely silent. Or we may do both, speaking from heart to heart and divulging the mystery of the spirit when we see a confidant and remaining silent, when we see one full of deceit and falsehood, for he is an enemy to spiritual life and his ignorance will turn on us and seek our destruction. We should patiently bear the gibes and scorns of such an ignoramus and extend civil words to him. This may be dissimulation, but it has divine authority. For it is but proper that a Sufi, as an exile in this world, should pay due regard to the character and capacity of the people among whom he lives. Also, patience shown to the unworthy purifies the worthy. It purifies the heart wherever a heart exists. But it must be true patience. According to the well-esteemed Sufi and Imam of the Prophet's time, Hasan of Basra, patience exercised for self-protection from the fire of hell, as in times of affliction or in renunciation of what the Lord has forbidden, is not true patience. Patience is true patience only when exercised for His sake, with no thought of self. The patience of Abraham when Nimrod cast him into the fire was true patience. It purified and gave resplendence to his heart. Similarly, the patience of the prophet Noah with the unbelief of his people, particularly of his wife, Wahila, whose plotting would seek to frustrate his missionary work served to polish his spirit's mirror.

THE HIDDEN TREASURE

The dervish must not be deemed to be a seeker of the treasure of divine attributes. He is lost in the treasure. He is the treasure himself. All the time, he is bowing before himself, contemplating nothing but the divine Essence and attributes reflected in the heart's mirror, which constitute his real self. For the true seeker is steeped in the object of his quest and is one with it. If He became naked or he saw in the mirror a solitary mite without any fantasy, nothing of him would remain. Both he and his fantasies would disappear. His knowledge of his mortal self would sink in ignorance. From this ignorance another knowledge would arise, saying, *"Lo, I am God,"* like the call received by Moses from the burning bush [28:30].

After Adam's bodily creation, the divine call came to the terrestrial angels, "Bow down to Adam, for in essence you are Adam. For a moment see yourself as Adam—God removed the squint from their eyes. The earth and heaven—worldliness and spirituality—became one. The horizon line was gone. All otherness disappeared. Unity blossomed forth.

Adam was contained potentially in the earth as a hidden treasure. His pure light shed its beams on the angels. In their attachment to the earth, they did not recognize the intimation of the divine mystery and the knowledge of the Names that was revealed in Adam's earthly body. Obeying the divine call, they paid obeisance to Adam. Their adoration of him was symbolic of the essential unity of all particular modes of being with the Absolute.

But the mystery of that unity is not to be told to the worldlings. Even if told, they will not understand. They can understand only the outward description of the dervish and the treasure, but not their reality. Their appetites are perverse. They are clay-eaters. The God-inspired perfect human being's fountain of wisdom will continue to flow unto everlasting, but with them it is closed. God has sealed their hearing, hearts and eyes. They are disbelievers at heart, and whether or not they are warned, they will not really believe. They have preferred this finite life to infinity. They have shut their eyes to the yellow meads of *asfadil* and opened them to this dust-pit, this world. It is a bad exchange for them.

Nevertheless, all hope is not dead. God, in His mercy, helps even them that despair. His logic no mortal can understand. He plucks forth the rosy dawn from the blackness of night. When Abraham wanted flour to feed his family or entertain his guests, he or his servant filled a bag with sand. God caused it to turn into flour. When David abandoned his intimates for His sake, the Lord, by way of compensation, made the mountains his musical accompanists [34:10].

THE DERVISH TURNS TO GOD

The dervish searched long for the treasure, but all in vain. It was to no gold or diamond mines to which the treasure scroll gave clues. The scroll, in fact, signifies the Koran which contains secret clues to the hidden treasure of gnosis. He at last turned to God and said, "O knower of the mystery, I, bedevilled by greed and covetousness, have been running hither and thither for the treasure and have gained nothing. I never said to myself that as uncertainty beclouded my path, I would untie this know by the help of Him who ties all knots."

One should seek the inner meaning of God's word, the Koran, directly from God and not go by his subjective opinion and alter its original meaning as if it were defective. Divine symbols, although seemingly simple, are not easy to understand. The knot He tied He Himself will untie.

"I repent of this egoism and thoughtless haste. I must renounce my dream of riches and again take to the dervish cloak—which is a sign of self-abasement and self-abandonment. I have no talent, personality or heart of my own. All these are but the reflection of You, O Lord. You Yourself are all. The bliss of release from self-consciousness is like the bliss of night in sleep when my knowledge and faculties leave the body and return to the unseen. Neither I remain, nor any merit or mine. The body is like a carcase. All otherness vanishes."

Identifying himself with the dervish and speaking in his own person Rumi says, "All night through, God is Himself uttering *alastu* and *bala*, as the primal covenant, that is, both asserting and acknowledging His absolute omnipotence. For who else is there to acknowledge it? Sleep has swallowed the all.

"When I return to self-consciousness, it is like morning time. This is the time when the sun flushes the orient and we are dispersed afresh into this world of scent and color. We offer grateful thanks to the Lord, saying, 'O merciful Lord, You have stored in the belly of night the treasure of mercy and all these delightful experiences. By means of night, which is like a dreadful scaly leviathan, You have given us rest, sharpened the eye, refreshed the ear, and made the body agile. Henceforth, with someone like You beside us, we shall never run away from situations of dreadful mien'—like the night of self-unconsciousness of self-negation whence the spiritual Light breaks forth. Moses saw fire in the burning bush, but it was the revelation of the divine light [28:29]. Pray give us an eye that sees things as they really are, so that floating rubbish or foam does not veil the sea of reality from us."

What blinds us is only means and secondary causes. The Sufis have no care for them, and, without them, attain spiritual perfection and bliss, except that without the divine grace which takes no account of merit or demerit, no attainment is possible.

"Even the unworthy need not lose hope and heart," continued the dervish. "For through the hand of Your mercy, not only the worthy, but also the unworthy, are released from the chains of servitude. In our pre-existence, how were we worthy to attain our present spirituality and knowledge? Yet, without our asking, You gave us concrete existence at the demand of need, and gifts without calculation, and also the capacity for their reception. We were but like a picture that is helpless before the painter and the brush."

God made the body pure, although it is but dust, the quintessence of dust. It is His house, His Kabah, which contains the heart which is His passageway. "The kingdom of God is within you," said Jesus. This body is a talisman of clay, guarding a hidden treasure of light, the spiritual essence of the human being. But the carnal or animal soul has infected the external senses and the mental faculties. Hence the dervish prays to God, "Cause our dust to be cleansed and become pure once again. Make our nothing to be something. You commanded this invocation from us, otherwise, how could this dust, these non-existences dare invoke You. You are alone are the supreme existence, the One containing the all. We have followed Your command from the beginning. Cause our prayer to be favorably answered.

"The sleep of unconsciousness has wrecked my understanding and senses. God has borne me into the sea of mercy. I do not know with what attributes or skill He will fill me and return to this world. This one He fills with the light of majesty and that one with idle fancy.

"If any judgment or skill belonged to me, my consciousness, senses and faculties would be under my control. They would never leave me without my bidding. I would always be aware of the soul's stages of travel. But I am destitute except for a pain-stricken heart. When I am unaware or forgetful, I have utterly nothing, not even power to seek anything. When I am aware, my portion is torment. This is the stuff of our sleeping and waking existence. Lay not on this nothing, another nothing, these worldly goods, which breed a hundred troubles. I seek relief from the narrowness of self-consciousness. I am better off possessing nothing. In my state of privation, O Lord, act in kingly fashion towards me. I will stand naked at Your gate, blind with weeping. Bestow on my tears spiritual growth from Your boundless pasture. If my eyes lack tears, give them abundant tears from the fount of Your munificence. Even the Prophet, despite his great fortune and majesty, sought tears from Your grace. How should I, an empty-handed pauper, not keep weeping blood-stained tears. Even the garden of paradise sought rain. We must never cease weeping tears of blood." Whether He accepts or rejects our prayer is His business, not ours.

THE MYSTERY OF THE HIDDEN TREASURE

In the midst of his invocation, inspiration came to him from the unseen. His difficulties were solved. It said, "You were told to put an arrow to the bow. You were not told to shoot with all your might. Your vanity led you to raise the art of archery to excellence. Your knowledge of archery and your reliance on it were your barrier. Abandon your trust in skill and strength. Just put the arrow of thought to the bow. Where it falls, dig up and search. Seek the treasure by means of tearful supplication. That treasure is near you. You have shot the arrow far afield."

God says in the Koran, "*We are nearer to him than his jugglar vein.*" Hence, we should seek His light within, not without. The philosopher wearies himself out with intellectual speculation. The more he speculates the further is he distanced from the treasure. The Lord spoke of those who "*have striven in (for) Us,*" [29:69] not of those who "*have striven away from Us,*" like Canaan, son of Noah, who, disdaining his father's counsel to embark on the ship, betook himself to the top of a great mountain. The further he went towards the mountain, the remoter he got from the refuge [11:36-48]. In the spiritual sea, the ark of Noah is the refuge, not any lofty mountain of intellectual thought which philosophers presume to upraise as a challenge to God-inspired teachers of the truth. As the Prophet said, "I am the ship in the universal sea." One must not set up shop over his master.

Most of those who are destined for paradise are simpleminded. In the words of the Prophet, "Most of the people of paradise are the foolish." As cleverness which teaches feints and tricks and is the means of worldly success and excites self-conceit and pride, is the very contrary of self-abasement and supplication, they have ceased to be clever. They have stripped themselves of exoteric knowledge and vanity, so that divine mercy may descend on them. The clever ones are happy with a skillful artifice, but the simple ones who observe their duty to God and will die to the phenomenal world like those who have surrendered to Him [3:102] and have abandoned all artifice and risen to contemplation of the Master artificer.[6]

16 THE MOUSE AND THE FROG

A mouse and a faithful frog happened to become friends on a river bank. Pledged to keep a daily rendezvous, they would meet in a nook every morning and play heartily with each other, tell stories, and exchange secrets, hiding nothing, interpreting in practice the Tradition, "A united party is a mercy."

Flow of conversation from the heart is a sign of friendship, while its obstruction a result of lack of intimacy. How should a loving nightingale that has seen the beloved rose remain mute? The effects of companionship with holy men are simply wonderful. When the friend is seated beside the friend, the disciple before the spiritual guide, myriads of mysterious are made known. For the brow of the spiritual guide is a guarded tablet (*lawh-i-mahfuz*), the archetype of the Koran on which is inscribed all the knowledge of the past, present and future. It plainly reveals to the disciple the secrets of both worlds.

While one is roaming about in quest of knowledge, his heart is a guarding tablet that guards and preserves the lessons of wisdom he learns from reason and intellect during the search, but when his intelligence is the gift of God, the gift of divine inspiration, or of the spirit of a prophet or saint or the spiritual guide, its fountain is in the midst of his soul, continually gushing, knowing no oldness, fetidness or impurity, and the guarding tablet becomes a guarded tablet. The other intelligence, his erstwhile teacher, which the spirit has not enriched, becomes his pupil. He was seeking wisdom, and now he has become the fountain of wisdom.[1] The inflow of what is from without can be stopped by blocking its passage, but not of what is continually gushing from the heart.

The spiritual guide is the guide par excellence on the path. The Prophet said, "My companions are the stars," the spiritual stars that show the way on sea and land. We should set our gaze on the face of a spiritual star and listen in silence to the voice of truth that comes from its divinely inspired self. Unless we be silent, how can he speak? The seeing eye is always better than a faltering tongue. Disputation or discussion will only stir up dust that will hide the reality of the star.

The saints and prophets and other holy men are exempt from error. When Adam became the theater of divine inspiration and love, his rational soul unfolded to him the knowledge of "Names." His tongue recited from the heart's page the name of everything as it really is in end and revealed to him through his esoteric vision the attributes and essences of all things from eternity to everlasting. Even the angels were bewildered by the amplitude of his knowledge. It was all truth.

Again, for nine hundred years, Noah treaded the way of Truth. Every day, he found a new sermon to preach. His lips drew their speech from the white pearl, the equivalent of the logos, that is in the hearts of the prophets, and not from the study of spiritual literature or learned commentaries. He learned the sermons from the fountain of revelations and from the exposition set forth by the spirit. It was from a wine so potent that when drunk, speech would outrush from the dumbest mouth and a new-born would become an eloquent divine and utter wisdom like the Messiah [19:27]. That wine even made the mountain sweet-lipped. From that mountain David learnt a hundred psalms. All the birds ceased their musical jug-jug and became his accompanists in song. The Lord's grace even made the iron supple and obedient in his hand [34:11].

An external teacher may not be obeyed if the disciple is not earnest. But the Lord's command is supreme and is heard, understood and obeyed even by the elements. Thus, as He willed, a fierce roaring wind became the destroyer of the tribe of Ad, who disbelieved in the judgement to come [69:4,6]. It served as a carrier to Solomon transporting his royal throne a whole month's journey every morning and every evening [34:12]. It also acted as his spy, catching and immediately wafting to his ear the talk of the absent, saying who said what at this moment.

THE MOUSE AS LOVER

The mouse loved the frog in his own way. The morning meetings were not enough for him. One day he said to the frog, "There are times when I long to talk with you, but you are busy frolicking in the water, unable to hear the wailing of lovers like me. There should be some means of communication between us whereby when I come to the river bank, my arrival will be made known to you, and, similarly, when you came to the mouse-hole, I would know that you had come."

The prescribed prayer is performed five times a day, but the lover's guide is the verse which says, *"They are constant at their worship"* [70:23]. That is, they are continually in prayer and always with the Beloved.

The plea of the mouse was plausible. For continual union with the beloved is the life and soul of lovers. "Visit once a week is not their ration." How should one separate himself from himself or visit himself only at intervals? The Lord's infinite grace is to lovers what water is to the fish. Fishes are at war with the many-colored forms on the dry land. Clear water alone is their life. Similarly, the gnostics, who are lovers of God, live by continual remembrance of Him. They have no love for this diffused shadow of the infinite, this dry variegated world of form and color. Without the divine sea, with its unicolor and purity, there is no delight for them, these spiritual fishes. Even its boundless waters are not enough for them. Their thirst is insatiable, as their object is infinite. There are always other heavens beyond the heavens they are contemplating. There is no limit.

A single moment of separation from the beloved is as a year to the lover. A whole year's unbroken union but a flying fancy. The beloved also craves to drink and seeks the lover who has a similar craving. When the thirsty soul moans for the water, the water also moans for the water-drinker. In fact, the initiative comes from the beloved. The thirst in our souls is nothing but the attraction exercised by the water. But for that attraction, no thirst would arise. There is mutuality between them, one following the other, as day follows night. Day is in love with night and has lost self-control. Night is even more in love with day. They are in mutual embrace for the sake of perfecting each other's task. Without the rest and energy provided by night, how should man feel refreshed and be able to work and earn during day?[2]

Esoterically also, the lover of God seeks the divine night of self-negation as it alone is the prelude to the dawning splendor of the vision beatific. Night loves self-extinction in the sea of light.

In the beloved's heart there is naught but the lover. In the heart of Adhra, it is always Wamiq.[3] Although God disapproves of all otherness, He approves of the union of human souls, which also excludes all otherness and has the element of unity and divinity in it. If the lover's heart has nothing but the beloved in it, there is nothing that can tear them apart. The two have become one. But it is not the kind of oneness which the discursive reason apprehends. It is the kind whose apprehension depends on one's dying to self. If one's reason could apprehend it, such self-negation or self-mortification would not have become a spiritual duty. Unless it was necessary, the king of intellect with such infinite clemency, would not have said, "Die to self" or "Die before ye die." Let us remember that lover and Beloved are two aspects of one Essence. They are a single reality, the reality or essence of love.

Continuing his humble entreaty as a devoted disciple, the mouse said to the frog, "You are my light and strength by day and rest and sleep by night. I am utterly restless without you yet you are indifferent to my longing love. During a whole day and night, you allow me access to you only at breakfast time. Admittedly, an ill-mannered wretch that I am, I am unworthy of your favor. But my reliance is on your universal grace, which, like the Lord's grace, does not seek merit to justify it. It is like the sun which shines on all alike making no distinction between saint and sinner, whose light loses nothing in the process. The sun warms the earth's belly, so that the earth consumes and assimilates all filth. God transforms the filth into herbage, narcissus and eglantine. In like fashion, God erases all evil actions. He bestows the robe of honor on the wicked. How great, how far beyond our perception, then, must be the recompense and bounty in the unseen world which the ever-observant, all-seeing Lord will lavish on the righteous for works performed with faith and devotion.

The Mouse as a Sinner

The mouse, now speaking as a sinner, says to the frog-spiritual guide who is God's deputy on earth, "Who are we to aspire so high and receive from God what the righteous receive? Come, O dear friend, and brighten my day with your goodly disposition. Look not at my ugliness or hatefulness. As God has planted me a thorn, how should I become a rose? Give to this thorn the spring-tide of the rose's beauty. I have reached perfection in evil and your grace in excellence. Grant me the boon I seek. When I die, your bounty, though exempt from need, will ignore my degradation, lament my death and weep for me out of kindness. It will sit long beside my grave with tears streaming from its kindly eye. Pray bestow on this grief-stricken self a little of the favors that you will later show to my dust."

The disciple, through such supplication to the spiritual guide reposes all his hopes on the boundless grace and bounty of the Lord.

The Sufi as The Son of the Moment

The mouse begs the frog not to defer the fulfillment of his

request, for there are dangers in delay. The Sufi—a role the mouse now assumes—is "the son of the moment," a technical term denoting the predominating spiritual state and rank of the Sufi at the moment. It also means the preservation of one's spiritual state.[4] Not yet the pure one, but imperfect, he waits for that "moment", that is , waits for the spiritual state, for spiritual ecstasy. When that moment comes, he clings to it as if it were his father which it is in the sense that it does not allow him to be driven to the necessity of looking to the future, but keeps him absorbed in contemplation of gardens and rivers of a mighty potentate, firmly established in His favor [54:54, 55].

The Sufi really does not belong to this dream-world where nothing is substantially real, but to the spiritual world, to the realm of God, with whom "is neither morn, nor eve," neither past, nor future, neither beginningless nor endless time—no divisibility of any kind. In that indivisible continuity, there are no temporal or spatial or any such unreal relations. All things co-exist in an eternal now.

When it is said that the Sufi is "the son of the moment," it is to be understood only as a denial of the divisibility of time. Divisibility implies duality and there is no duality in the spiritual world. It is like the statement, "God is one," which also is meant as a denial of duality, not as an expression of the real nature of unity. God is independent of number and is as remote for 1 as from 2.

The mouse said, "I am barred entrance into the water as I am of the earth. But you are the king or mercy and munificence. Grant me the favor I so passionate seek, so that I may enjoy the privilege of serving you at all times, instead of calling you on the river bank as at present and receiving no mercy of response."

After a long debate, it was settled that they should get hold of a long string of which one end should be tied to the foot of the mouse and the other to the foot of the frog so that whenever they liked, just by pulling the string, they could come together and mingle as the soul mingles with the body.

The mouse's idea was that by this device, he might be able to drag the frog to the dry land which would be the victory of the flesh over the spirit. The heart of the frog, as was natural, found the scheme distasteful. He thought that this devil, the wicked mouse, would land him in a trap.

THE FLESH AND THE SPIRIT

The tussel between the flesh and the spirit begins, and the inner meaning of the fable now begins to unfold. The body here is like a string that is tied to the foot of the spirit and brings it down from heaven to earth. The mouse is symbolic of the bodily nature to which the frog which is symbolic of the spirit is bound by the string of carnal reason. The frog-spirit or soul is happy when it escapes from the bodily nature into the water, which represents the sleep of unconsciousness, when each body is freed from the burden of actions and works, the burden of toil and trouble. But the body pulls it back from that happy slumber. The pulling is bitter to the soul.

MYSTICAL CLAIRVOYANCE

When a repugnant feeling gains entry into the heart of a good person it is not without significance. That feeling is not a vain fantasy. It flows from intuitive sagacity which is a divine attribute. It is something apprehended by the light of the heart from the universal or guarded tablet, which is an inviolable source of divine knowledge. It is something intuitively perceived.

Thus, Jacob had a foreboding of evil like the frog when the brethren of his son Joseph sought his permission to take Joseph out for frolic and play. Jacob's heart was divinely illumined and hence exempt from error. He could see with the eye of certainty. The foreboding that came to him—and he was a prophet—was decisive proof of their evil design, of the grief and anguish that lay ahead. But the divine destiny came, and, with its coming, the widest expanse is straitened. It muffles the eye of wisdom. Jacob was unable to understand what the foreboding meant. When told that the wolf had eaten Joseph, he suffered great agony and loss of vision through ceaseless weeping. Even Adam whom God "taught the "Names" failed to understand the plain meaning of "prohibition" and ate the forbidden fruit and suffered expulsion from paradise.

The heart knows and yet does not know the shifts and devices of destiny. God does what He pleases. That is the eye-binding spell of destiny, whose artfulness none can defeat. The heart may say to itself that as destiny's inclination is to cause this to happen, let it happen and it makes itself heedless of the happening. It bows to the inevitable. But the case of a prophet or saint is different. If he is check-mated by destiny, it is not check-mate, but tribulation that strengthens his soul and delivers him from a hundred tribulations. He is spiritually exalted by his total acquiescence in the divine fore-ordainment. A single fall uplifts him high on the spiritual spiral. Tribulation is truly the mark of holiness. It is purifying. Even a half-baked arrogant mortal whom the everlasting wine of love has relieved from his own kind of company is ultimately purified and becomes mature and spiritually discerning. The joy of sense, the delights of eye and ear attract him no more. He is freed from the feeble conventional faith of the worldlings and from the illusions of their unseeing eyes.

LIFE, A SUCCESSION OF THOUGHTS

Nothing is except God. All that exists in heaven and earth, including our empires and sovereignties, come from the trackless desert of not-being, from the world of the divine command, the world of the creative, "*Be.*" What is our conscious life but an unbroken succession of thoughts, fancies and experiences caravaning from non-existence into this material world? They are the phenomenal manifestation of an Essence that alone is unchanging and eternal, an objectivization of the divine mind. God creates them, determines their character, and causes their coming and going.

We are not stationery, but ever marching, some in one direction, some in another. Though unmoving in appearance, we should know that we are bound for a new abode, a new future for which, if we are wise, provision must be made in the present. Hence, a spiritual traveler has his eye and march set towards the future, even as our thoughts and fantasies are appearing and disappearing. Like all else, they appear from the same plantation. Otherwise, how should they be arriving all the time, without a break between any two successive ideas. They should be deemed as stars revolving in another heavenly orb. Coming from non-existence, they are like an arrow shot forth into the air, which cannot hang in the air. Their term is limited and they disappear. If one is lucky, and spiritual thoughts come to him, he should thank his stars. He should offer grateful thanks to God and perform charitable works which are the best expression of one's gratitude to Him. Ingratitude in a person is hateworthy. Although all bounty comes from God, He pulls us up if we do not thank the hand through which His bounty has come to us. If, however, sensual thoughts come, it is best to give alms, which is self-giving, and beg His forgiveness. Charity is a noble virtue, and with its basis in love, the noblest.

God who guides many and misguides many [2:24] has ordained that carnality and spirituality should pull us in contrary directions in order to test our spiritual calibre in this probationary existence. Also, duality is the very basis of manifestation. Hence not only good but also bad, not only carnal but also spiritual thoughts troop into our heart as if it were a guesthouse for passing travelers. They are like new guests, and should be deferentially treated, never with disdain, regardless their nature, for their coming is not without purpose. Thus, when the spiritual sense develops and becomes dominate, the carnal sense understandably pack off. Its term is up. Even the coming of a sorrowful thought is not without meaning. It uproots the old joy which has grown from evil, and reveals a new root that brings up a new joy which has grown from evil, and reveals a new root that brings up a new joy that grows from good. Whatever things sorrow takes away, it brings something better in exchange especially for those who possess intuitive vision, possess mystical clairvoyance and know that sorrow is the servant of those whose spiritual eye is open and who possess intuitive certainty.

One should seek to be like Job, a prophet who showed infinite patience during the seven years of tribulation that visited him as a guest from God so that the tribulation may thank him in His presence in a hundred ways. Good and evil are a part of life and they appear and disappear like the stars in their orbital courses.[5]

The thoughts, although passing, are relevant to any spiritual aspirant, for they hold the key to the secrets of the self. Everyone of them is a divine message, indicating His wrath or mercy. Not only mystics, but also lesser aspiring mortals, should meditate on its nature, investigate it in depth, as Solomon investigated every new plant that grew in the Farther Mosque (*masjid-i-aqsa*). As the study of the plants give us information about the hidden nature of the soil, meditation on the thoughts that troop into the heart will give us information about the secrets of the farther mosque of the heart.[6] As each thought is an objectification of its archetype in the spiritual world, through such meditation, real knowledge begins to grow in the heart. But mere meditation is not enough. The introoping thoughts must be evaluated and separated into good and bad thoughts—appropriate action taken on the good thoughts and bad thoughts thrown out of the kingdom of the body. But discernment between good and evil is not easy. A simple test—perhaps, not so simple in practice—is that if a thought is in harmony witall of duty in harmony with the voice of the conscience, which is the voice of God on the human level, untainted by any selfish consideration, it is a good thought. If, however, a thought is desire-toned, is related to the flesh and the devil, inspired by the glitter of gold or the pomp of power, it is a bad thought deserving of immediate dismissal.

This triple process of self-introspection, evaluation of thoughts and appropriate action must be continual if it is to lead us up the ladder of souls. Though the aspirant has to tread the path himself—none else can tread it for him—the star-light of the shaykh can guide him through the twists and turns of the wayless Way. Ultimately, when his heart is purified and the empirical self completely burnt out from the ashes of its shell will rise in radiance the phoenix of self. Dead is self-ignorance and self-knowledge, which is universal knowledge, knowledge of the divine in him, has been born. It is the birth of a new Messiah in the Bethlehem of the heart. The aspirant has found the changeless spirit in the changing flesh.

THE SUPPLICATION OF A SINFUL SOUL

Speaking as the earth-bound soul, the mouse says that we are powerless before the divine destiny, which brings good and evil fortune to all. He prays to God in all humility, "Illumine our tainted soul with your light. Deliver it from fantasy and vain imagination, free it from the dark well of the world, so that through Your loving kindness, my heart may clutch the rope of patience which Your grace lowers to favored mortals, and, by its means, rise above this clay and water and experience the joy of spiritual ascension."

"The seven lean cows are devouring the seven fat ones" [12:43], that is, the gross sensual qualities are devouring the subtle spiritual qualities. "The cheats of sense are ensnaring me. The wile of women are great (as if men are paragons of virtue). The first 'fall' of man was caused by Eve, a woman. The last fall was due to my mother's lust which cast me in the prison of her womb. Even Joseph of Egypt had to seek the Lord's protection from the cunning of women. Of whom shall I complain? Of women representing a type of the appetitive soul, representing the flesh that has caused my expulsion from Your favor, like that of Adam from the gardens of Paradise [2:35]? I have violated the primal covenant made with You and eaten the forbidden fruit.

"If the temptress Eve, or mother, is held guilty, can the tempted Adam or father be held exempt from all sin? Also, was the so-called fall really a fall into sin? Should it not be regarded as a fall into generation, necessary for the purpose of creation designed by God for Self-manifestation in order that He might be known? This fall was evidently a part of the eternal plan and that was the reason, perhaps, why so readily, He forgave the repentant Adam. God's ways are mysterious.

"Pray hearken to the lament of this fallen spirit, this Joseph in its fall from grace, and take pity on this Jacob, this rational soul. When I repented and found favor with You, I sought deliverance from satanic temptations, but to no avail. I could not exorcise the devil from my being. Nothing succeeds against destiny. Wondrous alchemies from His languid eye alone can transmute the evil eye into the good eye. That is, open one's spiritual eye which alone can see things as they really are. Then alone will die his love of outward gilded sense-objects, love of this false life which is a foil and no more. He will cry like Abraham, *"I love not them that set"* [6:77]. He will be content with nothing short of contemplation of God. The mystical soul goes after the king and itself becomes its prey. The two remain two and yet are one.

This is no airy dream or fantasy. The Lord has allotted to each of the five external senses, which are the faculties of the soul, a portion of the spiritual sense. It is distributed amongst them and is king over them. When the senses are delivered from the body, they unite in one sense which bears one aloft to heaven. To each sense is thus given the means of access to the world of the unseen, to God Himself. The spiritual sense to which the Lord has given lordship over all senses and faculties, is immediate vision and recognition of the divine.

THE END OF THE MOUSE AND THE FROG

The mouse-body or rather the earth-bound soul kept pulling the string in the hope of winning over the frog-spirit. Ever since the end of the string, that is, the prospect of success manifested itself to him, his heart and soul, he said, had become pale and wan in constant contemplation of the hoped for union with the frog. But of a sudden, at the appointed hour, the raven of death came and carried off the mouse into the air. Along with him, the frog also was dragged from the water, its foot entangled in the string of carnal reason. Death seizes and destroys the soul also that is tied to the flesh.

When the people wondered how the raven could enter the water and carry off the water-frog, the frog said that this was only a natural retribution for one who mixes with a base friend or a rascal. One should always seeks a good companion.

SPIRITUAL CONGENIALITY, THE TRUE BASIS OF FRIENDSHIP

The mouse and the frog are incongruous in appearance, but real friendship can exist between those even more incongruous in form like water and bread and the human being. Friendship depends on congeniality between two beings. Congeniality is spiritual in origin. It is independent of the outward form or face. Form is like the mineral or the stone. Nothing inorganic knows congeniality.

The spirit is like an ant and the body like a grain of wheat or barley which the spirit picks up and carries because it knows that when the grain is eaten it will be transmuted and becomes homogeneous with it. But the barley or wheat does not come to the ant. Nor does the barley come to the wheat. Both are inorganic. But the ant comes to another ant because it is its congener. The outward forms are like the grain. They are moved by the spirit. No grain moves along without a grain-mover. One should behold the mover, not that which is moved, if he wants to know the initiator of the movement.

Just as the ant is the carrier of the grain, the frog typifying the soul is the carrier of the body, so that is the frog that is the actor. The body does no more than carry out the intentions of the soul speaking or acting as the soul speaks or acts. We see the pen that writes, but not the pen-wielder. This exonerates the earth-bound mouse, the body, of all blame. The culprit is the string that binds the soul to the body. Representing the flesh and the devil, it pulls the soul away from spirituality towards sensuality. When death comes, the body and the sensuous soul both are destroyed.

Blessed is the eye whose ruler is reason, the eye that sees the end and is wise and at rest. It is from this eye, the eye of reason that one learns to discern the difference between good and evil, not from the undiscerning fleshly eye that is deluded by "the verdure on dung-hills." The eye that sees only what it sensually desires without bringing it to the touchstone of reason, is the bird's ruin—the eye that sees the trap, the alluring falsity of the delights of senses and knows the end is its savior.

But while reason can perceive the difference between good and evil in the world of form, it can have no knowledge of the unseen, no knowledge of the absolute unity of God, as it cannot deliver itself from the duality of the subject and object of thought or see or know the nature of mystic union. Such knowledge comes by immediate experience as love alone can utter the explanation of lover and loverhood. It comes by divine inspiration and is revealed to the prophets and saints for transmission to mankind as it was revealed to Jesus. His form was human like ours, but who was homogeneous with the angels, and was, therefore uplifted by the celestial bird, the Archangel Gabriel, the holy spirit, above this fretted heaven—unlike the raven of death that carried the fallen frog-spirit to the dusty grave.[7]

17 THE DERVISH AND THE POLICE INSPECTOR

A certain dervish had a bountiful allowance from the police inspector of Tabriz, Badr al-Din Umar by name. Relying on his never-failing generosity, he had recklessly incurred debts to the tune of nine thousand pieces of gold. He went to Tabriz from outlying areas, full of hope and rejoicing in spirit in the thought that his generous patron would clear his debts.

Though only a police inspector, at heart he was an ocean of bounty. He was like a kinsman to poor strangers. He had cleared many debts of the dervish. Regardless of what he gave or how much he gave, he felt it was utterly nothing and was ashamed of it. If the celebrated Matim Tayyi, whose generosity is legendary, had been alive, he would have become a beggar to him, and laying his head before him made himself as dust at his feet.

Tabriz is no mean city. It is a city of noble spirits, of spiritual guides and saints, whose favor leads the soul to peace in nearness to God. It is a garden city with the splendor of paradise. Delightful scents diffused by the spirit from above the empyrean waft down upon the inhabitants of Tabriz. It is the abode of peace of the Sufi's quest.

But when the poor dervish sought the police inspector's

house, whose door he knew so well, he was told that, sated with this world of woe and wail, he left for heaven the day before yesterday. His shadow was the refuge of the needy, but the sun rolled it up in great haste.

This tragic news broke the dervish. He shrieked and fell down unconscious. They sprinkled rose-water on his face to revive him, weeping over his piteous plight, but to no purpose. He lay unconscious till nightfall, when his soul returned half-dead from the unseen.

ALL GIFTS ARE FROM GOD

When he regained his senses, he turned penitently to God and said, "I am a sinner, O Lord. I rested my hopes on a created being, equalling him with You. The Khwaja (police inspector) had indeed shown great generosity, but compared with your munificence, it was almost nothing gave me an allowance. You life and animate existence. He gave me a house and You gave me the heaven and the earth. He did not create gold or bread. They were Your gifts to him. You also gave him generosity and compassion the display of which increased his joy. And yet, I made him my *qibla* ignoring the original *qibla* Maker.

It was for the human being that God created this dome of heaven, this carpet of earth and all that is folded therein. Adam, the father of mankind, is an astrolabe, a reflector, of His attributes, and his nature a theatre for His revelations. Whatever is seen in him is His reflection. God gave the prophets knowledge of spiritual astronomy. Every perfect human being whose inner eye is open like theirs can observe like them the secrets of the unseen. Lacking such an eye, the dark worldlings, fall into the well of the world, this well of error and illusion. What one sees therein is from outside. It is a reflection. Not knowing this, he is like the lion in the story of "The Lion and the Beasts"[1] where he is misled by the stratagem of the hare who tells him that another lion, his rival, is at the bottom of the well. He must go into it and take vengeance. He looks into the well and sees his own reflection. Fancying it to be his enemy, he jumps into the water and drowns. He did not know that what appeared in the water in the well was not produced by the water, but was from outside.

One who seeks to wreak vengeance on another is in error. He sees his own fancies everywhere. He does not know that the sole source of all actions, of all that is, is divine energy, the divine Essence and attributes. And what he sees as enmity in the enemy is from God and is derived from His attribute of wrath. A sin in another is only a reflection of his own sin. People are mirrors of one another. It is one's own hypocrisy, iniquity and arrogance that are reflected in others. One does not break the mirror because he sees his own ugliness in it. Why then hate or curse any creature?

Evil passions are only shadows of divine wrath. They are passing. He must look beyond them, as he must look beyond everything external, to the world of reality. When one pours earth on the reflection of a star in the water, fancying it to be the star itself, and the earth hides the reflection, he thinks that the unlucky star is no more. But he is in error, for that star is in the sky. And the ill-luck in this quarter is only a reflection of the ill-luck in the quarterless quarter.

All gifts are the gifts of God. All that appears in this world is a reflection of the gifts. The gifts of worldlings may be endless, but they cannot be carried to the other world. They will all remain behind. After all, how long can a shadow stay in sight? We should practice contemplating the source of the shadow, the source that is everlasting.

Those who supplicate God in need are blessed by Him with bounty and a long life. He makes the gift and the recipient ever-living. He resuscitates the dead. The gifts of God mingle with one like the spirit, as if they were he and he was they. Do not seek bread and butter for Him. For if without them your bodily fatness goes, He will bestow on you spiritual fatness which is concealed in the bodily leanness. To the fairy, He gives sustenance from scent, and to the angel from spirit. Why then depend on the animal soul? God makes us living by His love. It is the life of love that we should beg of Him. We should ask of Him spiritual provision, not bread and water.

GOD IS REFLECTED EVERYWHERE

This creation is as pure and limpid water wherein the divine attributes are shining. Our knowledge, our justice and learning, our clemency are like the reflection of a heavenly star in flowing water. Kings are the theatre for the manifestation of His sovereignty and the learned, the mirror of His knowledge and wisdom. Generations have come and gone. This generation is new, but the justice and the learning are the same. The moon is the same, but the water in which it was reflected is not the same water. It has been changed in this water-bed many times, but the reflection of the moon and the stars of the divine attributes, is unchanging. For the foundation of the reflection, as stated earlier, is not in the flowing water. It is in the vast firmament of heaven. The beauteous ones are the mirror of His beauty. Love of them is a reflection of love for God. For what creates love in man for a woman is not her ravishing face or figure, but the spiritual and divine qualities in her. And it is these qualities that cause the true lover to go beyond this reflected beauty and seek union with the true beloved, its essential source, the phenomenal thus serving as the bridge to the Real. The cheek and mole return to their source at the end. How should a fantasy dance in the water for ever? All these pictured images, these phenomena in the river water are a passing reflection, but seen with the spiritual eye, their basis is in God. They are He as He sees Himself in external guise. This myriad splendored creation is but "the time-vesture of the eternal." We must not see two where, in reality, there is one.

KHWAJA, THE PERFECT HUMAN BEING

The poor debtor's reason reprimands him for seeing double, for seeing the khwaja as one apart from God. The khwaja had gone past the ninth celestial sphere. He was not homogeneous with these worldly darklings. He was spirit, not gross body, marrow, not bone. A true seeker of God like him loses himself in the object of his search and becomes one with it. Self-negation, he is no more creaturely, as commonly understood. No more an individual worshipper, he has become the subject and object of all worship. He is essentialized.

The khawja may appear like any other reflection, but, in reality, he is not a reflection. He is not God, but may be said to be "the appearance of God in the likeness of a reflection." The exalted saints lose their creaturely attributes and are transmuted. They must not be reckoned among the created beings. The *qibla* of divine unity, that is, the object of worship, cannot be two. When the terrestrial angels worshiped Adam, they did not worship clay, but the divine attributes, the light of Muhammad, revealed in the earthly body of Adam. The perfect human being contemplates nothing but the divine Names and Attributes reflected in his heart, which constitute his real self, his basic reality. He sees nothing without seeing God in it.

It is said in the Koran, *"Whoso obeys the Messenger, obeys God"* [4:80]. Also, God said to Muhammad, *"You did not throw when you threw"* [8:17], the handful of gravel which, in the battle of Badr, routed the numerous army of his enemy—the Quraysh. The perfect human being, a spiritual successor of the Prophet, is like him, only a passive instrument of divine action. His hand is the hand of God. To see such a person is to see the Light of God. To serve him is to serve God. The divine attributes reflected from him give spiritual food to his believers, to those who do not deny the Truth when it comes to them, nor are deaf and dumb to His revelations [6:5, 39].

The perfect human being receives the light directly from God, not through the atmosphere or the six directions, not through our visible sun or stars, but by a secret channel. He is inwardly illumined. Clouds may darken the sky, but they cannot bar the way by which light strikes his heart, for that way is unknown to them as to other people. There is a hidden link between the Lord of man and the human spirit.

The maker seeks and kills all unreal existence. When He

reveals Himself in His glory, the illusion of self-existence vanishes. We should not say two or call two, but regard the slave as effaced in the master. The khwaja is dead and buried in his Creator. Let his spiritual eye transcend his clay and see him as one *qibla* as one object of worship. To see two *qibla*s is a sign of double-seeing or strabism. It is to remain deprived of both aspects of the one, His transcendence and imminence, of His inward and outward aspects.

The police inspector's bailiff was distressed by the grief of the dervish whose indebtedness had become notorious. He went round the city to raise donations for him. He recited his piteous tale to attract compassion from people. But all that the devoted beggar could get by begging was a paltry sum not exceeding a hundred dinars. The bailiff took his hand and went with him to visit the grave of that wonderful khwaja, the police inspector, and said to the dervish, "When a servant of God receives the divine favor so that he extends hospitality to another man, he sacrifices his wealth for the latter's benefit. To be grateful to the benefactor is to be grateful to God, for it was His favor that enabled him to show beneficence. To be ungrateful to the benefactor is to be ungrateful to God. Always be thankful to God for His bounties. Offer thanks and praise to your benefactor. God has said, '*Do you bless him (the Prophet)* [33:56]' for Muhammad was one to whom God had transferred the attribute of His providence."

At the resurrection, God will ask His servant what he had done with what He gave him. The servant will say that he gave grateful thanks to Him with all his soul, for He was the source of his bread and sustenance. God will say, "No, you did not give thanks, as you did not give thanks to him who was a habitual benefactor. You perpetrated wrong and injustice on a generous soul. Did not My bounty come to you by his hand?"

On reaching the grave of that noble benefactor, the poor indebtor burst into tears and loud lamentation. He said, "You were the refuge of the righteous. You were like parents to the poor in meeting their expenses, taxes and debts. You tenderly cared for me and a hundred like me like your own children. You were our cash and property, our pride and fortune. You are not dead. It is our fortune and our happy life that is dead. The generous Hatim Tayyi gave countless material goods to the spiritually dead worldlings, but you are momently giving a life that is lasting and is like gold coins that are beyond calculation and exempt from depreciation. Your grace is a loving shepherd like Moses, guarding all created beings from the wolf of pain." The munificence of the saints is boundless.

It is said that once a sheep fled from Moses, and, in searching after it, his feet were blistered and his shoes fell off. It was nightfall by the time the sheep was found. It was in a state of exhaustion. With no trace of anger or irritation on his face, but full of love, pity and tears, Moses caressed its back and head, as a mother caresses her child, and said, "I can understand you having no pity on me, but why was your tender nature cruel to itself?" At that moment, God said to the angels that Moses was full worthy of prophethood.

The Prophet has said that God did not bestow prophethood on one who had not been a shepherd in early life. He himself was a shepherd for a long time. He makes them shepherds so that they should display the prophet's calmness and fortitude before He invests them with prophethood. Every prince who performs the task of shepherding mankind in a manner conforming with the Lord's commandments, and shows foresight and understanding is inevitably invested by Him with a spiritual shepherd's office exalted above the moon's sphere.

IN LIFE AND DEATH, THE SAINT IS WITH GOD

Continuing, the poor debtor said, "O khwaja, I know that in recompense for your shepherding the poor with such perfection, God will bestow on you everlasting sovereignty. In hope of your bounty, I incurred heavy debts. Where are you that you may redeem my debts, showing munificence as always. I know that even when you were here, you were beyond this world. Only your body was on earth. Your spirit was not translated to heaven after death, but was already translated while you were alive. The spirit is from the command of the Lord, and of its knowledge, we have been vouchsafed but little [17:85]. Whatever is said about it cannot be the truth. His spirit is shining in heaven, but is hidden in the void. But where is that ruby lip, I wonder, that would unlock perplexities and utter sweet words? Where, oh where?

"How long shall I keep crying 'where,' 'where,' like a ringdove seeking her nest? The khwaja is where his heart and thought always dwelt, where one hope always turns in the hour of anguish and illness, He is beyond 'where,' 'where,' beyond the infinitudes of space. He is with God. Would that I had asked myself, 'Where are we?' and realized that it is only through self-negation that we can rise to the world beyond time and space and find him again. Oh where is our reason that even within the spatio-temporal world it may perceive the myriads of splendor that flash forth from the divine epiphany on the spirits of the elect? Now that God has withdrawn the khwaja from the earth, I am left in debt and torture. I am leaving this sweet dust in despair. I must also go to God. He is the assembly place. *"All are brought into Our presence,"* God has said [36:32].

Every moment, God imprints new ideas on the mind's tablet, erasing the old. Now anger is imprinted and acquiescence removed. Now stinginess replaces generosity. Never are my ideas free from such imprinting and erasing. God erases what He will and establishes what He will. The potter is ever working at the pot of itself. The pot cannot become broad and long, or assume any shape. At every moment we are being filled and emptied by Him, as we are in His ever-working hand. On the day the eye-bandage is removed from the eye, with what intensity will the work be enamored of the worker, the master-craftsman? If one has an eye and an ear, he should practice seeing with his own eye and not through the eye of another, and harkening with his own ear and not depend on other ears. His thinking should be guided not by any convention or tradition, but by his own reason. Seeing, hearing, and thinking must be direct, not through the blinding veil or any external authority or any intermediary.

The bailiff took the poor debtor to his house, gave him viands to eat, apart from the hundred dinars, and told him stories that filled him with hope, and also, how in his own case the experience of adversity was followed by prosperity. Midnight passed, and amid story-telling, sleep fell upon them both, transporting their spirits to spiritual fields.

The Bailiff's Dream

The bailiff dreamt that he saw the khwaja seated on a pedestal in the heavenly palace. The khwaja said to him, "O good bailiff, I have heard all you said, but I was not commanded to answer. Here our lips are sealed so that the mysteries of the unseen are not divulged to earthly mortals and the veil of heedlessness of God completely rent causing mankind to turn from this world of grief and woe to the other world and through neglect, let this world, which God created for Self-manifestation go to ruin. This would defeat the very purpose of creation. We are all ear, though our material ear is deaf. We are all speech, though our lips are sealed. The material world is the veil, the spiritual world is the vision. We sow seeds in the earth and that is the season of toil and concealment. We reap here what we have sown there, and this is the season of recompense and manifestation.

The khwaja had not forgotten his poor friend, the debtor, when he departed this earth. He now revealed to the bailiff how the debt was to be repaid. He had packed up rubies and other jewels in a vessel on which the debtor's name was inscribed. He had stored it in a certain vault. He wished to hand over these jewels to him with his own hand, but death nullified his intention. The sale proceeds of the jewels would be more than ample to repay the debt, but he should be careful of swindlers. As the Prophet taught his followers, three days time should be taken to decide whether a particular offer should be accepted or not. Only kings knew the worth of this treasure. The position should be explained to his heirs, with his greetings, in order to ensure that the entire sum of gold is delivered to his friend. If the good dervish said that he did not need so much, all of it should still be given to him, and he should be left free to give away as much as he liked to whomsoever he liked. He needed nothing back. "The milk never returns to the nipple." Should the poor dervish accept nothing, let his heirs lay the entire bounty at his door so that every passer-by may carry the gold away. He had kept these jewels in store for two years and vowed to God that they would be his. If his heirs took any part of them, and thus vexed his spirit, they would suffer great loss and a hundred tribulations. He wished the dervish to remember him.[2]

The bailiff sprang up from sleep, joyous, drunken. He said to the dervish, who was wonder-struck at his strange state, that he had dreamt a mad dream in which he saw the khwaja, that giver of things, who had given up his life for the vision beatific. Drunkenly, he kept recounting the dream, till losing his reason and consciousness, he fell and lay flat in the middle of the room. People gathered round him. At last, he rose from his spiritual intoxication into a state of sobriety and started expounding the doctrine of correlated opposites. He said, "O ocean of bliss, You have secretly enclosed contrary in contrary—forms of consciousness in unconsciousness, a wakefulness in sleep, wealth in the humbleness of poverty, life in death. Riches are never diminished by alms-giving. On the contrary, charity is enriching, both materially and spiritually. As the Prophet said, 'O possessor of wealth, munificence is a gainful trade.'" As is said in the Koran, in the prescribed prayer, there is preservation from lewdness and iniquity [29:45]. Within this body of clay there is a prince, a treasure, hidden in a ruin, so that satan may only see the animal body, not the king or the treasure. That treasure is the treasure of the divine attributes, which is found not in the treasury of queens and kings, but in the ruin of self-negation.

Great is the munificence of saints. The debt of the good dervish is paid, not by anyone living, but by the dead police inspector, the khwaja. In truth, the khwaja was not dead. As is said:

He that died and found rest is not dead.
The truly dead is he who among the materially living
    is spiritually dead.³

18 THE THREE PRINCES

There was a King and he had three sons. All three were sagacious and discerning. In generosity and battle, each was more praiseworthy than another. They were the delight of their father's eye.

The king instructed them to journey through his empire and establish certain arrangements in certain places and appoint certain viceroys in certain places.

They equipped themselves for the journey, kissed the king's hand, and bade him farewell. But before leaving, the king said to them, "Go joyously where ever your inclination takes you. But for God's sake, do not visit or wander around one fortress whose name is the robber of reason. Its towers, roof and floor are adorned with exquisite pictures and images—like the chamber of Zulaykha, which was so cunningly decorated with pictures of her that wherever Joseph looked, he had no choice but to see her face. Keep well away from it."

Anxious for their spiritual well-being, he wanted his sons to keep away from deceits of sense, those false delights which only lead to woes that are not false. One should know that all that one has drawn from heaven and earth is only a loan that has to be paid back—all, except the spirit, which God has breathed into the human form [15:29]. The spirit is not on loan, but comes from His munificence and is everlasting. One should cleave to the spirit. All other things are vain—vain in relation to the spirit, not as creations of His perfect craftsmanship.

Nothing that He has created is without a purpose though it may not be manifest to us.

The gnostic, in his wisdom, keeps away from this abode of delusion, this world where things are not what they seem, and seeks replenishment from the fountain-head of eternal life within his soul. As the fountain is the source of all things, it makes him independent of all fountains flowing without, of all things external. Reliance on them only slackens one's quest for the eternal fountain. One should take a leaf from the gnostic and not quest for water and earth or heart's sorrow will be the price he will have to pay, for, early or late, age, ill-health or death will cause their vanishing. Our work should be from within the soul, if we are seekers of eternal life and bliss.

God has made all the six directions a theatre for the manifestation of His signs to the mystical seers and has told them, "Wheresoever you turn, His Presence is there," so that whatever they look upon, animal or plant, they see His beauty. But from the profane eye that beauty is hidden. When one who is not a lover of God drinks water from a cup, he sees his own image in the water, but when a clairvoyant mystic drinks water, he sees God in the water. As his self, his image is negated in Him, whom else should he see in the water except Him. As a Sufi said, "I never saw anything without seeing God therein."

GOD'S ZEAL

God is zealous. Through His zeal, the selfless mystic's spiritual eye sees His beauty reflected in every form, earthly or heavenly. His zeal is directed only against His lovers, against those who have seen Him, but go after another, equalling him with God, preferring him to Him, when another is negated. He alone is and is the All and is always with them. It is not directed against human devils and beasts whose gaze is confined to shows and shadows. But if through His grace, the devil becomes His lover—God does whatsoever He wills, independent of cause or means. He becomes like Gabriel a guide to the righteous on the spiritual path, and his devilish nature dies. But one should not count on such a rare possibility. We must not be sense-bewitched and let vain desire waylay us, but strive against sense and self and aspire quality for His loving jealousy, which may save us from retrogression.

THE FORBIDDEN FRUIT

The forbidden castle was remote from the other fortresses and the main highways. But for the king's prohibition, the princes would never have thought of approaching it. But the attraction of the forbidden fruit aroused in them a craving to investigate its mystery. A prohibition causes the pious to hate what is forbidden, but incites the sensual to covet it. By the same means, God guides many, and leads many astray.

The princes said to the king, "Far be it from us to deviate from your commands. We will carry out the services entrusted to us. It would be shear ingratitude to forget your kindness."

THE MEANING OF "IF GOD WILL"

The princess relied on themselves to carry out their father's injunctions and did not mention the saving clause—the words "if God will." They were proud of their intellects and believed in causes and means. They were blind to His contrivance and omnipotence. It is of course not the mere omission of the words "if God will" but a harness of heart, an unawareness of His Almightiness which leads to their omission that is important. Many do not pronounce these words, yet their souls are in harmony with the spirit of the clause which renders its verbal utterance unnecessary. If one shoots an arrow to the right and finds that it has gone to the left or chases a deer and makes himself the prey of a hog or has dug pits for others and seen himself fall into them should he not inquire who the changer or turner is? And as he is not visible, would it not be a celestial being? Would it not be God?

In another story, "The King and the Handmaiden," to which the poet makes a passing reference here, the best exoteric physicians are unable to cure a love-sick maiden because of their conceited reliance on their own knowledge, intelligence, and omission of the saving clause. She is a last cured by a divine physician.[1]

The lesson is clear. One should not place total reliance on means. One should be suspicious of them. The Lord can render them ineffective. He is the turner of eyes, hearts and thoughts. This realization and the prudence and precaution to which it leads is the essence of the saving clause. One should no be too sure of oneself.

Nor is this just sophistry. It shows that the real existence of things is not in the things themselves, but in God. To deny the realities or to think that all this here is illusion, both are sheer fantasy. All things exist as ideas in the eternal knowledge of God. He determines the actual differences in their character and individuality in this shadow world—which is a true copy of the divine original. He gives them the desire and the receptive capacity for the concrete existence He bestows on them. They may be shadowy and ephemeral, but that which gave them life is everlasting Reality. They are full of God. The essence, the divine in them is real. No true copy or symbol is wholly without reality.

Defying their father's wise injunction, the princes came to the forbidden fortress, that purple-lined palace of sweet sin. It was richly adorned with pictures, portraits and designs. It had five gates to the sea and five to the land—the latter five, like the five external senses, facing towards the material world of scent and color, and the former five, like the internal senses, seeking the mysterious world of spirit.

The princes were bewitched and made restless by those thousands of pictures and decorations. They were doubtless of surpassing beauty, but were only like ornamental cups, just phenomenal forms—the love of which is emblematic of sensual love. The cup may have wine in it, but it is not distilled from the cup. It is alien to it. It comes from without. A wise man opens his mouth to the giver of the spiritual wine. It comes only to one whose heart is pure and is ready to receive it. He does not open his mouth to the material cup. As God said to Adam, "Abandon the forbidden wheat and seek My heart-enthralling reality."

FORM AND THE FORMLESS

Form is created by the formless like smoke by a fire. The least fault in that which has form is irritating, but formlessness has no fault and is utterly bewildering. Instruments of countless types are born from non-instrumentality, hands from handlessness, the human being in the fullness of form from the soul of the soul. The soul belongs to the world of unity, but is created to reflect God's diverse attributes, thus fulfilling the purpose of God, which is Self-manifestation.

The cause never resembles the effect. The cry of anguish does not resemble the loss that caused it. The cry has a form, but the loss, its cause, is formless. What resemblance does the exertion of the laborer bear to the money he receives in payment for it? Even where the effect is in the other world and the cause is in this world, the two are not of the same complexion. When a man prostrates in prayer, his prostration here becomes paradise in the other world. His renunciation of desire becomes a river of water there, his love for God a river of milk, his delight in devotion a river of honey, his spiritual intoxication a river of wine. None knows except God how He has connected particular effects with the particular causes.[2]

God's working is formless. It sows the seed of a form or idea in pre-existence, differentiating the souls in His eternal knowledge. From that seed grows up a body, with senses and a reasoning faculty. The original ideas, according to their own nature, determine the state of the body as good and evil, and are the motives to all bodily action. If the idea be of beneficence, the body turns to thanksgiving. If of a city, it journeys to the city. If of a beauteous face or figure, it revels in enjoyment. If of the unseen world, it practices religious seclusion.

All the ways of life, all the crafts, are but the shadow or reflection of thought-forms. What are the walls or a roof of a building? Nothing, but the though-form of the architect, though, in his thought, there is no material brick or mortar, no stone or wood. The action that results from his thought-form is manifested in outward concrete form, but the thought-form that emanates from the spirit or mind and motivates the action is unmanifest, and the two are correlated as cause and effect.

Again, the ideas that arise from the cheering cup at a banquet result in unconsciousness, which is pre-existent in the divine mind and is the final case, which is formless. So is knowledge which is the goal and final cause of physical attendance at an academic institution; the goal of the material form of sword and shield is victory, and victory is formless. When the formless goal is reached, the external form of the idea is abandoned as no more relevant. It was an accident in the first instance, not the substance.

All these forms are the slaves of the formless and cannot deny their benefactor. They have their very existence from Him. Even the skeptic's disbelief in God is reflected from Him, as all thought is framed by Him, the thought of atheism or infidelity not excluded. This does not mean that God is infidel. The ordainment of infidelity is knowledge. In relation to the ordainment, it is no infidelity. Infidelity is the thing ordained; it is born of our ignorance. Infidelity as ordained is like the display of the ugly by the artist, the display of his versatility. It is not the artist's ugliness.

Formlessness is both the source of action and its result or end and objective. If we are going to a city or to a friend—both have form—it is because we are attracted thither by a formless feeling of pleasure. We are going to experience that which has no locality, which is timeless and placeless, for pleasure is different from time and place or form. We are ever going to the formless world, though we may not know that that world is the real object of our journey. In truth, we worship God. For all our wayfaring is for the sake of the pleasure of which the Formless One is the ultimate source. All our desires, beliefs and actions have no real object except God, as these grow from the pre-dispositions He has sown in us and which eventually carry us back to Him. Even earthly love can be educative and lead us to spiritual love at the last. As the poet Jami sings:

> Drink deep of earthly love; so that thy lip
> May learn the wine of holier love to sip.

In fact, the first stage of every human being is the form. The spirit, which is beauty of disposition, comes after the form. The fruit comes first and then its delicious taste. Though the outward form is flying crookedly, it will lead us to the inward meaning in the end.[3] Above these seekers of earth and heaven, of course, is one who has lost all sense and consciousness, for whom this earth and heaven do not exist, who is reduced to nothing. By losing all and being completely negated, he has sped toward the whole and gained all.

Everyone receives from God his pre-determined portion of good and evil ideas which are the stuff of which God has fashioned paradise and hell. Though troops of fantasy are marching in perpetual succession from non-existence to occupy our hearts, none—except God—knows the way to His rosaries nd furnaces. If one did, he would bar entrance to every unlovely fancy.

THE CASTLE CASTS ITS SPELL

In the pavilion of the castle or fortress, among the numerous portraits, they espied one whose majestic beauty intoxicated their senses. The castle, "the robber of reason," wrought its spell. Love of that pictured form was burning them like a flame of fire. They were weeping tears of blood and gnawing their hands, crying, "Alas! Now we see what our father had seen at the start. How often did he counsel us to keep away from this castle?"

The prophets have done us a great favor by making us aware of the end. They have warned us against the perils of worldly pleasure which lures only to leave, and exhorted us to follow their guidance, so that past this world of illusion, we may attain into His presence.

The root of sin is in us. It is not to know our own divinity; not to know that the prophet is "thou"—we ourselves—not the unreal "thou" to whom there is no other world than this, so that there is no escape from this visioned show, but the real, essential "thou," which is buried in the unreal "thou," all "thou's." It is the perfect human being, the shaykh within who has seen this "thou," when it was just an idea in the divine mind and who was made acquainted with every material form before it was robed in materiality, and who speaks in His name.

The three brothers said, "We have flouted the king's admonitions and commands and paid little regard to his incomparable favors. We trusted our own intelligence and wisdom, imagining ourselves to be perfect, and, in consequence, have fallen into affliction. We now know our weakness. A single feeling of contentment is better than a hundred expansive banquets. The shadow of a spiritual guide is better than God's glorification by one's ignorant empirical self."

Moved by the anguish of sensual love, they began to inquire whose portrait it was, of which paragon of beauty that had drugged them like opium!

After much inquiry during their travel, they came upon a shaykh of deep spiritual insight. He unveiled the mystery to them, not by speech, but in silence, by inspiration that flashed from universal reason. He said, "This is a portrait of the princess of China—the divine beauty—who is the envy of the Pleiades and is hidden like the spirit, and kept jealously guarded in a secret bower and palace. No man or woman has access to her presence. She is not to be sought by any cunning or intellectual contrivance, but by dying to self and to all contrivings, and dependence on the divine favor."

The three began to discuss what plan they should adopt to gain their end. They were comrades in one thought and in one passion, weeping tears at one moment and emitting burning sighs at another.

The eldest prince said, "We have always preached patience and fortitude to others, inspired them with courage in moments of danger, removed a hundred fears and anxieties from their hearts. Now that pain has become our guest, how is it that we become distracted, and are crying, 'Alas' like cowardly females, forgetful of our previous manliness? We were always leaders before; we must not become laggards now. We must restore ourselves to our normal state of spiritual strength and natural vigour."

THE QUEST FOR THE DIVINE BEAUTY

After much discussion, the love-intoxicated brothers decided to set out for China, the mystical Orient. The way to union with the beloved is barred. For the human being can go near the light of God, when self-negated and unconscious of any personal existence, but he cannot become God. He is not His congener.

"I am the Truth," said the martyr-saint Hallaj. "There is no God except I," said the eminent Sufi Bayazid. Such seemingly blasphemous utterances are wrung from God-intoxicated lovers by their uncontrollable love of Him. One in ecstasy does not know what he is saying or doing. All claim or talk of one's union with God, even God's saying about His friend that "I am he" or "he is I," should be understood as being subject to the over-riding truth that the divine and human natures cannot commingle, and that He alone is, and none else has the right to say "I am."

As the princess of China typifies the divine beauty, which is the source of all beauty, earthly or heavenly, the three princes could not possibly attain to union with her. Nevertheless, it is laudable to get as close to her as one can.

The spiritual journey is said to consist of two steps—step out of self, step into Self, or step out of duality, step into unity, unconscious of separate self. With the first step, the seeker gains whatever is to be gained. It is a different step, or rather a difficult stage. Words falter or fail when describing anything spiritual.

The princes commenced the journey to the spiritual land of China, the divine realm. They chose fortitude as their guide. Their inward eye was opened and they became seers, "true witnesses." Like Abraham ibn Adham, love parted them from their parents, banished them from the throne, tore them from self. When one in love casts himself into a fire, like the prophet Abraham, God cherishes him in the fire, and destroying the secondary cause, the fire, turns it into a rose-garden.

NOTES

Most of the notes are citations to the six books of the *Mathnawi* indicated by Roman numerals following the M for *Mathnawi*. The Arabic numbers indicate the verse in the *Mathnawi* to which the note refers.

Introduction
1 M.I.2654-2655.
2 M.I.1727-1730.
3 M.VI.2.
4 M.IV.755.
5 Nicholson, p. xiii.
6 Koranic verses citations refer to the numbers of the translation of the Koran by Abdullah Yusef Ali.
7 M.III.1149.
8 M.IV.2880.
9 M.IV.3558-3559.
10 M.V.1891.
11 M.III.2109.
12 M.II.1753.
13 Commentary, M.VI. Notes on 4876.

1 Prophet Moses and Pharaoh
1 M.I.3486.
2 M.I.1615-1619.
3 M.III.1721-1745.
4 M.III.22.
5 M.II.2307-2308.

2 Prophet Solomon and the Queen of Sheba
1 M.V.200.
2 M.I.2467-2470.
3 M.I.2003.
4 M.I.2648-2649.

5 M.IV.807.
6 M.I.2654-2655.
7 M.VI.3239.

3 Prophet Joseph and Zulaykha
1 M.VI.4118.
2 M.II.127, M.IV.3662-3664.
3 M.V.2594.
4 M.II.1276-1279.
5 M.IV.673-674.
6 M.VI.3637-3639.
7 M.IV.1423.
8 M.VI.3390-3391; M.I.1765, 1768.
9 M.II.3782.
10 M.V.3806-3808.
11 M.VI.2792.
12 M.I.3205-3209.
13 M.VI.4829.
14 As readers may know, Joseph and Zulaykha is one of the most popular love romances and it has many renderings. The most celebrated of these is that by the great scholar and mystic poet Jami (1414-1492 CE), said to be the last great classical poet of Persia. The Koran has a whole chapter on Joseph. In Rumi, the story has a mystical coloring.

4 Prophet Muhammad and the Sick Companion
1 M.III.4166-4170.
2 M.II.301.
3 M.IV.91-93.
4 M.I.1995-1997.
5 M.I.2905, 2914-2916.

5 The Old Harper
1 See Hujwiri, *Kashf al-mahjub*, pp 393-420.

7 Daquqi: His Visions and Miracles
1 M.I.69.

8 The Lawyer of Bukhara
1 See Commentary on M.III.2281.
2 M.II.1770.
3 M.III.3686-3699, 3789-3921, 4377-4420, 4615-4623, 4664-4748.

9 The Story of Ayaz
1 M.IV.887-890.
2 M.II.1049-1053.
3 M.IV.2613-2615.
4 M.II.1192.
5 M.II.167.
6 M.II.1049-1052; M.V.1857-1891, 1918-2149, 3251-3285, 3351-3355, 4025-4032.

10 The Breaking of the Pearl
1 M.I.3507; M.II.173.
2 M.V.4035-4119, 4153-4210.

11 Compulsion and Freewill
1 M.I.1497-1499.
2 M.VI.385-434.

12 Shaykh Muhammad Sarrazi of Ghazna
1 M.V.2667-2733, 2749-2811.

13 The Story of Bilal
1 M.II.1720.
2 M.VI.888-1110; M.III.172-177, 3517.

14 The Sufi and the Judge
1 M.I.2143-2144.
2 M.II.158-159.
3 The physical father is only the husk or shell. When all things are eternally decreed, one cannot wonder why some are good and others bad. Or how can the many, this vast ever-renewing world of endless opposites, issue out of the one

unmanifest eternal, who, in essence, transcends all plurality and variableness?
 4 M.VI.1293-1382, 1483-1655, 1720-1757.

15 The Dervish and the Hidden Treasure
 1 M.I.2000-2003.
 2 M.II.1345-1346.
 3 M.VI.1939-1942.
 4 M.I.1578.
 5 M.I.598-599.
 6 M.VI.1758-1766, 1834-2006, 2026-2043, 2257-2375.

16 The Mouse and the Frog
 1 M.I.1063-1065.
 2 M.III.4417-4420.
 3 Wamiq and Adhra are the hero and heroine of an eastern love romance versified in Persian by the 11th century poet, Unsuri, no longer extant.
 4 Hujwiri, *Kashf al-mahjub*, p. 13 footnote.
 5 M.V.3676.
 6 M.IV.1314-1318.
 7 M.VI.2632-2815, 2941-2973.

17 The Dervish and the Police Inspector
 1 M.I.900-1372.
 2 It is said that Rumi's reference here is to the completion of the *Mathnawi* two years before his death and his wish that it should not be anyone's monopoly, but be available to all spiritual seekers in his orison.
 3 M.VI.3014-3028, 3106-3219, 3248-3344, 3518-3582.

18 The Three Princes
 1 M.I.36.
 2 M.III.3445-3447, 3461-3463.
 3 M.III.526-528.